"Rescued from obscurity, Clark's vivid account of trials and travel in the American West offers witness to the overland trail, the oft-forgotten conflict between Utah's Latter-day Saints and the U.S. government in 1857–58, and the tragic Mountain Meadows Massacre, with strong contextual support from the editors."

—ROBERT CLARK, editor of *Overland Journal*

"William Clark's measured account of his extraordinary overland journey has long been a vital, if hard to consult, source for anyone seeking to understand the North American West at the eve of the Civil War. In this first scholarly edition of Clark's narrative, William MacKinnon and Kenneth Alford provide essential context that allows contemporary readers to understand the importance of once-famous figures whose significance has faded from popular memory. Their thorough research illuminates the arc of Clark's life before and after his trip to California, as well as how his account came to be. They guide us to a fuller understanding of nineteenth-century commercial freighting on the plains, the intricacies of the Utah Expedition, and the precariousness of life in the Mountain West."

—GEORGE A. MILES, retired William Robertson Coe Curator of the Yale Collection of Western Americana

"MacKinnon and Alford have transformed an already wonderful account of an intriguing adventure in the antebellum West into a scholarly gem that paints the strange Utah War episode with all its color and accompanying grit."

—GENE A. SESSIONS, coauthor of *Camp Floyd and the Mormons: The Utah War*

"William Clark's compelling account of having survived hardship and danger on the western trails is here brought out of obscurity and expertly contextualized by two of the foremost authorities on the Utah War of 1857–58. The book is a model of careful editing, sensitive handling, and informed research."

—CHARLES E. RANKIN, editor of *Toward a More Perfect Union: The Civil War Letters of Frederic and Elizabeth Lockley*

On the Overland Trails with William Clark

A TEAMSTER'S UTAH WAR,
1857–1858

Edited by William P. MacKinnon
and Kenneth L. Alford

Foreword by Howard R. Lamar

University of Nebraska Press
LINCOLN

© 2025 by the Board of Regents of the University of Nebraska

All rights reserved

The University of Nebraska Press is part of a land-grant institution with campuses and programs on the past, present, and future homelands of the Pawnee, Ponca, Otoe-Missouria, Omaha, Dakota, Lakota, Kaw, Cheyenne, and Arapaho Peoples, as well as those of the relocated Ho-Chunk, Sac and Fox, and Iowa Peoples.

Library of Congress Control Number: 2024033370

Set in Whitman by A. Shahan.

Frontispiece: William Clark (1834–1920). The only known photo of Clark, probably taken in the late nineteenth century or early 1900s when he was in his sixties. This image ran in an Iowa newspaper with an account of his "pioneering" western adventures on November 3, 1905. Courtesy *Des Moines Iowa State Register and Farmer*.

For Sherilee Bond Alford (1959–2022)
An inspiration to the author-editors of this study
even as she completed the arduous journey
to her final destination.

From here [Utah] we drove into San Bernardino, arriving there on the thirteenth day of January 1858. It was warm and delightful weather and the grass was green . . . the ship that landed us safely out of *Utah*, no matter what the cost, was welcome to all it got, for now we could breathe easy.

WILLIAM CLARK, "A Trip Across the Plains in 1857"

Contents

List of Illustrations	ix
Foreword by Howard R. Lamar	xi
Acknowledgments	xiii

Part 1. Understandings

Editors' Introduction	3
Editorial Decisions	7
Background and Context: The Utah War	11

Part 2. William Clark's Edited Reminiscences ("A Trip Across the Plains in 1857")

Section 1. "We Had an Eye on California": Signing On, Starting Out	17
Section 2. "I Was Starving with a Train Loaded with Provisions": Sick unto Death	27
Section 3. "They Make the Earth Tremble": Into the Buffalo Range	32
Section 4. "Consider Yourselves Discharged": Sunday Confrontation	37
Section 5. "Grand and Beautiful Scenery": Wolves along the North Platte	47
Section 6. "A Sage Brush Country": Crossing the Continental Divide to Green River	54
Section 7. "The Boss, Seeing They Had No Show, Surrendered": Meeting Lot Smith	57
Section 8. "Into Winter Quarters": An Agonizing Crawl to Fort Bridger	60

Section 9. "Saddle Up and Be Quick about It":
        Into Captivity with the Latter-day Saints   67

Section 10. "Difficult for a Man to Escape
        Their Vengeance": Life in Salt Lake City   74

Section 11. "We Started, Badly Scared Inside":
        From Salt Lake through Utah's
        Southern Settlements   81

Section 12. "Enough to Make a Man's Blood Run Cold":
        Crossing Mountain Meadows and Beyond   88

Section 13. "Back to Wisconsin": The Fate of
        Sherwood and Tuttle   100

Appendix A: The Pomeroy and Kingston Story   103

Appendix B: William and Cora Clark's Later Years   106

Appendix C: William Clark's Obituaries   112

Appendix D: Status Differences among Teamsters   115

Part 3. Meaning

Editors' Epilogue   121

Editors' Conclusions   157

Notes   167

About the Editors   211

Index   213

Illustrations

1. Howard Roberts Lamar	x
2. Army bull train on the Overland Trail	1
3. Map of William Clark's travels, 1857	6
4. "Yoking a Wild Bull" by William Henry Jackson	15
5. William H. Russell, Alexander Majors, and William B. Waddell	20
6. Wagon master Chatham Ewing ("Chat") Rennick	23
7. "Grub Pile" by William Henry Jackson	29
8. "A Bull-Whacker" by Frederic Remington	34
9. "Yoking Up" by William Henry Jackson	41
10. Forts along the Oregon and Mormon trails	50
11. William Adams ("Bill") Hickman	70
12. Army bull train on the Great Plains	73
13. Bull whacker self-portrait by William Henry Jackson	79
14. The Center Plaza, Pueblo of Los Angeles	87
15. *Harper's Weekly* Mountain Meadows Massacre woodcut	95
16. Map of William Clark's travels, November 1857–January 1858	98
17. Bird's-eye view of Ames, Iowa, 1875	107
18. Grave marker for William Clark	113
19. "Bull Whacker" by Charles M. Russell	119
20. The Utah Expedition's march through Salt Lake City, June 26, 1858	125
21. Spanish Fork, Utah Territory	129
22. Lieutenant "Chat" Rennick, 1864	132
23. William Clark's mining paraphernalia	135
24. Corner of Main Street and Clark Avenue, Ames, Iowa	143
25. Newspaper ads for William Clark's Ames grocery store	146
26. Holograph manuscript of William Clark's "A Trip Across the Plains in 1857"	150
27. Utah Expedition supply wagons corral on the Great Plains	165

FIG. 1. Howard Roberts Lamar (1923–2023), Yale's president and Sterling Professor of History. He was a founder of the Western History Association and for decades an inspiration for students seeking to explore the American frontier with the preeminent teacher and mentor in the field. Courtesy Michael Marsland/Yale University.

Foreword

HOWARD R. LAMAR

Only a few of the overland trail accounts of the mid-nineteenth century are classics. What sets them apart from hundreds of others is their authors' perceptiveness, eye for colorful detail, and ability to transform trailside drudgery into a compelling narrative about the American West. William Clark's essay "A Trip Across the Plains in 1857" is one of the few such texts to emerge from the U.S. Army's Utah Expedition.

Who was this twenty-three-year-old who set out on a cross-country odyssey in the company of a very mixed bag of soldiers and camp followers? The character of the former ranged from lads destined to receive the Medal of Honor to deserters of the worst stripe. The civilians supporting them included Jim Bridger, the nation's premier frontier scout, as well as William C. Quantrill, a teamster, camp cook, and card sharp who would soon become the Civil War's most savage guerrilla.

Of William Clark, historians until now have known virtually nothing except his name and the high quality of his manuscript, a document published with scant explanation in the pages of an obscure journal a century ago. Now come William P. MacKinnon and Kenneth L. Alford, historians driven to present Clark's essay anew and provide answers. They succeed by furnishing perspective and context enabling twenty-first-century readers to appreciate the heroes, villains, and ordinary folk with whom Clark trekked to Utah Territory. Thanks to the collaboration of Alford and MacKinnon, we also have an unusual view of the Latter-day Saints as glimpsed by Clark while he was a prisoner of war and later a fugitive among assassins. As with the pages devoted to Clark's proximity to the army and its civilian teamsters, his view of Latter-day Saint society sweeps in a range of people and experiences including not only unspeakable violence but the courage of some church members to risk their own safety to protect Bill Clark and his traveling companions.

Foreword

If you are one of the few people who has encountered these reminiscences as first published in 1922, enjoy rereading them to appreciate who William Clark was and what he experienced. If you come to Clark's record for the first time, be prepared for an account of life on the overland trail and in Salt Lake City quite unlike any other. In the midst of killers, heroes-in-waiting, and American yeomen on both sides of the Utah War, you will see William Clark grapple with illness, thrive, mature, and develop an unusual ability to write. Along the way, watch for such Clark intimates as George B. Tuttle, a young teamster soon at odds with army provost marshals, and assistant wagon master Frank McCarthy, a tough hombre forced to fight his way out of a Fort Bridger gambling den at the cost of a dead infantryman. This was Bill Clark's world as he headed west.

We are indebted to Messrs. MacKinnon and Alford for surfacing Clark's narrative in a way that enables us to imagine it all.

Acknowledgments

Just as William Clark made his way west in 1857 with the help of comrades, the author-editors of this study have benefited from a great many kindnesses. In our case, assistance during our long trek to publication took the form of inspiration, apt suggestions, and tips for locating key documents and information. Our thanks to those who provided such help, but especially to the family members, professional colleagues, and organizations acknowledged below.

Chief among these benefactors was the late Howard Roberts Lamar, who in his ninety-ninth year provided the foreword for this study. It is perhaps the last such piece he wrote, and we deeply appreciate his willingness to share thoughts about William Clark's story while encouraging its republication. Both of us have long admired Howard's ability to explore the American West and lead a great university; one of us was fortunate to have him as mentor, teacher, and friend since 1958. When Professor Lamar died on February 22, 2023, he was reading the biography of a nineteenth-century western photographer. It was a selection reflecting not only his still-formidable intellect but also his commitment to the field in which he had labored so effectively since the mid-1940s.[1]

Many of the professionals acknowledged below helped us to improve pieces of what became this book. However, Richard E. Turley Jr. of Farmington, Utah, went the extra mile in reading the entire manuscript and offering suggestions based on his deep understanding of territorial Utah and his long run as assistant historian of the Church of Jesus Christ of Latter-day Saints. We are grateful for the way he brought his unique competence to bear on our behalf.

Among those who led us to a better understanding of William Clark's traveling companions and their postwar fate was genealogist-historian Ardis E. Parshall of Salt Lake City. Similarly, the late Curtis R. Allen of Centerville, Utah, shed light on the struggles of Clark's "chum" George B. Tuttle to extract his brother Ira O. Tuttle from his onerous enlistment

Acknowledgments

in the Utah Expedition's Second U.S. Dragoons. Key biographical information about Clark himself and his wife, Cora, came from the Ames, Iowa, newspapers of the early twentieth century; Alex Fejfar, exhibits manager of the Ames Historical Museum, led us to these unexploited sources. In the city administration of Ames, our thanks go to Mayor John Haila and public information officer Susan Gwiasda for their help in obtaining a photograph of the street sign for Clark Avenue, the Ames thoroughfare named in honor of the subject of this book. Images of William Clark's gold scales were obtained with the assistance of Jodi Evans, registrar, and Kay Coats, collection coordinator, at the State Historical Society of Iowa. Eric A. Grunwald and Dan Morford provided fast and helpful assistance with additional images from the Scotts Bluff National Monument.

With respect to understanding the migration of William Clark's manuscript from his family to the editor of the *Iowa Journal of History and Politics*, we are indebted to Susan K. Harris, regent of the Sundial-Solomon Dean Chapter of the Daughters of the American Revolution in Ames. It was this organization that purchased William's reminiscences from his widow in 1920 and then donated them to the State Historical Society of Iowa for eventual publication. The society's registrar in Iowa City, Jodi Evans, provided us with information about the manuscript's current location and fragile condition. When we serendipitously discovered that a heretofore unknown holograph variant of the manuscript was held by Texas A&M University's Cushing Memorial Library, College Station, curator Anton DuPlessis and library specialist Vaprrenon Severs of that repository went the extra mile to help us examine it and study its provenance.

In terms of our own manuscript, we acknowledge the guidance and support of W. Clark Whitehorn, the University of Nebraska Press's executive editor, for his key role in transforming our years of research and writing into a book worthy of William Clark's reminiscences. Charles E. Rankin of Helena, Montana, first suggested editor Whitehorn and Nebraska as receptive "midwives" for this process. He has our thanks for doing so, as well as for his support for our earlier books with another publisher. For crafting an index that makes *On the Overland Trails with*

Acknowledgments

William Clark a more readily useful study, we are indebted to Galen Schroeder of Fargo, North Dakota, a consummate professional of the front rank.

Our thanks also to Nguyen Hang, reference librarian of the State Historical Society of Iowa's museum in Des Moines for images of the scales and poke William Clark took to California and back to weigh and transport gold dust. That Clark carried this equipment across the Great Plains, Rockies, Great Basin, and Mojave Desert in the midst of a military campaign speaks volumes about his optimism and tenacity in pursuit of an El Dorado on the Pacific Coast.

We appreciate the efforts of Elayna Smith and Tiea Paschal, student research assistants at Brigham Young University, Provo, who performed a variety of tasks contributing to the final result, and Beverly Yellowhorse, manager of BYU's Religious Education Faculty Support Center.

Finally, we acknowledge with gratitude the role of the late Sherilee B. Alford and Patricia H. MacKinnon, our wives, in making this study possible. Sherilee did not live to see William Clark's manuscript republished, but, as she endured the final phase of a long illness, she knew the nature of our plans and offered thoughts, perspective, and exemplary courage more helpful than she probably realized. Pat MacKinnon, one of Sherilee's admirers, provided her own wisdom along the way, as she has done for all our historical collaborations. Our cup runneth over.

On the Overland Trails
with William Clark

PART 1

Understandings

FIG. 2. Army bull train (probably RM&W's) in motion on the Overland Trail, 1858. *Frank Leslie's Illustrated Newspaper*, January 8, 1859.

Editors' Introduction

Readers have easy access to a mountain of published trail stories from California's gold rushers, but there are relatively few available accounts of their younger brothers' adventures with the U.S. Army's Utah Expedition a decade later. On the eve of the Civil War, these lads marched toward Salt Lake City as soldiers or civilian teamsters, mule skinners, bull whackers, and drovers. With five thousand troops under orders for Utah Territory during 1857–1858, supported by thousands of camp followers, there should be a plethora of material describing their trail experiences. That there is not reflects a national amnesia about the Utah War, compounded by Americans' understandable preoccupation with the Civil War soon to follow.

To address the gap, this book surfaces and republishes one of the very best such accounts—the reminiscences of William Clark, a young teamster hired by the firm of Russell, Majors and Waddell, the West's greatest freighters. Decades later, Clark assembled his trail notes, consulted his memory, and wrote a narrative he titled "A Trip Across the Plains in 1857." In 1922 the *Iowa Journal of History and Politics* published this manuscript posthumously. With a tiny print run and few technologies for reproduction, the article's availability was long limited to university libraries and a few historical societies. Even with the relatively recent boon of the internet, "A Trip Across the Plains in 1857" remains difficult to find; its title lacks key search terms like "Mormons," "teamster," and "Utah Expedition." Searching electronically for the author's name tends to lead researchers not to our man but rather to the more famous Capt. William Clark of the Lewis and Clark Expedition. For one hundred years, then, this has been a valuable but obscure document—one hiding in plain sight but practically inaccessible except to the most enterprising chroniclers of the overland trails and Utah War.

While working to make Clark's essay available to a broader readership, we have also aimed to improve its relevance by providing material entirely missing from the original printing: an explanation of the Utah

War's origins and prosecution; maps to chart Clark's travels; illustrations to enliven major players; and annotations to clarify the sometimes arcane people, places, incidents, and issues mentioned. Also included for the first time is an account of the manuscript's colorful provenance.

Why read William Clark's reminiscences? The short answer is perspective and pleasure. There is no other primary source that provides an up-close view of such colorful western characters as William Adams ("Bill") Hickman, one of Brigham Young's "b'hoys" and among Utah's most brutal gunmen, and Chatham E. ("Chat") Rennick, Clark's wagon master and soon lieutenant to William C. Quantrill, not only a Utah War participant but the Confederacy's most notorious guerrilla.

By the same token, Clark provides a near-unique account of the non-Mormon prisoners held by the Nauvoo Legion at mountain bivouacs and in Salt Lake City. Finally, we note that Clark's reminiscences also include one of the few credible firsthand descriptions of the killing field at Mountain Meadows in southern Utah. He crossed this site three months after the unprecedented atrocity there of September 11, 1857, a reminder to readers that the Utah War was hardly bloodless and that Clark's travels swept in not only the Great Plains of his title but the Rockies, Great Basin, and Mojave Desert as well.

Clark presents this information through an engaging style that ranks with the most appealing of the reminiscences written by other fluent military and civilian veterans of the Utah War who trekked west.[1] His narrative, like theirs, is a pleasure to read, with insights and observations that go far beyond the typical trail diarist's preoccupations with the availability of water, wood, grass, and safe river crossings.[2]

Inexplicably, when the editor of the *Iowa Journal of History and Politics*, Benjamin Franklin Shambaugh, published Clark's reminiscences, he left readers at sea as to who Clark was. Other than stating his name, year of death, and identity as a short-time mayor of Ames, Iowa, Shambaugh chose not to explain anything else about Clark's background. And so for one hundred years there has been no understanding of when and where Clark was born, whether he married and served in the Civil War, and what he did for a living and where during the sixty-two years after his flight from Utah to California while running a gauntlet of hostile tribes and Anglo assassins. In 1922 this information would have been easily available from Clark's surviving family, then living in Iowa, but for unknown reasons the original editor chose not to pursue this source. By adding such information here, we hope to provide context by which modern readers can appreciate Clark's extraordinary adventures in a way not previously possible.

A man who went to such effort in old age to create an invaluable trail narrative and insider's view of the Utah War deserves rescue from further neglect. As explorers of the American past, we need William Clark's help to enrich our own trek west.

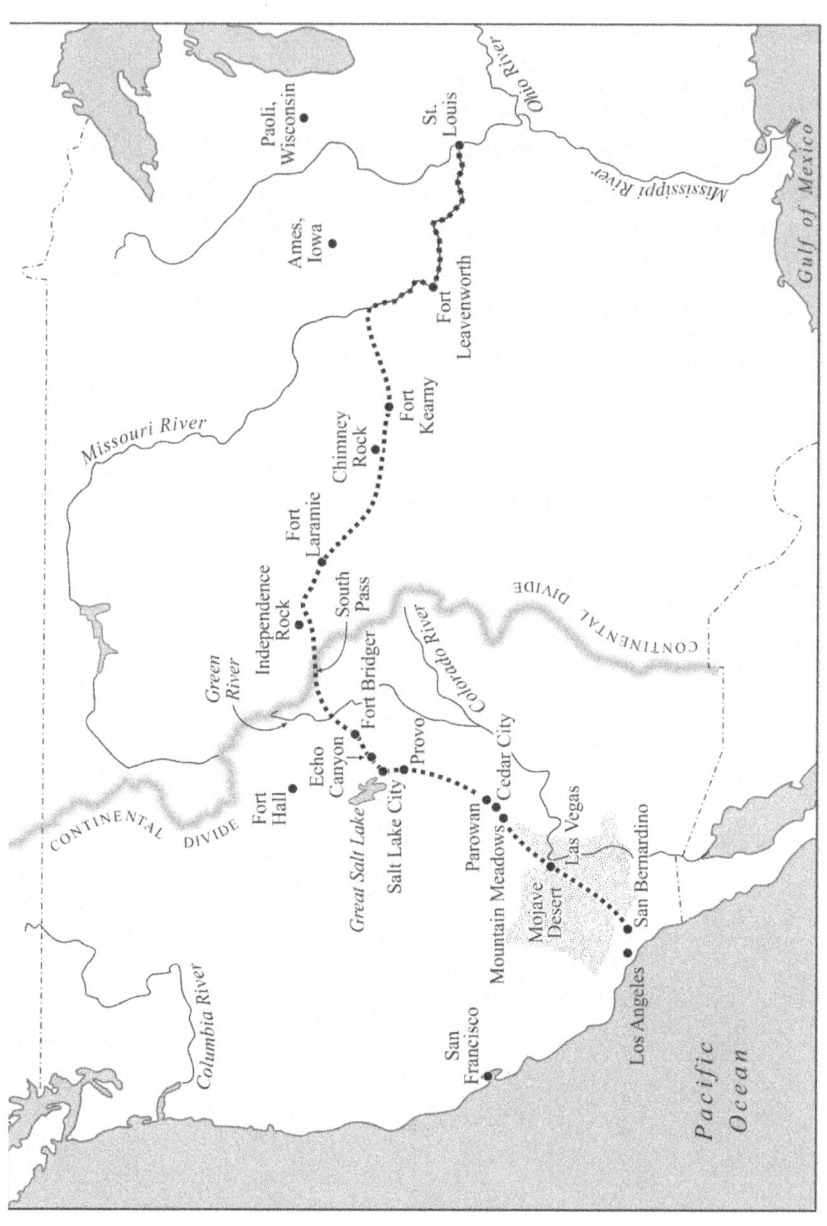

FIG. 3. William Clark's travels, St. Louis to Salt Lake City, summer–fall 1857. Created by Mary Lee Eggart, Baton Rouge.

Editorial Decisions

Confronted by a long manuscript unbroken by chapters and lightly edited, we set out to make William Clark's story more useful to modern readers. We did so by dividing what he wrote into thirteen chapter-like subsections, to which we gave appropriate titles. We also replaced many of the original footnotes with new references to the best scholarship of the intervening one hundred years, while adding a substantial number of new notes about the people, places, and issues Clark mentioned but about which the original editor was silent.

A good example of such new information would be the background of "Chat" Rennick, the wagon master under whom Clark and his chums labored over twelve hundred miles of trail. Only now can readers realize that Rennick went on to become one of the most notorious Confederate guerrillas of the Civil War. It is understandable that Bill Clark did not anticipate his boss's destiny, but there is no reason for his editors then and now to deprive readers of an awareness of Rennick's reputation. Before leaving Clark's wagon master, we should note Clark consistently spelled Chat's last name as "Rennick." While "Renick" more frequently appears in the U.S. Census and other records, the editors have chosen to follow Clark's usage.

Beyond the relatively brief information appropriate for footnotes, we have provided more substantial context for some of the characters, events, and circumstances appearing in Clark's story. Such editorial comments take the form of italicized introductory paragraphs at the beginning of each of the book's thirteen subsections. Our hope is that such material will better enable readers to enjoy and appreciate Clark's work.

A few other editorial decisions warrant mention. One such judgment runs to how best to describe the Church of Jesus Christ of Latter-day Saints and its members. "Mormon" is a long-standing nickname derived from the title of one of the religion's principal scriptures, the Book of Mormon. During much of the nineteenth century, the church's leaders chafed under this term, often writing it in quotes to signify their discomfort with this informality and undue familiarity. Several years ago, in order to strengthen its identity as a Christian organization, the church's leadership decided that the use of "Mormon" was to be discouraged and that the organization's formal name was the preferred form of address. The somewhat slangy term "LDS" was also to be avoided. Accordingly, outside of Clark's original text, "Latter-day Saint" is used in place of Mormon or LDS whenever appropriate. Conversely, because of its sometimes pejorative flavor, we have also chosen to avoid using "Gentile," the old term in Utah for nonmembers (even Jewish ones). The current editors—one a Latter-day Saint and the other Presbyterian—jointly view these decisions as a matter of respect for our readers and their religious affiliations, if any, rather than a matter of "political correctness."

One other quite different matter of terminology should be explained. In the hierarchy of the overland trails' job titles, William Clark was technically a "bull whacker," by virtue of his assignment to move wagons powered by yoked oxen. (Similarly, his peers driving mule teams were dubbed "mule skinners.") Probably because of bull whackers' image as rough, dirty, and profane men working in the bottom regions of the freighting world, Clark eschewed calling himself what he was. Instead he opted for the more socially acceptable job title "teamster."[1] To honor his preference and use a label more familiar to modern readers, the descriptor "teamster" appears throughout this study, including its title.

In addition, we have followed the practice of the U.S. Geological Survey and State of Wyoming in spelling the names of rivers and streams without the traditional apostrophe. Accordingly, tributaries of the Green River are presented as Blacks Fork and Smiths Fork.

Writing when he did, Clark identified Albert Sidney Johnston as a "general" throughout his reminiscences, which would have been natural for the times. Johnston was a Confederate general when he died at the battle of Shiloh on April 6, 1862. As the senior officer—North or South—killed during the Civil War, Johnston would have been well-known to most of Clark's readers in 1922. The fact, though, is that during most of the Utah War Johnston was a colonel in the U.S. Army. It was only when he signed his new oath of office at Camp

Scott, Utah, in April 1858, that he became a brevet brigadier general, with promotion from colonel retroactive to the previous November. To avoid confusion, we—like Clark—have chosen to refer to Johnston as "general" throughout this book.

It should also be noted that in editing the concluding portion of Clark's reminiscences dealing with his passage through the desert just east of Las Vegas during December 1857, we extracted the several paragraphs dealing with the story of one of the Pomeroy brothers' mishaps and moved it to a new section we designated appendix A. We did so because essentially this material was a distracting digression dealing not with Clark's own experiences but rather with a tale he later heard secondhand in California from former mail carrier C. L. Kingston. This material was worth retaining, but not in its original location in Clark's manuscript.

Perhaps the most interesting editorial decision to be made came near the end of our work with the surprising, serendipitous discovery that in the fall of 1915 William Clark gave a complete holograph copy of his manuscript to the editor of Ames's *Evening Times*. This newspaper proceeded to publish it unmodified, in installments appearing in twelve successive issues during November and December. The text of this version is verbatim to the one that appeared seven years later as an article in the *Iowa Journal of History and Politics* without reference to its earlier appearance in the *Evening Times*.

What to do with such a discovery? In the end, we chose to note the existence of the 1915 variant and to publish in our epilogue section the brief introductory material provided by the editor of the *Evening Times*. In effect, in editing and republishing this manuscript as *On the Overland Trails with William Clark*, we have worked from the 1922 version, using, where warranted, the footnotes that appeared in the *Iowa Journal of History and Politics* plus additions of our own. A more complete discussion of the provenance for these variants (and that currently held by Texas A&M University) appears in the "Editors' Epilogue."

Finally, we note that for purposes of brevity and simplicity, this volume does not contain a bibliography. Our belief is that since William

Clark's manuscript is autobiographical rather than a narrative history, the array of new footnotes provides ample information about the monographs, journal articles, and manuscript materials used to bring his reminiscences alive for twenty-first-century readers. The book's new, comprehensive index should also be helpful.

Background and Context
The Utah War

In brief, the conflict involved the armed confrontation over power and authority between the civil-religious hierarchy of Utah Territory led by Governor Brigham Young, president of the Church of Jesus Christ of Latter-day Saints, and the administration of President James Buchanan.[1] In the spring of 1857, soon after his inauguration, Buchanan perceived rebellion and set out to restore federal authority in the territory by replacing Young as governor and installing a successor to be escorted west by a large army expeditionary force. It was a change Young contested through his Nauvoo Legion and the use of hit-and-run guerrilla tactics. The result was a conflict that brought not only casualties but federal treason indictments for Young and hundreds of other Latter-day Saints. For the former governor and a few others, there would also be indictments for murder. With tens of thousands of troops and camp followers involved, including William Clark, it was the nation's most extensive and expensive military undertaking during the period between the Mexican-American and Civil Wars.

At the heart of the conflict was the disconnect between the two leaders' radically different philosophies of governance. Young viewed Utah as a millennially focused theocracy operating under his prophetic, authoritarian leadership. The U.S. government saw Utah as one among multiple federal territories intended to function under republican principles and, until statehood, as a ward of Congress through a federally sworn governor appointed by the president, confirmed by the Senate, and supervised by the U.S. secretary of state.

The war did not well up abruptly in the spring of 1857 because of a single critical incident. Instead, it arose from ten years of accumulated issues, with Utah-federal relations steadily deteriorating after the Latter-day Saints' 1847 arrival in the Salt Lake Valley, then a part of Mexican

Understandings

Alta California, after they had endured persecution in Illinois, Missouri, and elsewhere. A failed attempt by President Franklin Pierce to replace Young as governor during 1854–55 was emblematic of both the growing tensions involved and the fecklessness of Buchanan's predecessors in dealing with them.

By the time of Buchanan's inauguration on March 4, 1857, virtually every area of contact between Utahns and the U.S. government had become a contest of wills. Conflicts that arose over administration of departmental matters such as mail service were aggravated by public uproar over three emotional issues: the church's official acknowledgement of polygamy in 1852 after years of denial, the new Republican Party's adoption of an antipolygamy presidential platform plank in 1856, and perceptions that Brigham Young was seeking independence outside the Union while arranging antifederal alliances with multiple Indian tribes. The latter issue was especially volatile because of the potential for bloodshed and blockage of the transcontinental emigration trails to the Pacific Coast, compounded by the fact that Young had long doubled as Utah's U.S. superintendent of Indian affairs.

The catalyst for President Buchanan's decision-making at the end of March 1857 was a series of complaints by Utah's federal appointees, virtually all of whom (except Brigham Young) would flee the territory in early April. Theirs was the second such exodus in five years. These officials portrayed Utah as a violent territory led by a disloyal, out-of-control governor prone to incendiary rhetoric disrespectful of the U.S. government. In the Latter-day Saint view, such provocative language from their civil and religious leader was simply an assertion of Utah's constitutional rights in the face of congressional and executive branch behavior perceived in the Great Basin as colonial, corrupt, and ineffective.

Because of enduring controversies enveloping the Utah War's historiography, understanding what the conflict *was not* is important to grasping what it *was*. Despite Latter-day Saint complaints of religious persecution, the Utah War was not a federal attack on the Church of Jesus Christ of Latter-day Saints or its religious tenets. As unpopular as the polygamy issue was across the country, in 1857 there was no U.S.

statute barring the practice of plural marriage. For a lawyerly James Buchanan, the issue in Utah was the need to restore federal authority, not the eradication of polygamy or its practitioners. His orders to Gen. Albert Sidney Johnston, commander of the Utah Expedition, and the new governor, Alfred Cumming of Georgia, reflected this emphasis.

If the Utah War was not a religious crusade, neither was it "bloodless." Such a trivialization obscured the enormity of the September 11, 1857, Mountain Meadows Massacre; it was an atrocity in which Nauvoo Legionnaires and their Southern Paiute auxiliaries disarmed and killed about 120 Arkansans emigrating to California through southern Utah, one of the greatest blood-lettings of the entire American overland trails experience. This atrocity plus a plethora of smaller-scale killings produced casualties roughly equivalent to those occurring in the same years in the territory's eastern neighbor, dubbed "Bleeding Kansas."

Four days after the tragedy at Mountain Meadows, Brigham Young proclaimed martial law, an illegal decree that barred civilians and the U.S. Army from entering, crossing, or even leaving Utah Territory without his authorization. News of this draconian move and shock over the massacre interrupted migration to California and Oregon, an intolerable problem for a westering nation accustomed to the freedom of unrestricted travel.

In mid-October Brigham Young issued secret orders to the Nauvoo Legion authorizing the use of lethal force against the Utah Expedition if it moved west of Fort Bridger toward the Salt Lake Valley. With this escalation, which followed the appalling loss of life at Mountain Meadows, the destructive raids on the U.S. Army's livestock and supply trains, and the imposition of martial law, Brigham Young crossed a Rubicon in the fall of 1857. By so doing, in the eyes of federal officials he changed the character of his dispute with the U.S. government from a series of nasty provocations to armed rebellion.

During the third week of November, the Utah Expedition reached Blacks Fork of the Green River after crossing the Continental Divide at South Pass and enduring Latter-day Saint attacks, agonizing cold, blizzards, and a massive loss of beef cattle and draught animals. There, near the ruins of Fort Bridger, a civilian trading post burned by the

Nauvoo Legion in October, Albert Sidney Johnston concluded that he could not force the snow-clogged mountain passes into the Salt Lake Valley only 113 miles to the southwest. At an altitude of seven thousand feet above sea level, he took his exhausted command into winter quarters, designating the vast cantonment he established as Camp Scott in honor of the army's general in chief. Here, William Clark and his chums elected to be paid off by Russell, Majors and Waddell and set off in the snowy wilderness, first for Salt Lake City and then California.

PART 2

William Clark's Edited Reminiscences ("A Trip Across the Plains in 1857")

FIG. 4. "Yoking a Wild Bull" by William Henry Jackson (1843–1942), 1866. Here Jackson depicts the bruising ordeal of all new bull whackers in the corrals of RM&W outside Fort Leavenworth, an initiation Jackson underwent nine years after Clark's. Alexander Majors claimed these teamsters, once seasoned, could catch and yoke their oxen in sixteen minutes. Drawing by Jackson, courtesy Scotts Bluff [Nebraska] National Monument.

SECTION 1

"We Had an Eye on California"

Signing On, Starting Out

Editorial Notes

These are the reminiscences of William Clark, who was born to Samuel and Anna Clark on April 26, 1834, in Java, Wyoming County, New York, an agricultural community just southeast of Buffalo. William was one of seven children and the second of five sons enumerated in the 1850 census.[1] *As such, he was unlikely to inherit the family farm. This circumstance, or any number of other factors, may have prompted him to leave home in the mid-1850s to strike out on his own soon after he came of age. In the aftermath of the Mexican War and the discovery of gold in California, Bill Clark joined tens of thousands of other young Americans moving westward along the country's roads and rivers.*

Because only one photograph of Clark has surfaced, and that taken in old age, we have no idea as to his physical appearance in the late 1850s, although in one autobiographical snippet he revealed that he was tall (6'1"). While trekking west—probably during 1856—Clark stopped in southern Wisconsin near the new hamlet of Paoli. There he found work with Pliny Clark (no relation), a Vermonter who had homesteaded eighty acres in 1848. During an extended stay with farmer Clark and his herd of Spanish Merino sheep, Morgan horses, and Durham cattle, William Clark honed his skills at handling animals. He also began a friendship with his prosperous employer's daughter, Corphelia Jane ("Cora") Clark, a girl twelve years his junior. When the subject of romance arose, Cora's father suggested William seek his fortune elsewhere and return to press his suit when she was of marriageable age. Accordingly, Bill Clark again headed west, this time bound for gold rush California. Neither Clark's reminiscences nor his first editor mentioned this background, although early in the twentieth century an Iowa newspaper reporter with an eye for a good story captured the outline of the prolonged cross-country Bill-Cora courtship.[2]

Because of the way Clark began his manuscript, some readers may conclude he was a native of Freeport, a town in northern Illinois near the Wisconsin border, although, as discussed above, he was an upstate New Yorker. This was not a casual mistake. Throughout Clark's telling of this story in the twentieth century, he left people with the misimpression he was from Freeport.

Similarly, the manuscript leads readers to believe that the three lads Bill Clark befriended in St. Louis—Edwin Leach, George B. Tuttle, and Martin L. Sherwood—were from Peoria, Illinois, and Oshkosh, Wisconsin. In fact, census enumerations and obituaries indicate that these young men had more complex backgrounds than that. Leach was a native of Sherman, Fairfield County, Connecticut, who subsequently moved to Illinois with his parents, probably to a farm near Carlyle, Clinton County, rather than Peoria. Tuttle was a native of Wayland, Steuben County in upstate New York; since 1851 had lived with his parents and siblings in Ripon, Fond du Lac County, Wisconsin. Sherwood's roots remain a mystery. That Clark misidentified their hometowns and sometimes mangled Tuttle's middle name reflects the likelihood that he was writing from memory decades after the Utah War. Alternately, these young travelers may have deliberately obscured the details of their backgrounds from Clark and others, as many gold rushers assumed aliases. Their behavior was so common that it spawned a song popular in California saloons and mining camps throughout the 1850s: "Say, What Was Your Name in the States?"[3]

If Clark's account of this foursome's origins was opaque or misleading, his description of their entrée to the freighting firm of Russell, Majors and Waddell near Fort Leavenworth, Kansas Territory, was highly accurate. And so Clark shares his revulsion over the poor quality of meals provided and the bruising experience of breaking the company's untrained cattle to the yoke. In this and many other ways, Clark's record tracked with accounts left by Utah Expedition teamsters and drovers who preceded and followed him on the overland trail. Also credible was the animosity Clark recorded between "Yankees" like him and those of the Russell firm's teamsters with Southern sympathies—the so-called Missouri pukes. With sectional animosities over race, culture, and politics this intense, small wonder that the Civil

War erupted less than four years later and was at its most violent along the Kansas-Missouri frontier. It was a region in which former Utah Expedition camp followers—Bill Clark's peers—campaigned as guerrillas, riding rough shod over the civilian population.[4]

A TRIP ACROSS THE PLAINS IN 1857
by William Clark

[ORIGINAL 1922 NOTE:[5] This account of a trip to Salt Lake City and California was written by William Clark, originally in the form of notes made during the journey. Years later these notes were rewritten and the original scraps of paper were destroyed. The footnotes have been added by the editor, and occasional alterations have been made in capitalization and in the spelling of words and place names. The manuscript was secured and presented to the Society by Mrs. Louis Bernard Schmidt of Ames, Iowa. Mr. Clark died in February, 1920, in Ames, Iowa. He had been twice Mayor of that city. —THE EDITOR][6]

I started from Freeport, Ill., about the middle of June for St. Louis, Mo., not knowing where I would finally make a stop for any length of time, as I was undecided what I would do. The first night in St. Louis, by chance, I fell in company with three young men: one from Peoria, Ill., by the name of Edwin Leach, a bright young man of about twenty-one years of age, and George Tuttle and Martin Sherwood from Oshkosh, Wis. These two were chums and had come down the Mississippi from the pinery on a raft and were very agreeable young men.[7] We started together to "take in" the city. In the morning we strolled along the levee and went aboard several boats—one soon to start up river to Leavenworth City.[8]

It was suggested by some one that we all go up to Leavenworth on this boat, which was agreed to at once, and we gathered up our baggage, got aboard of her, and paid our fare to Leavenworth.

On this boat were bills posted stating that Majors, Russel & Waddel [sic] wanted several hundred young men to drive ox teams across the

FIG. 5. Partners in Russell, Majors and Waddell, Clark's employer and the West's greatest freighting company. All Missourians with years of experience on the Great Plains, they were l. to r. William H. Russell (finances and contracting), Alexander Majors (operations), and William B. Waddell (office). In the early 1860s Russell plunged the firm into bankruptcy through ruinous financing arrangements and an overextension of operations. Photo from Raymond W. Settle and Mary Lund Settle, *Empire on Wheels*.

plains to Utah, and would pay $30 per month for the round trip or $40 and take our discharge at Salt Lake City.[9]

We all concluded we would hire out to them and make the trip.

After landing in Leavenworth, we disposed of our luggage and started out to get what information we could in regard to the trip we were about to undertake.

We learned that the government was going to establish three military posts in Utah Territory and that Majors, Russel & Waddel had a large contract to deliver their beef cattle and soldiers' supplies to these posts.[10] That Col. Vanvliet had gone on ahead with an escort of twenty men to hunt out and locate them and be ready to receive the soldiers and supplies when they arrived;[11] and that Majors, Russel & Waddel's contract would require twenty-six trains of twenty-six wagons each and require six yoke of cattle to each wagon. The cattle were nearly all wild steers, four and five years old and each team would be allowed only two yoke of gentle cattle. The men would have to load their own trains, would have to stand guard half of every other night, and do their own cooking; and it was rumored that we would be made to drive Sundays. We concluded to go to one of the contractors, William Russel [*sic*], to make our bargain, and not trust to an agent. We made our bargain with him and enrolled ourselves for the trip, with the express understanding that we should not be asked to drive Sundays, unless for the want of grass or water. We pledged ourselves together to stand by our bargain, and not to be run over by our train boss, as we had learned that they would undertake to force us when out on the plains, so as to make extra time and give them notoriety for making a quick trip.

We learned that most of the men, or teamsters, and all of the train bosses were southern men and most of them were hired in the south to come to Kansas to drive the free state people from the polls and carry the election in the interest of slavery. Most of the teamsters in our train had their expenses paid and were armed, and some paid as high as one hundred and sixty dollars in cash for this purpose. This was shortly after the Jim Lane trouble in Kansas, so there was not the best of feeling between themselves and the "Yanks" as they called us.[12]

It was, I think, about the 24th of June [1857] that we commenced our work of loading our wagons for the trip. Our loading was done at the Fort, a short distance out. We carried one hundred pound sacks of bacon, sugar, and rice and loaded up the wagons. When night came, we were a dirty greasy looking set of "tender feet" as we had handled one hundred pound sacks all day on the run for we worked as though every thing had to be done in one day. In the morning we got up sore and lame from our work the day before, as we had not been used to work for some time. But they sent us to the corral to help brand a lot of cattle. After the *buccaro* had roped the cattle we would have to help hold them to be branded with a hot iron used for that purpose.[13] It was no easy job, as we were jerked about unmercifully which did not help to rest us much.

We ate our meals at the outfit house—bacon, saleratus bread, and stewed apples, all cooked by a man who, I do not think, ever cooked many meals before and did not care whether he ever cooked many more.[14]

The next day was Sunday, and we were to start on our trip Monday [June 29, 1857].

We were a sick and sore set of fellows, but determined not to give up the trip before us, as we had an eye on California.[15]

We passed the day as best we could, getting things ready to take with us. As we were not allowed to take our trunks, we concluded to take what clothing we needed in a grain sack. I sent my trunk with my best clothes to an uncle at Lawrence, Kan., to care for till I called for them, which I did ten years later.[16]

We went to bed at the outfit house and Monday morning at three o'clock, they called two of us to get up and go to the Company's store to get our guns and blankets that the Company furnished and charged to us, as every man had to be armed with a rifle at least.[17]

We all four got up but the boss said they needed only two of us. We told him we all went in that train or none of us went, as that was our bargain with Russel. So when they found we were determined, they gave in.

Then we were taken in a wagon four miles out to Salt Creek, from which place we were to start. We got there at day break.

Our cattle were soon driven into corral for us to yoke.[18] Our train crew [consisted of] of a wagon boss, by the name of Chatham Rennick—a big, six foot two inch man, an assistant wagon boss [Frank McCarthy], twenty-six teamsters, and two extra hands, making thirty men in all. But we had ten extra men to help us get the train started.

We went into the corral with three lasso ropes to catch our cattle and fasten them to a wagon wheel to put their yokes on, as they were so wild it was the only way we could get them yoked. We would then chain this one to a wheel till we got another and so on till each team [of two oxen] was yoked. Then to get them hitched to a wagon tongue was another big job, but at two o'clock in the afternoon we succeeded in getting them all hitched on and started to break corral, and a lively time we had.[19] Now the fun began, not for the teamsters, but for the lookers on. It was life [dangerous] work for us to keep our wagons right side up. Twenty-six teams of nearly all wild cattle going in every direction—three hundred and twelve head of crazy steers pitching and bellowing and trying to get loose or get away from the wagon, and teamsters working for dear life to herd them and keep from upsetting or breaking their wagons; and every now and then a wagon upsetting, tongues breaking, and teams getting loose on the prairie.

FIG. 6. Wagon master Chatham Ewing ("Chat") Rennick (1827–1865). William Clark's bull train boss photographed early in the Civil War, probably when a sergeant in Company C, Third Battalion of a pro-Confederate Missouri militia unit. At age thirty, Rennick had been to California and would have been considerably older than William Clark or the other teamsters in his train. Photo from Watson and Brantley's 2008 book *Confederate Guerrilla Sue Mundy: A Biography of Kentucky Soldier Jerome Clark.*

It kept every extra man on the jump to keep the cattle moving in the right direction.[20]

Fourteen men on horseback and twenty-six teamsters had a lively experience that afternoon and evening, and finally, at nine o'clock that night had succeeded in getting nine wagons two miles from starting point and getting the cattle loose from the wagons in a demoralized condition. Some of the teams had one or two steers loose from the yoke, and the others were dragging the yokes. Everything was in confusion.

The rest of the train was strung over the prairie—some wagons tipped over, some with broken wheels, and some with the tongues broken; and, in fact, were in rather bad condition for a journey of twelve hundred miles in a wilderness.

The men had had nothing to eat since four o'clock in the morning, and were all nearly played out; but we went to work to get some "grub," as we called it, to stay our stomachs. I could hardly wait for it to be cooked. I found a settler that lived close to where we were and asked him to bring me some milk and bread for which I gladly paid him, and we four chums made our supper of bread and milk.

We were ordered on guard the first part of the night. Chat Rennick, our wagon boss, stationed each man on guard. It fell my lot to go down the valley and keep the cattle from a piece of timber. Tuttle was stationed on the west to keep them from going over the hill, and was furnished a mule to ride, as his beat was considered to be the hardest. Ed Leach on the east near the wagon[s] and Mart Sherwood on the north had little to do, as the cattle were determined to go to the timber or over the hill.

It kept me on the run as hard as I could to keep them from the timber, and Tuttle was worked equally hard to keep them in from the west.

About midnight Tuttle came over on the run as fast as his mule could go, met me, and turned back on the jump up the hill, and his saddle girth broke and let him off, saddle and all.[21] His mule got away and ran off and he had to take [after] it on foot. We both worked as hard as we could to keep the cattle until our relief came, which did not come till two o'clock in the morning. As the men did not go to bed till about eleven o'clock that night, the boss concluded he would divide the time with us.

When Rennick came with the men to relieve us, I had just reached the spot where Tuttle's saddle lay, and I was so exhausted and completely tired out, that I fell to the ground, and dropped to sleep in a moment. It was with difficulty that Rennick and Tuttle could awaken me and get me to the wagon to bed, as I would drop as soon as they let go of me. I would beg of them to let me sleep where I was, but they got me to camp, and I knew no more till seven or eight in the morning.

This was a fine morning, and Rennick had sent back to Leavenworth for more wagons, wheels, tongues, etc. to repair what was broken the day before, and also a lot of teamsters as over half of his men had skipped out, and left only eight or ten out of twenty-six teamsters.

Those of us who were on guard the night before were allowed to take it easy that day and rest up.

Rennick succeeded in getting more men and extra help, and gathered up the balance of the train and got it up to camp that night and ready for another start.

The next morning we commenced another day's work and succeeded in getting four miles that day and getting all the wagons into camp; although several wagons had been upset and [there were] some breakages. But we were prepared with several extra wagon tongues and some other repairs and a kit of tools to mend any ordinary breakage.

We pulled out the next morning and worked hard all day with the usual mishaps, and made five or six miles, and, in six days we reached Grasshopper, forty miles from Leavenworth.[22] There was not a day without some mishaps or breakages.

The next day was Sunday, and, I think, the Fourth of July.[23]

After breakfast, we changed our clothes, cleaned up, and washed our clothes, and were lying around to rest ourselves as best we could, after our hard week[']s work, as we were nearly worn out, when the boss concluded it was "time to hitch up" and snake a short drive.[24] We four Yanks told him the rest could drive if they wished but that we would not. We had done enough for one week.

The rest seemed willing to go, but, as we would not, he did not urge very hard.

That day I ate my first frogs' legs. "Old man" Clark from Cape Jerdo, was in our mess.[25] He was fond of fried frogs' legs and he caught and cooked some, and gave me some, but I can not say that I liked them very much; although they are considered a very choice dish by some people.[26] But I had not much of an appetite then for any thing that was in reach, for the overwork and poor "grub" began to tell on me, as I was not used to the kind of food we had—bacon, saleratus bread, boiled rice, and dried apples. As none of us were cooks, we would take turns in cooking. Our bread would be black and solid, not fit to eat. I began to get so I could not eat half a meal.

We rested all that day and in the morning made another start and drove all day with but one or two upsets and a broken tongue or two.

We went on with the usual mishaps all of that week and camped Saturday night on the Big Blue [River], near where Crete, Neb., now stands.[27]

We had fine weather all the week and we traveled over a beautiful country, mostly prairie with an occasional belt of timber along the streams, and now and then a claim shanty which was a welcome sight along these prairies.[28]

SECTION 2

"I Was Starving with a Train Loaded with Provisions"

Sick unto Death

Editorial Notes

Although accustomed to handling his oxen ("the cattle") by years of farm work, Clark had great difficulty coping with bad water along the trail and the unappealing food prepared by his unskilled mess-mates from the flour, bacon, and coffee provided by Russell, Majors and Waddell. Without women or experienced cooks in the train, Clark was traveling with a group quite different in demography and skills from most of the family-intensive emigrant trains around him. It was an adjustment—one that nearly killed him—that dominates this section, together with harbingers of trouble from his pro-slavery, Southern-oriented peers and their wagon boss, Chat Rennick. Aside from these sectional tensions, Clark also provides an early glimpse of what would become a major conflict further along the trail, the issue of whether the train and its teamsters would work on Sundays.

The shanties were particularly welcome to me for I was starving with a train loaded with provisions, such as they were; but I had got so that the sight of this kind of food was sickening to me. It was with the greatest difficulty that I could swallow any thing except a little coffee, and my chums would go a mile to get me a little milk, sweet or sour, as that was all we could find that I could relish. Any-thing we did not have I craved, but what we had to eat my stomach revolted at sight of, and I had become very weak, so much so that my chums would yoke my oxen and hitch them on for me, and each would favor me all he could by letting me ride and they keeping my cattle in the road. As Tuttle was ahead of me and Sherwood and Leach behind, on fair roads they could herd my cattle along, but it was so hard for them to run back and forth to look after my team that I would sit on the tongue and do all I could to keep them up.[1] All this time I went on guard every other night for half of the night, as the boss was rather cranky; but my chums would not allow me to do any herding—only sit on my beat, and they would do the running for me.

There were two claim shanties near so that I got my supper of milk and also my breakfast Sunday morning, which strengthened me and gave me new life, and I felt quite well, only very weak.

My chums did the usual Sunday chores and we four went up the creek a short distance to see if we could not get a fish or two for me.

After a short time Rennick sent a man to call us to go and drive up the cattle and hitch up as he was going to make a drive the rest of the day. But we told him that they could drive as far as they liked, but we did not drive on a single rod, and that, if we thought he was going to ask us to drive every Sunday, we would unload our traps [personal gear] and stop right here, as this country suited us very well, and we didn't hire to drive Sundays nor be dogged about by any body. We were willing to do our duty but drive Sunday we would not and that we might as well settle that question today for the rest of the trip, as we rather liked the looks of this place to stop. He gave us to understand that he would not ask us to drive on Sundays any more, unless actually compelled to for the want of grass or water, and this settled the question for the time.

But we heard occasional remarks from some of the men, stating what they would do with the "Yanks" when out on the plains but paid no attention to them, concluding to do our duty as men, and trust to luck, as trouble would come fast enough without borrowing any. We thought Chat Rennick had sense enough to know who of his men did their work the best; for nearly all of his Missourians were a low, shiftless, and quarrelsome set, always in a jangle among themselves, and kept him scolding them half of the time.[2] We concluded the remarks of such men would have no weight with him. The assistant boss [Frank McCarthy] was little better than the rest.

"I Was Starving"

FIG. 7. "Grub Pile" by William Henry Jackson, 1866. The monotonous, poorly prepared meals cooked over a fire of "buffalo chips" at this trailside camp were no better than what a few years earlier had reduced William Clark to "starving with a train load of provisions." Drawing by Jackson, courtesy Scotts Bluff National Monument.

The next day we drove all day without anything of interest happening, as by this time our cattle were fairly well broke in.

I missed the claim shanties, the last one being at Big Blue.

I had eaten nothing since morning, but I tried hard to eat down a little supper, but could force down very little. Nothing exciting occurred for several days.

I could not gain my appetite and consequently grew weaker all the time. My chums had the most of my work to do. Although very hard for them, they did it cheerfully. There were two extra hands for the purpose of driving when needed, but their time was occupied, either in favoring some of their kind or feigning sickness.

I had told Rennick that I was not able to drive and he could not have helped knowing it, for I had fallen away thirty or forty pounds, and was a mere skeleton, just able to crawl. Finally, Bill Eads, one of the extras came and drove my team part of the time for two or three days, and my chums would do the rest. They were willing to do all they could and the others were willing they should.[3]

The day we reached Rock Creek, I was scarcely able to walk and had ridden all day.[4]

That night the boys fixed me a bed on the ground near the camp fire. Then they got supper and begged me to eat a little, but the very sight of it made me sick and it seemed to me I would break in two in the middle.

Here Mr. Rennick began to show a little sympathy for me. He said I must eat something. I told him I couldn't. He said I would not live till morning if I did not eat something.

They handed me some bread and coffee. I took a swallow of coffee and a bite of bread, chewed it and tried to swallow it, but could not do it any more than I could swallow an ox team.

I craved cold water. We had bad water all the way. They commenced to hunt through the train for something I could eat, and finally found some corn meal which a fellow by the name of Albert Frank had.[5] He brought it to me and asked me if I could not eat a little gruel. They made some and I drank it. It tasted good to me. In ten minutes I felt better. It stopped the pain in the small of my back. They gave me a little several times during the night. In the morning I felt quite smart, only very weak. The boys made more gruel to take along in the wagon and I took a little quite often during the day.

That night we camped close to a spring of good cold water. I slid out of the wagon, cup in hand, and managed to get to the spring before Rennick saw me. He came running up, telling me to stop drinking or I would kill myself, but before he got to me I had swallowed two or three cups of water. I never had water taste so good before, and I told him I would like to die feeling as good as that water made me feel. Rennick led me back to the wagon and they let me have a little water often, which, with my gruel, made me feel quite cheerful.

In the morning I was considerable better, and Rennick let me have his individual two-gallon keg which the boys filled with this cold spring water. Then they wet a blanket, wrapped the keg in it and put it in the wagon for me. It kept cool all day. I drank my porridge often and by night I had a little appetite for bread and coffee.

The next morning I felt better. My appetite began to come to me, and I could eat a fair allowance of bread and bacon.

The boys had improved in bread making and made quite good bread by this time.

In a day or two I got so I could drive my team and eat a square meal of such food as we had. In fact, I thought it good enough for anyone, as, by this time I had a wolfish appetite and could eat six times a day and relish my food.

SECTION 3

"They Make the Earth Tremble"
Into the Buffalo Range

Editorial Notes

With this section, Clark takes his narrative northwest into a description of Nebraska Territory's sand hill region and the migration of its immense buffalo herds. Of all the phenomena experienced by westering soldiers and civilians on the Great Plains, this movement of bison was the most dramatic, dangerous, and providential (supply-wise). Accordingly, it was also the one about which travelers always commented in their letters, diaries, and reminiscences, although inexplicably Clark's original editor made no comment about buffalo.[1]

While Clark also described at some length the Sioux bands encountered near Fort Kearny, he virtually ignored the Cheyenne, other than to mention them briefly as targets for Sioux raiders. It is a strange imbalance, especially in view of the fact that on August 2, 1857, twenty-eight miles west of Fort Kearny, Cheyenne warriors descended on an unguarded herd of U.S. Army beef cattle and stripped it of 824 head the Utah Expedition could ill afford to lose. At about the same time Cheyenne also attacked a Russell, Majors and Waddell train near the confluence of the South and North Platte Rivers at Ash Hollow.[2] *One possible explanation for Clark's tribal emphasis is that by the time he wrote his reminiscences, the Cheyenne may have receded from national awareness, while memories of a Sioux threat remained vivid due to the clashes and spectacular massacres involving the tribe in Minnesota (1862), at the Little Big Horn, Montana (1876), and Wounded Knee, South Dakota (1890). It is also possible that, with the passage of time, Clark confuses the Pawnees (a tribe driven by the Sioux and others from the north plains into Texas) for the Cheyenne.*

Clark's description in this section of the salutary effect of a few items temporarily added to his diet while visiting Fort Kearny reminds readers of the monotony and deficiencies of a teamster's daily fare.

Everything went nicely till we reached the sand hills, eight or nine miles from Fort Kearny.[3] Here were about three thousand Sioux Indians, camped a short distance from the road.

The Sioux and Cheyennes were not on very good terms. The Sioux had gathered near the Fort and would send their warriors out from here to plunder and steal from the Cheyennes.

They were friendly to the whites while near the Fort, but forty or fifty of them came and met us and begged tobacco and anything they could get, bothering us considerably. They would try to get into our wagons—would climb in behind to steal what they could. We had to watch them, and pulled them out of the wagons often. They followed us till near the Fort, where we camped for the night, then we made them leave.

Here I succeeded in buying some bottled pickles and a few beans of the soldiers. After getting them I went straight to camp and put on a kettle of beans to stew, and had a fine supper that night. I got enough for two or three messes, so I had a little change from bacon and bread, but anything tasted good now.

In the morning we started on and, after going five or six miles, we came across a few scattering buffalo.

Mr. Rennick and the mounted men—four in all—started after them, running them a while, but did not get any.[4] At noon we camped near a large herd. As soon as we had unyoked our cattle, Ed Leach took his gun and started out after one. He succeeded in getting near enough to one to get a shot. The buffalo was pawing and throwing the dirt in a buffalo wallow when he shot him. He fell but got up again. Leach loaded again and gave him another shot and run for camp very much excited and told what he had done. Three or four of our mess went back and found the buffalo badly wounded. They shot him two or three times before he fell. He was a large old bull and some distance in advance of the herd.

FIG. 8. "A Bull-Whacker" by Frederic Remington (1861–1909). Remington's teamster was in sharp contrast to the youth and rougher wardrobe of the bull whackers drawn by Charles M. Russell and William Henry Jackson, both of whom had worked among the real thing for an extended period of time. Drawing in *Century Magazine*, April 1902, courtesy McCracken Research Library, Cody WY.

Several of the men now started out for more, but did not succeed in killing any.

We dressed [butchered] this fellow and divided it up with the train crew. We had a fine feast of buffalo meat[,] the first taste of fresh meat we had had since we left Leavenworth. We all decided it was the best and sweetest meat we had ever eaten.[5]

We had just got into the buffalo range. The grass was nearly knee high before we struck this range, but here it was quite well fed down.

That afternoon we saw several large herds some distance off along the sand hills.

The next morning was fine, and we were in sight of thousands of buffalo.

There was one large herd after another all along the sand hills as far as the eye could reach.

This range of sand hills extends along the south side of the [South] Platte River, from one to four miles from the river. Every now and then a big herd of buffalo, moving north, crossed the river, and we could see large herds across the river.

As the atmosphere is clear and dry here, we could see many miles. It was a beautiful sight. I had never dreamed there were as many buffalo in America as we saw that day. We were not out of sight of thousands of them half an hour at a time all day long. We killed several and were loaded down with buffalo meat, and we had some salted down for future use.[6]

The next day was the same—drove after drove all day long. We thought best not to kill any more as we could not use them.

Every little while a big herd would start down toward the river to drink, two or three miles ahead or behind our train. They went on the run and would make the earth tremble several miles away.

That night we camped near the Platte River. The men on guard were cautioned to keep a good lookout and not let our cattle get near the buffalo, there being several large herds in sight but none nearer than half a mile. Rennick had planned our camp so as not to be too near for fear of losing some of our cattle among the buffalo. An extra guard was placed to herd the cattle.

About midnight the whole crew was aroused. There was a big herd of buffalo moving towards our cattle, going to the river. We all got around our cattle and, while some drove the cattle out of the way, others went to turn the course of the buffalo and by shooting into the herd, we finally succeeded in changing their course and driving them around our cattle.

There had been several instances where parties, crossing the plains in the season of the great buffalo move, lost their cattle by the buffaloes getting in contact with the cattle and stampeding them.

It seems that we were in the great move north, as trains a week ahead of us or two weeks behind us, saw very few buffalo.

The next morning we started on our journey and drove to Plum Creek and camped.[7] We were still in the same buffalo range. We had a fine camp ground.

SECTION 4

"Consider Yourselves Discharged"

Sunday Confrontation

Editorial Notes

In this section, Clark's narrative brings together three of Russell, Majors and Waddell's most colorful field agents. Each of them had already established a reputation among freighters on the Great Plains and Oregon Trail; all would go on to even greater notoriety during and after the Civil War.

Frank McCarthy was, of course, working as assistant wagon master of Clark's train under Chat Rennick. When the Utah Expedition went into winter quarters at Camp Scott near Fort Bridger during late November 1857, General Johnston required Russell, Majors and Waddell's trains to stay with the expedition. It was an order that forced the company to discharge and pay off its teamsters, several hundred of whom enlisted for nine months military service as volunteer troops. The rest headed back to the Missouri-Kansas frontier or remained at Camp Scott as either quartermaster employees or unemployed idlers. Under these circumstances, McCarthy remained in the Fort Bridger area to protect Russell, Majors and Waddell's interests, especially its wagons, their freight, and any surviving draught animals.

In this violent, unstable garrison society awash in alcohol, McCarthy found trouble during late November 1857, as reported by war correspondents for the New York Times *and Horace Greeley's* New-York Tribune: *The stringer for the* Times *filed a dispatch from Camp Scott reporting, "Mr. McCarty [sic], a wagon-maker [master] of Russell & Waddell, was put on trial for shooting a soldier a few days since. It seems that a party of drunken soldiers attacked him with stones, and struck him several times. He finally, in self-defence, shot one of them, and it is supposed the soldier cannot live."[1] As a civilian, McCarthy was tried on homicide charges in the makeshift court established near Fort Bridger rather than by an army court-martial. He was acquitted.*

Either from disgust over this incident or concern about retribution from the dead soldier's comrades, McCarthy left the train in early December 1857 to return to Kansas. Accordingly, he drops from Clark's narrative at that point.

Frank McCarthy's penchant for quick decisions and summary justice was not unusual among Russell, Majors and Waddell's wagon masters. A New York war correspondent traveling with one of the firm's caravans described a similar affray that took place on the plains en route to Salt Lake City:

> A soldier was shot through the breast on the 13th by a swaggering wagon-master of one of Russell's trains named White, without just cause. Had it not been for military discipline Mr. White would have met a speedy reward, and in the absence of civil justice the act would have been as justifiable a case of retribution as any that has happened in the most palmy days of Judge Lynch. Five shots were fired, one of which was mortal. Despotic authority in some cases is a mighty good thing.[2]

Sometimes the wagon master was the victim, as with Dave Wagner, an experienced, well-liked trail boss for one of the Russell firm's bull trains. He was "dry-gulched" in Utah's Echo Canyon by teamster Charley French, a "half-breed Sioux" anxious to settle a lingering grudge at trail's end. One of the late wagon master's other employees, German immigrant George W. Beehrer, recorded just before his boss's assassination that Salt Lake City "is a rendezvous for the vicious," where teamsters "squandered not only their money, but also their souls. Within three days, three of my train comrades were dead. Antonio was stabbed in an affray over a bar-maid. Johnny Bull was shot at a gaming table; and Red, the Missourian, was murdered in a saloon brawl."[3]

Sic transit gloria.

The second of Russell, Majors and Waddell's field men mentioned by Clark in this section was Chat Rennick, wagon master and Frank McCarthy's boss. Rennick, of course, has been introduced to the narrative earlier, but in this section comes Bill Clark's first description of Dwight J. McCann, a somewhat mysterious operative to whom Clark refers only as the firm's "agent." Based on his background, McCann may have been the most highly educated person in Russell, Majors and Waddell's train; to the editors he comes across as what in modern businesses would be a headquarters staff person or senior financial person representing the company's owners. At age thirty, McCann may have been not only senior in organizational authority to McCarthy and Rennick, he was also older than they were. Born in Erie, Pennsylvania, in 1827, Dwight McCann spent most of the 1840s as first a student and then an administrator at Erie's premiere private academy. In 1849 he relocated to New Orleans to serve as principal of a similar school, and then abruptly changed career direction to study medicine in Baton Rouge at what would become Louisiana State University. When Clark first encountered him on the plains in 1857, Dwight McCann was on the verge of starting a prominent banking career in Nebraska City, the new operations base on the Missouri River for Russell, Majors and Waddell. Also in McCann's future was his controversial role in the congressional investigation of the so-called Indian Ring during and after the Grant administration.[4]

The reason for Clark's discussion of McCarthy, Rennick, and McCann in this section was the practical dilemma he and his "chums" posed by their refusal to work on Sundays, a decision that threatened the forward movement of the entire twenty-six-wagon train. It is unclear whether this decision was a religious matter of observing the Sabbath in traditional fashion or simply a case of young men asserting what they believed to be their previously agreed-upon right to a weekly day off to rest. What the chums had to support their position was not only the verbal assurances from partners William H. Russell and Alexander Majors at Fort Leavenworth but the printed Rules and Regulations their firm issued to each wagon master and many of the teamsters, including an admonition that "the use of profane language is strictly forbidden. We expect our trains to observe the Sabbath, and whenever an opportunity occurs to hear preaching, embrace it."[5]

Apart from the military pressures of the Utah War, this Sunday work matter was a serious issue that each company of emigrants debated and needed to resolve throughout the four decades the overland trails were used. Among emigrants, the standard rule was that if one was not at Independence Rock along the Sweetwater River by July Fourth, the risk was high of snowy weather in the mountains ahead. By any measure, the Utah Expedition and its wagon trains were dangerously late, as they had left Fort Leavenworth during the third week of July 1857 due to late decisions in Washington.[6]

Resolution of the Sunday work issue for Chat Rennick's bull train was a local and temporary matter. Depending upon the pressures of trail conditions, weather, and the calendar as well as the rapport between wagon masters and their crews, Alexander Majors's ban on Sunday travel might not be honored any more faithfully than his prohibition on swearing. In 1858 a New York reporter described the behavior in his mule train: "There is no Sabbath on the plains. The men work right on, not knowing whether it is Saturday, Sunday, or Monday. The day of the month is inquired about, but not the day of the week. We drove on as usual."[7] A more relaxed approach was recorded by James H. Mills while working as a bull whacker with a small group of families crossing the Oregon and Bozeman Trails eight years later. Mills noted that his train voted to rest on Sundays unless movement was necessary to find a better campsite, and so managed to "lay by" all or part of the Sabbath two-thirds of the time. During these breaks, "Some washed. Some bathed[.] Some mended and played cards and checkers, some went hunting, some sang songs, others hymns [and] a few read a little in the testament." Teamster Mills commented about one Sunday, "Laid by to day and rested [but] whether we kept it holy or not is another question."[8]

Nothing unusual occurred that night. The next day was Sunday. We got our breakfast and did our washing. Then we ran some bullets, cleaned our guns, and put them in good condition for use.[9]

Frank McCarthy, the assistant wagon boss, came riding up on his mule and ordered us to put up our traps and go and help drive the cattle up, and yoke up, for they were going to make a drive. We told him we would not. He then said, "You can consider yourselves discharged."

We told him he had better send some one around that had authority to discharge us. Then he rode off after the cattle.

Albert Frank now came over to where we were with his gun and clothes and said that if we were discharged, he would go with us.

It was evident that they intended to show us right here what they would do with the "Yanks when out on the plains" as we were seventy miles from the nearest settlement which was Fort Kearny.[10]

"Consider Yourselves Discharged"

FIG. 9. "Yoking Up" by William Henry Jackson, 1866. This drawing depicts a bull train breaking camp on the Oregon Trail with the recently-completed transcontinental telegraph line in background. During Clark's trek west, the telegraph ended east of the trails in Boonville MO. Drawing by Jackson, courtesy Scotts Bluff National Monument.

An agent of the Company's, Mr. [Dwight J.] McCann, had come up and camped with us the night before.

Soon the cattle were driven into the corral. Mr. McCann was at the entrance of the corral guarding that gap while the men were yoking the cattle.

They all grabbed their yokes to yoke their cattle except us five.

As we were in the front mess of one wing of the corral, it brought us close to where McCann stood.

Chat Rennick came and ordered us to go and yoke our cattle.

We told him we would not yoke an ox that day.

He said we could consider ourselves discharged from the train.

We told him all right, that we would as soon have our pay and go back from here as to go the whole trip. He said that we could never get back, that the Indians would kill us.

We told him we would take our chances on that. Then he said he would not let us take our guns along. We plainly told him that we had them and before they got them from us, they would be liable to get the charge that was in them, and that they were loaded for buffalo too.

Mr. McCann spoke up and said that there were men enough to make us drive.

At this George Tuttle told him to repeat those words again and there would be one less Missourian, and drew his rifle. We all had our guns in our hands.

Rennick now spoke up and said[,] "Hold on there, I don't want any of that kind of work."

Then we told him what brags had been made by his men; that now was a good time to settle it, as they had us out on the plains. There were men enough to massacre us but not enough in that train to make us drive a single rod, and we meant just what we said.[11] Then we told them that they might as well begin quickly and get the job off their hands as soon as possible, as they might have another that would need their immediate attention.

Rennick said he did not want any trouble with us, but wished we would drive, as the other men found no fault about driving Sundays.

We told him that he could go on as fast as he wished, as these Yanks wouldn't bother him. We would go our way and they could go theirs. That we were discharged and did not belong to his train any longer. Then we proceeded to pack up our things and put them in shape for our homeward trip.

Rennick now began to urge us to put our things back into the wagon and go along and they would make but a short drive.

We told him he had discharged us without a cause, and asked him if he had any men in his train that did their work any better than we had.

He said, "No not as well, only you will not drive Sundays."

We said we were glad to hear that, and that there was a law in regard to a train boss discharging a man over twenty-five miles from a settlement, and that the Company was responsible for the acts of a train boss. We had a more paying job than to drive a team for him any longer. As he had acknowledged that we had done our duty better than any other men he had, for we had hired to William Russel with the understanding that we were not to drive Sundays.

Then he began to get real good natured, and, I think, a little uneasy; for, if five men left, there was no show to get anyone to drive our teams through. McCann was going on the next day to catch up with the train

"Consider Yourselves Discharged"

ahead. Even if the two bosses and the two extra men drove, it would leave one team without a driver and no one to look up camping grounds.

Rennick now began to argue the case with us for a compromise of this difficulty. We spent an hour or two before a settlement was reached. He made several propositions to us before we accepted. Finally he asked us if we would put our things back into the wagon and get in and ride to camp and McCann, himself, and the extra men would tie their mules behind the wagons and drive our teams that afternoon, and we should not be asked to drive again on Sunday unless actually necessary for want of grass or water.

We accepted this proposition.

As we had lost a couple of hours since the cattle were yoked, we could not get far.

We all got into our wagons and rode to camp, except Tuttle.

Soon after starting, I was taken quite sick with a violent chill. Tuttle went to Mr. Rennick to get some medicine for me, as the company had sent a chest of such medicines as thought necessary on such a trip, in care of the train boss. Tuttle took Rennick's whip, and he came to my wagon, found the condition I was in, and went and got me some quinine and such other medicine as he thought I needed.[12]

Tuttle then told Rennick to get on his mule, and he would drive the rest of the day. Mr. Rennick did so and went ahead to hunt a camping place, and in a short time we camped.

Mr. Rennick showed considerable sympathy for me, coming often to my wagon to see how I was getting along, and began to take quite an interest in us. In fact, he was naturally a good man, although he had listened a little too much to some of his worthless men. I think he began to see his mistake, and, from this time on, I would not wish a better boss. He worked hard for the interest of his Company and began to appreciate his best men.

In a short time he came into our mess and stayed with us all the way through.

Monday I was not able to drive and he furnished a man to drive for me.

We travelled all day in sight of large herds of buffalo. In the afternoon we saw a very large herd, reaching more than a mile, coming directly towards us, and as we could not drive past before they came upon us, we doubled up our train in as small space as we could and as quickly as possible. We were none too soon for by the time the men got their guns out the leaders were within ten rods of our wagons and still coming. The men fired at them, killing nine in their tracks and wounding many more. Some of them still acted as though they would not be driven off, and Martin Sherwood ran to my wagon, put a [percussion] cap on my gun, and, pointing to a big buffalo which stood defiantly not more than ten rods from my wagon, said, "Clark, shoot that big fellow."

As I had not shot a buffalo yet, I turned over, put my gun out of the wagon and fired. I did not even hit him. I was so sick I did not see my gun barrel—only the buffalo.

Albert Frank had his gun reloaded by this time and shot him just back of the fore leg. He bellowed, then turned and ran back into the herd. By this time the other men had reloaded and fired into them again. The wounded turned and ran back into the herd, parting them, and they charged by before and behind us.

We were here some time before they all passed. There were thousands in this herd.

After they had passed the men took their knives, and, cutting a strip along the back bone, cut out the tender loin of a few of those lying nearest us and left the rest, as we had more buffalo meat than we could use.

Nothing particular occurred during the rest of the day. I began to get better and the next day drove part of the time.

We were still in the buffalo range, but they were not as plenty as before.

We camped that night about six miles from the crossing of the Platte, and drove in the next morning, camped, got an early dinner, and prepared for crossing.

We hitched on to about one-third of our wagons with fifteen yoke of cattle to each wagon, but started into the river with only three wagons.

Mr. Rennick had ridden across the river to see how the ford was, and found the river was full of holes, some a foot deep and others seven or eight feet deep. Unless we zigzagged from one sand drift to another, it would be impossible to cross, as the whole bed of the river was a shifting bed of sand.

We had driven but a few rods before we stalled, with our wagons in four or five feet of water. We swung our cattle up and down several times and tried to make a start, but it was of no use, as the sand began to settle around our wagon wheels. So we sent out and got six yoke of cattle more for each wagon. By the time we got them hitched on for another pull, the sand had drifted around our wagons till they were hub deep in the sand, and the cattle were knee deep. The men would have been in the same fix had they not kept stepping around.

We swung our cattle and made a pull but we were [stuck] fast and could not move. We had to get our shovels and shovel around the wheels and oxen. Then we took another pull and this time got the wagons on the move, but only for a short distance, when we stalled again. It was such hard pulling, the cattle could go but a little way at a time. Every stop the sand would gather as before, and it was almost impossible to get another start. Occasionally a chain would break and we would have to get another or repair it with a link made on purpose. It was impossible to get more than eight or ten rods in an hour. Some of our cattle began to get discouraged which made it still worse. The river is about eighty rods wide at this point.

We finally succeeded in getting three wagons across and our cattle back to the balance of the train by nine o'clock that night. You can guess we were a tired and wet lot of teamsters, after being in the water ten hours, part of the time waist deep.

After changing our clothes and having our supper we were glad to go to bed, except those who had to stand guard.

We left three men on the other side of the river and Rennick sent three more over on mules to stay with them. In the morning we drove all our cattle into the corral and yoked three teams of eighteen yoke each, of the oldest and best cattle and started across.

As we had zigzagged across the river for several rods up and down in crossing the day before, we had learned the best route.

We got across with these wagons without much difficulty. In the course of the day we got the balance of the train across and made a short drive and camped.

SECTION 5

"Grand and Beautiful Scenery"

Wolves along the North Platte

Editorial Notes

In describing the wolf-infested North Platte Valley and several of its topographical oddities (Ash Hollow and Chimney Rock), Clark's narrative mirrors the reactions of overlanders who preceded and followed him. Puzzling, though, is his decision to pass over any reference to the battle at Blue Water Creek near Ash Hollow. It was a clash that had taken place only two years earlier and had become General Harney's signature military accomplishment; its brutality even spawned Harney's enduring nickname, "Squaw Killer." This battle was the opening conflict in the Great Sioux War that plagued Nebraska Territory for decades thereafter. It is difficult to imagine that Russell, Majors and Waddell's teamsters and the troops they accompanied were oblivious to such a major event as they negotiated their descent into Ash Hollow.

Similarly, it should be noted that Bill Clark also chose to ignore at least two other trailside landmarks he encountered in this region: Court House Rock and Scotts Bluff. While neither formation was as dramatic as Chimney Rock, both were stunning candidates for discussion. That Clark would have seen them again in 1868 while eastbound to claim his intended bride makes it all the more unusual that his reminiscences omitted reference to these rock formations.

Even stranger than these omissions was Clark's failure to describe or even mention his brief sojourn at Fort Laramie, Nebraska, the most significant settlement between Fort Kearny and Salt Lake City. He mentions the Laramie Mountains, but not the military post and adjacent trading establishment that bore their name. Once the Utah Expedition and the bull trains of Russell, Majors and Waddell departed Fort Laramie, they were on their own and beyond help should they need it.

We had not been molested by Indians so far. We had met parties of twenty or thirty at different times, but had been cautious. When they came riding near us, we would double up our train and prepare for them, and they would soon ride away apparently friendly.[1]

This day, after crossing the Platte, we met an Indian trader with quite a train, loaded with buffalo hides that he had bought of the Indians and was taking to Leavenworth to sell.

He told us that the Indians had attacked the train which was two days ahead of us at Ash Hollow, our next camping place.

Having had no trouble with the Indians, the boss had become careless and had allowed his train to string along, the wagons being some distance apart.

At Ash Hollow there is a steep hill, and, as the head teams were going down this hill, the Indians ran in and cut off the three hind wagons from the rest of the train and stampeded the cattle, upsetting two of the wagons. They killed the two teamsters and plundered the wagons. The third teamster got his gun and jumped behind his wagon, and succeeded in keeping the Indians off till the front teamsters came up and drove them away, wounding several.[2]

This made us a little nervous and still more careful.

In the morning we drove to the top of the hill and closed our train up as close together as we could, and while going down the hill at Ash Hollow, kept a good guard out, for we could take only two or three wagons down at a time. It was a very bad hill to get down with such heavy wagons, and took us some time to get our train down, but we finally got down all right, and camped near the North Platte.[3]

Here William McCarthy, a brother of Frank McCarthy, our assistant boss, met us.

He had been sent out by Majors, Russel & Waddell in charge of a herd of eight hundred beef cattle to drive them to Salt Lake. He had eight men, and a team and wagon to haul their supplies.

At Plum Creek, where we had our mutiny a week before, while they were getting their dinner a party of Indians, apparently friendly, came into camp, stayed a short time, and went away. Soon after they left, McCarthy, fearing some mischief, got on his mule and started to go out around his cattle. Another party of Indians came charging towards his cattle. McCarthy put spurs to his mule but they got between him and the cattle and stampeded them.

As soon as McCarthy had got a little way off the other Indians fired into camp, wounding two of the men. They returned the fire, wounding several Indians, then ran towards the herd to meet McCarthy who, by this time, was making toward camp as fast as his mule could run, with several Indians in hot pursuit, one quite close. As he came to a little slough, his mule stopped. The Indian fired and shot his collar off on one side. He then wheeled in his saddle and shot the Indian, and got his mule started again.

As the other men were coming to his rescue, the other Indians turned and started toward the cattle, and the men went back to the wagon.

The two men at camp were only slightly wounded, one through the leg and the other in the side.

They dressed the wounds and concluded to stay here over night, as their cattle were gone. About sundown they were made glad by the arrival of one of the Company's trains.

Majors and Russel by this time had their twenty-six trains on the road only a day or two apart.

In the morning McCarthy put his outfit in charge of this train, then got on his mule and started on ahead, going from one train to another till he reached ours where his brother was, and stayed with us till we reached Fort Laramie.[4]

These two Indian scares made us more cautious. We kept good guard around our wagons at night. We were now in the worst Indian country on the route, and we kept close together.

The next day was Sunday and we did our usual chores, but were not asked to drive.

Monday morning we moved on. In the afternoon we saw quite a large party of Indians riding toward us. The boss stopped the head team and commenced to corral. The extra men came charging back, ordering us to corral as quickly as possible, for the Indians were coming upon us.

Every man hurried his team up, and we got them corralled with the cattle inside. Then every man got his gun, and got inside the corral, ready for them, except Rennick and the mounted men.

But before the Indians got to us they began to slow up. They came up and appeared friendly. Whether it was because we were so well prepared for them or not, we never knew. They chatted awhile with the boss and rode off.

We strung out our teams and moved on for the rest of the day without further trouble.

About noon the next day we came in sight of Chimney Rock. It looked but a short distance from the road, but we traveled the rest of that day and till noon the next, and camped right opposite of it.

As soon as we had our [mid-day] dinner, three or four of the boys took their guns and started out, saying they were going to climb Chimney Rock, as we were going to rest here an hour or two.

They started out and traveled till the middle of the afternoon before reaching the rock. It being so late, they did not climb the rock but made tracks for camp, fearing the boss would be after them. It was just dark when they reached camp, so we had to stay here till morning.

We heard afterward that it was seven miles out to Chimney Rock from where we camped, but it did not look to be over a mile. The atmosphere here being so dry and clear that it made objects in the distance look very much nearer than they were, and travelers were often badly deceived.[5]

This country was quite different from that we had passed over. From Leavenworth across to where we struck the Platte River near Fort Kearny, it was a fine, beautiful country mostly prairie, with an occasional belt of timber along the streams. But up the South Platte it was comparatively a level, grassy plain from the river back to the sand hills, with no timber,

FIG. 10. *opposite*: Forts along the Oregon and Mormon trails, May–June 1858. A year after Clark and his bull train passed through Fort Leavenworth, Kansas; Forts Kearny and Laramie, Nebraska; and Fort Bridger, Utah (top to bottom), these photos—the first taken along the western trails—were made by Capt. James H. Simpson's detachment of army topographical engineers bound for Utah. Montage by author-editors from 1858 photographs by Samuel C. Mills and Edward Jagiello. Courtesy Library of Congress, Manuscript Division, Lee-Palfrey Collection.

and here we had to substitute buffalo chips for fuel. After reaching Ash Hollow we began to get some scrubby wood.[6]

The whole appearance of the country had changed. It began to be more wavy and rocky, and occasionally there were some scrub cedars, scattered among the rocky hills. The tops of the waves were covered with rock in all the shapes the imagination of man can picture.

After leaving our camp near Chimney Rock, we traveled in the midst of this grand and beautiful scenery a few days, undisturbed by Indians, much to our relief. We now came to Fort Laramie.

The country along the North Platte was nearly the same all the way, although it changed a little as we neared the Laramie range of mountains. There were more of the scrub cedars on the rocky bluffs.

The Laramie Mountains were quite bald, there being little timber except in the canyons.

From Laramie we moved on up the river without any excitement, and, arriving at Horse Shoe Creek, camped close to the Laramie Mountains at Horse Shoe Bend.[7] Here the creek runs in the shape of a horse shoe, and we camped at the mouth of the bend, turning our cattle down in the bend—a nice place to herd. At the lower end of the bend was some timber.

George Washington Tuttle, Sherwood, and myself were on guard the first part of the night.[8]

After Rennick had come out, as was his custom, to see if every man was on duty before he went to bed, and had gone back, we told Tuttle and Sherwood to go to camp and to bed, as they were not feeling well. As we had so far had no use for our guns while on guard, we sent them to camp by the boys. We were not allowed to fire a gun at night unless at Indians.

After the boys had been gone a short time, George Washington fell asleep. He was on the side next the timber. The cattle started into the timber and I ran around to head them off and wake him up. We drove back what we could find, and as we were standing by George's camp fire, we heard more tramping around in the timber. I went into the timber for them while George watched those we had. It was very dark in there. Just as I reached the cattle a pack of wolves set up an unearthly yell close behind me. The cattle jumped and ran as fast as they could, and I was as close behind them as I could keep. The wolves ran after us, yelping at every jump. The cattle ran into the bed of the creek, it being dry, and up toward our camp, leaving the creek opposite my camp fire and running into the herd. I stopped at my fire badly scared. The wolves stopped within a rod or two of the fire, keeping up their howling.

I stuck close to my fire, occasionally throwing a fire brand at them, as they came near, when they would run off a few rods only to return again. I kept them off in this way till our relief came. They were the big gray timber wolves, and there were ten or fifteen in this pack. While standing by my fire, I wished I had my gun. I should have fired it, even though I disobeyed orders in doing so. After this I kept my gun when on guard.[9]

We had not got out of sight of camp in the morning before ten or fifteen of these ravenous beasts came into our camp ground to pick up our crumbs.

We moved on for several days around the Laramie Mountains to where Fort Fetterman now stands, with but little change in the scenery. Occasionally we met an Indian trader with his train of furs and buffalo hides going toward the States.[10]

SECTION 6

"A Sage Brush Country"

Crossing the Continental Divide to Green River

Editorial Notes

With this section, William Clark's reminiscences finish up what could be thought of as his "travelogue" across the Great Plains, preparatory to relating in section 7 the Utah Expedition's first major interaction with the Nauvoo Legion and the realities of guerrilla warfare in the Rockies.

As with the sections that precede this one, the material in section 6 is full of Clark's wonder over the constantly changing terrain and the challenge of moving his bull train across it. Having said this, it is again noteworthy that he wholly omits mentioning his passage through South Pass to Pacific Springs as well as what he heard about the unsuccessful descent there by six Nauvoo Legion cavalrymen on the Tenth U.S. Infantry's mule herd during the night of September 24–25, 1857. Both events were remarkable in quite different ways. That Clark chose not to mention them in even a minimal way sets him apart from the thousands of Utah War participants for whom crossing the Continental Divide and experiencing a nocturnal attack by armed fellow Americans were noteworthy events.[1]

Our course took us through near where Fort Casper now is. Here the country is different. Occasionally a strip of sand, then some sage brush and alkali spots.

We left the river here for Pacific Springs. The boss told every mess to fill their water kegs before leaving the river, as we would have a dry camp before reaching the Springs. Our mess and some of the others obeyed, but there were two messes who were always short. Each man was afraid he would do more than the others. They did not get any water. We told them that we wouldn't go dry to furnish them water and that they had better fill their kegs, but they did not.

Before we had gone far they were begging [for] water. We gave them water to drink all day, but when night came and supper to get, the whole train was short of water, and only those who had filled their kegs had any for cooking. When these poor fellows came for water to cook with, they were refused. But they would not take "no" for an answer, and came in a body and were going to get it by force, when the muzzles of several rifles were leveled at them. They went away, after receiving some good advice from Rennick.

They went back to their messes, and to bed hungry, but wiser men. They were very thirsty before reaching Pacific Springs the next day.

Here we had the worst thunderstorm I ever saw. The wind blew a perfect gale and the rain came down in sheets. The first storm we had had on our trip. In the morning we had quite a job to find our cattle, as they had stampeded in the storm. This was in a sage brush country.

We traveled for some days through a rough hilly country to the Sweetwater River.[2] Here we drove down a long hill into the bed of the river and traveled some distance down the river close to Independence Rock.[3]

This rock was covered as high as men could climb with names of men who had crossed before us—some as early as 1848.

It was rough rocky traveling in the bed of the river and we were glad to strike a dry road again.

Not far from here we came to Soda Lake.[4] This "lake" was a bed of soda or alkali, white as snow, four or five inches deep. We tested the quality of this soda in bread making and it took the place of saleratus very nicely.

Here was the largest sage brush that I ever saw—five or six feet tall. We saw our first elk here and tried to shoot him but failed. We had seen very little game except buffalo and a few antelope which were very shy.

We traveled up the Sweetwater some distance, and camped by the river one day, and, finding plenty of fish, we improvised a seine by taking a wagon cover and attaching an ox chain to it for a sinker.[5] We seined the river awhile, catching nearly a bushel of fish—mountain shiners—and had a grand feast. We passed the Rattlesnake Hills and Sweetwater Mountains and crossed the Rockies at South Pass.[6]

We drove on the west slope of the mountains till we reached Dry Sandy Creek. Here we had poor water and heavy, sandy roads, and our cattle were getting weak from the long journey. It was slow traveling down this stream, and we would have to double our teams to get through the sandy streaks.

We went from here on down Big Sandy Creek, and across to Green River near where Granger now is.[7]

We had quite a hard time in crossing this stream.

Here we found a sort of trading post, and they had farmed a little. Rennick found some potatoes here and bought some. They were the first vegetables we had had since leaving Leavenworth, and it was a treat to us all.

SECTION 7

"The Boss, Seeing They Had No Show, Surrendered"

Meeting Lot Smith

Editorial Notes

With this section, Bill Clark introduces readers to the Nauvoo Legion's first major attack on the Utah Expedition, a hit-and-run cavalry raid in early October 1857 that destroyed three twenty-six-wagon supply trains owned by Russell, Majors and Waddell. Unlike the small-scale attempt to stampede a regimental mule herd a few weeks earlier, this thrust was a spectacular success. It took place on the night of October 4–5 in Utah's Green River district (now Wyoming) and destroyed irreplaceable rations, equipment, uniforms, and wagons with an estimated value of a million dollars. The raid immediately followed the Legion's incineration of two Latter-day Saint way stations on Blacks Fork—Forts Bridger and Supply.

The Nauvoo Legion's willingness to burn the Latter-day Saints' own settlements was a graphic example of Brigham Young's seriousness about his "Sebastopol Strategy," a focused destruction of Utah Territory's infrastructure inspired by Russia's scorched-earth tactics during the Napoleonic Wars and the recent conflict in the Crimea. At the same time the ability to destroy a significant number of the army's unguarded supply trains signaled Latter-day Saint military effectiveness and its underestimation by the Buchanan administration, the Utah Expedition, and the Russell firm.

News of both thrusts, as well as of the Mountain Meadows Massacre and Brigham Young's proclamation of martial law, reached the Atlantic Coast nearly simultaneously in mid-November. There soon followed word of General Johnston's capture of Nauvoo Legion directives ordering this guerrilla campaign. That such events were happening so brazenly and at the hands of fellow Americans created a shock wave with national impact not unlike that of the Japanese attack on Pearl Harbor eighty-four years later. That the cost of the Utah War was about to escalate in terms of blood and treasure in the midst of the country's worst economic downturn in twenty years only added to the public's alarm at the events unfolding in Utah Territory.

From his reminiscences, it is clear William Clark knew the name of the Latter-day Saint cavalry officer who led the audacious destruction of his employer's three supply trains at Big Sandy and Green River—Maj. Lot Smith. By the end of 1857, the entire nation knew Smith's name, and he was well on his way to becoming perhaps the most mythic Latter-day Saint military figure of the nineteenth century.[1]

Here we laid over, as we were in no hurry now. Colonel Vanvliet had gone into Salt Lake City, and Brigham Young refused to allow the soldiers and their supply trains to enter the city. The Mormons had an armed force stationed along the road out, nearly to old Fort Bridger, one hundred miles from Salt Lake City, and they were building fortifications to keep the government trains out. There were twenty-five hundred armed Mormons stationed along this road.

Colonel Vanvliet came back, and when he met the first train, ordered them to turn back to Ham's Fork and stop till further orders. He left part of his escort with them, exchanged part of his mules, and rode back to Fort Laramie as fast as he could, changing mules at each train and ordering each train to stop at Ham's Fork.

We were twenty-six miles from the Fork when he met us.

We rested here a while, then drove in and camped near the other trains. There were four trains ahead of us. This was about the last of September.

There was a fine camping place with plenty of good water and fine grass for our cattle.

Other trains kept coming in every day or two.

After we had been here about a week, Oct. 4, I think it was, Lot Smith, a Mormon captain with two hundred mounted men came riding into camp, stopped awhile, then rode off toward Green River. About seven miles out, he met one of the Company's trains. He stopped them and ordered them to go back. The boss, seeing that they had the advantage of him, said that his cattle were nearly worn out, and that he would have to rest them before he could go far. Smith allowed them to camp and rest up, and then he and his men rode on. When he was out of sight they yoked up and came on to Ham's Fork.

Smith reached Green River just as another train had unyoked, and drew their guns and demanded their arms. The boss, seeing they had no show, surrendered. Smith's men set fire to their train. The boss plead for their private property—clothing, bedding, guns—and the mess wagon with their provisions which they finally allowed them, but burned the twenty-five wagons of government goods before their eyes. Smith then ordered the men to take good care of the cattle till he came back after them.

He and his men went from here to the Sandy and came upon two trains close together, camped for dinner, the next day, and burned the wagons, allowing the men their private property and mess wagons and cattle to haul them back to the States. They drove the rest of the cattle back to Green River, where the others were, and left them there.

The boss of the Green River train, with his assistant, came to Ham's Fork the next day.

In a couple of days Rennick and four or five men from each train, with ten soldiers that Vanvliet left, went to Green River, got these cattle, and drove them to Ham's Fork. Then we moved up the Fork two or three miles to shift camp as our herd was now so large and trains were still coming in. We stayed here a few days and moved again.

Rip Van Winkle, boss of one of the trains that was burned, was in charge of the cattle while moving this time.[2] As they were driving the herd along about a half mile behind the wagons, Lot Smith came charging up, took all the men prisoners, and drove off the whole herd of thirteen hundred cattle. He turned the prisoners all loose that day except Rip Van Winkle. They kept him two days before turning him loose.

We now moved camp every day or two on account of grass.

SECTION 8

"Into Winter Quarters"
An Agonizing Crawl to Fort Bridger

Editorial Notes

In this section Clark describes the frustrations of the Utah Expedition's march and countermarch along Hams Fork in an unsuccessful search for a northern (Bear River–Soda Springs) approach to Salt Lake City to avoid forcing passage through Echo Canyon. He then turned to the agonies of the army's immediately following crawl to the charred ruins of Fort Bridger while beset by blizzards, snow drifts, subzero temperatures, and a massive loss of draught animals. The soldiers and teamsters who endured the rigors of these twin disasters compared them to the hardships of Napoleon's retreat from Moscow in the winter of 1812. If anything, writing from the comforts of a half-century later, William Clark muted the horrors of what he experienced in northeastern Utah during October and November 1857.

In his diary, Capt. John W. Phelps of the Fourth U.S. Artillery recorded the rigors of attempting to march cross country up Hams Fork without a road while trying to manage a battery of brass field howitzers. On October 6, as Phelps and his Light Battery B prepared to strike out for the elusive northern route, he wrote, "There was never a military command in such a position as ours—so far from resources, these and free intercourse with home about to be shut out by the snows of winter, our [ox]trains in the rear and the grazing in front being assailed with fire by the enemy, that enemy outnumbering us five to one; and our governor and the officer assigned to the command absent together with their instructions and an uncertainty as to when they will arrive. The order to the troops however is clear—it is to establish a fort at or near Salt Lake City, and this should be attempted whatever may be the consequences." One of Captain Phelps's exasperated artillerymen summarized the march and countermarch that followed with a verse from a Mother Goose rhyme: "Orders to return, the command divided into three divisions . . . 'The king of France marched up the hill. And then marched down again.'"

When Albert Sidney Johnston caught up with his command near Hams Fork's juncture with the Green River on November 3, the trek toward Fort Bridger resumed. Then a blizzard struck. Johnston's adjutant and tent mate, Maj. Fitz John Porter, recorded what happened: "It was one magnificent struggle from the beginning to this place [Bridger]. One more day's march and our meat ration—beef, horse, and mule—would have been diminutively small for the winter. The last company of the 10th infantry, escorting the last of the supply-trains to Fort Bridger, reached this camp at 10, P.M., on the 22nd; thus requiring six days to move our little army and its supplies less than six miles. . . . The men have borne their trials without a murmur . . . not a word of complaint have I heard."

On November 19 the expedition's rear guard, a battalion of Lt. Col. Philip St. George Cooke's Second U.S. Dragoons, followed their comrades into the ruins of Fort Bridger. Half of Cooke's troops had lost their horses to starvation and exposure. His report to Albert Sidney Johnston described what he saw on the road from Hams Fork as "hundreds of dead and frozen animals which for thirty miles nearly block the road; with abandoned and shattered property, they mark, perhaps, beyond example in history, the steps of an advancing army with the horrors of a disastrous retreat." It was an experience unmatched in American military history until the withdrawal from the North Korean reservoirs during the winter of 1950–1951.[1]

Once at Fort Bridger, Clark and two of his four "chums"—Edwin Leach and Martin L. Sherwood—lay plans to continue their trip to California notwithstanding General Johnston's ban on westward travel through Utah. George B. Tuttle dropped out of the group at this point in a quixotic attempt to extract his underage brother, Ira, from an unwise five-year enlistment in the Second Dragoons. Albert Frank had apparently had enough adventure for one winter and decided to risk a return trip across the plains rather than press on to California with Clark or spend the winter at Fort Bridger as either an unemployed teamster on short rations or an infantry private *in the battalion of volunteer troops then recruiting troops at General Johnston's behest.*

In about two weeks Colonel Alexander came up with one thousand soldiers, but with no orders.[2]

The Mormons burned the grass ahead of us for several miles.

After the teams had all arrived, Colonel Alexander concluded, as the Mormons had Echo Canyon route so well fortified, he would have to take the Soda Springs route, down Bear River and in by the northern settlements.[3] So he ordered us to move up to Soda Springs, eighty miles north.

The Mormons had, before this, captured four teamsters and escorted them into Salt Lake City.[4]

While preparing to move, and after tying up my bed which had been under some willows, I stepped back for my gun which had been under the bed. I took hold of the muzzle, and, as I raised it, the hammer caught on a twig and I got the charge all in my hand which made an ugly wound, disabling me for driving.[5]

We moved on, and in a few days reached Soda Springs. It was now quite cold, and we had some snow before reaching the Springs. In a day or two after eight or ten inches of snow fell and it was very cold weather.[6]

After we had been there about a week an express messenger from Colonel Albert Sidney Johnston came riding into camp with orders for us to move back to the crossing on Ham's Fork, and stay there till he arrived.

We started back. It was very cold and our cattle were weak. We could make but eight or ten miles a day. We left some of our poorest cattle at each camp, they not being able to travel. We arrived at the crossing in eight days.

Two days afterwards [on November 3] Colonel Johnston came in with his men.

Some of them rode out to old Fort Bridger, and, after looking it over, came back and ordered us to move on to Bridger, and they would go into winter quarters there.[7]

By this time several mountaineers had fallen in with us and traveled in our company for protection, as the Mormons had killed one or two already.

These mountaineers all had squaws for wives, some of them quite nice looking. The men had some of the finest buckskin suits I ever saw, made by their squaws. The seams were welted and fringed and the coats were trimmed with otter fur around the collars and cuffs, down the front, and around the bottom.[8] Across the shoulders and on the sleeves were patterns wrought in beads of various colors. The pants and vests were also trimmed with beads in fine taste.

A company of Dragoons came up to camp before we started.[9] This made about two thousand five hundred men—soldiers and teamsters.

It was a bitter cold day that we started. The train was six miles long. The last of the train did not leave camp till noon, and it was dark when they got into camp that night.

It was a very cold night and the herders could not stay with the cattle. In the morning we found we had lost one hundred and sixty head which had strayed off in the storm, and sixty head of government mules had died in camp. This weakened our teams so that we could move only a part of our train at a time, many of the cattle left being too weak to work.[10] We were six days getting this train twenty-six miles to Fort Bridger.

Here Charley Morehead, Major & Russel's pay master, came in to pay off the teamsters that wanted to stop here.[11] Many of them took their pay and volunteered to go into the army. Others went back to the States, being fitted out with teams by the Company.[12]

It was two weeks before our loads had been turned over to the government officers.

Then my comrades and myself took our pay.

Sherwood, Leach, and myself had decided to try to go through Salt Lake City and on to California.[13]

George Tuttle had found a brother here among the Dragoons that had run away from home and enlisted. He was under age, and George said he would stop here and try to get him out.[14]

A Prisoner by the Mormons

Utah was under martial law.[15] The troops had captured four Mormon prisoners, among them "Doc" Hickman, a brother of "Bill" Hickman's.

The Mormons had plotted to kill Hurt, an Indian agent that was stationed near Spanish Fork, south of Salt Lake.[16] He had taken to the mountains and came to the soldiers' camp for protection. He brought the news of the Mountain Meadows Massacre and the Parrish murder, also that the Mormons had the Aikin brothers and comrades in prison.

Chat Rennick had long before this got to be a warm friend of ours. He tried to persuade me to go back to Leavenworth with him and said he would guarantee me a train in the spring at one hundred dollars a month if I would go. But I was determined to try to get to California.

Colonel Johnston had forbidden any one going into Salt Lake City, and had his pickets out five miles.

The Mormons had twenty-five hundred soldiers stationed between here and the City. There was no other way of going except through the Mormon camps.

We each bought an Indian pony. Leach and Sherwood got saddles also, but I could not get one, so I had to use my blankets for a saddle and had rope stirrups.

We went to Colonel Johnston for a pass to go through their lines, but he refused us, and also forbid our going. We asked him what we should do. He told us we could either volunteer or go back to the States. He would give us fifteen days' rations to take us to Laramie where we could get another supply.

This was about the middle of November and very cold weather.

We were not the kind of boys that turned back. We did not care to be soldiers and winter here on quarter rations as it was evident they would have to do. Seventy-five wagon loads of provisions had been burned, we had lost twenty-five hundred head of cattle by the Indians and Mormons and those that strayed off. Colonel Johnston had sent Colonel Marcy across the country to [New] Mexico with pack mules for supplies.[17]

We concluded to take the fifteen days' rations and make sure of that, and then try for California. As Rennick had crossed to California the

"Into Winter Quarters"

year before, we concluded to make a confidant of him, tell him our plans, and ask his advice. He tried to discourage us, saying the Mormons would never let us go through. If they did not kill us themselves they would put the Indians on us.

But as he could not discourage us, he gave us what information he could as to how we could get around the pickets, and helped us to some provisions on the sly. Then we started, as was supposed, for the States.

We went fifteen miles toward the States, then struck across the bench to a stream called the Muddy, and got down the bluff just at night. It was a very cold night, but we found wood and very good grass on the hill sides, and hobbled our horses for the night.[18]

Then we made some coffee and thawed out our frozen bread and ate supper.

The next day we traveled down the stream, keeping close under the bluff, till night, and camped close to thirty head of our cattle that had run off the night we left Ham's Fork. Here we felt easy.

We built a good fire, mixed some bread in the top of the [flour] sack, and baked it in the ashes, as our cooking utensils consisted only of a coffee pot and three tin cups.

After supper we concluded we could make a little stake by driving these cattle back to the soldiers' camp. The soldiers were so short of food that we thought we would be well paid for them. So the next morning we mounted our ponies and drove the cattle to camp and turned them over to Rennick. He said that we should get good pay for that work. Rennick delivered the cattle to the quartermaster who said he would settle with us the next day.

He came with several wagon bosses the next day to decide on a fair price to pay us. Most of the men thought that two dollars a day would be enough, but Rennick told them that we ought to have big pay, no wages about it; that we had taken big chances, lost three days in the dead of winter and our provisions; and these cattle were fifteen hundred dollars clear to the government, and the soldiers needed them badly, but the cheap men prevailed. They concluded to pay us fifteen dollars apiece. Mr. Rennick was so provoked at this that he gave us more provisions and got a pass for us to go and hunt more cattle. He went with us out past the pickets and got us into our camp that night, then went back to the fort.

We traveled all next day and reached the crossing of the Bridger road, thirteen miles from Bridger, just at dark. Here we camped.

Soon it began to snow. We stuck up some sticks and stretched a wagon cover which we had brought with us, to shield us from the storm.

SECTION 9

"Saddle Up and Be Quick about It"

Into Captivity with the Latter-day Saints

Editorial Notes

With this section, William Clark begins the story of his captivity by the Nauvoo Legion and strange, weeks-long relationship with Lt. William Adams Hickman. Although he was one of the Legion's junior officers, Hickman, along with Capt. Orrin Porter ("Port") Rockwell, was among the most famous of Brigham Young's operatives known as his "b'hoys."[1] By the time of the Utah War, reporters' and editors' frequent use of the adjective "notorious" had made it virtually part of Hickman's name. Called simply "Bill" during the Utah War era, after the near apotheosis of James Butler ("Wild Bill") Hickok in the 1870s, historians and other writers began to dub Hickman "Wild Bill" while also using the descriptors "Danite" and "Destroying Angel."

Within the Nauvoo Legion's command structure, Hickman certainly took orders, but, because of his proximity to Young, he developed a freewheeling, independent style that belied his relatively low-level military rank. Accordingly, in early 1858 when Brigham Young set out to create a new military force to be called the "Standing Army of Israel," apostle George A. Smith explained to his brother in England, "Porter Rockwell and Wm. Hickman are getting up two independent companies. All the men selected are well mounted, expert riders, and dead shots,—armed with Rifles and Revolvers."

Bill Clark's time spent as Hickman's prisoner in the fall of 1857 was bracketed by the latter's murder of ammunition trader Richard E. Yates in Echo Canyon on October 18 and that of the Aiken party in Utah's southern settlements during November. Clark's recollection of his whimsical banter while riding alongside and drinking with Bill Hickman provides a view of both men not found elsewhere.[2]

After supper Captain [William] Maxwell, a Mormon officer, with twenty-eight men came riding up, and ordered us to saddle up and go with them, and be quick about it too. We had footed it all day through a foot of snow to save our ponies, and were very tired. We asked permission to stay where we were till morning. He said he didn't want any back talk. So we packed our ponies, mounted, and rode six miles as fast as our ponies could go, with about half of the men in front and the others behind us, to the Mormon camp where there were two or three hundred more men.

They took our ponies for the night and in the morning sent us with an escort of five men to Bear River.[3] Here Leach and Sherwood traded horses with the Mormons and gave their guns to boot, as guns were of no use to us now. They got good strong ponies.

Here they amused us for some time by asking questions. We answered them as we thought best. Finally, when bed time came, they sang some of their Mormon songs and had prayer. But such a prayer I never heard before. They prayed for the destruction of Johnston's army and for the torture of all Gentiles—not excepting present company even.[4] Although hard to listen to we stood it like majors, as we knew there was no other way, and kept as cheerful as we could. We joked with them and made ourselves quite at home, although, I confess, we were very badly scared. Below is a sample of their songs—one verse only:

> Squaw killer Harney's on the way,
> Duda duda day,
> The Mormon boys for to slay.
> Duda duda day.
> Come let us be on hand,
> By Brigham Young to stand,
> And if our enemies do appear,
> We'll sweep them from the land.[5]

Next morning they sent five men with us to their big camp at the entrance of Echo Canyon. There were nine hundred soldiers here. This is a very deep canon. The road ran close to the rocks and wound along the stream. The Mormons had stone fortifications all along on top of the mountains. They could get behind these and shoot the soldiers as they passed through. It was a very strong position.[6]

The Mormons were armed with every conceivable kind of guns from a toy pistol up.

They had prayer here also before retiring.

These were the poorest specimens of humanity that I had ever seen together, nearly all English, Danes, and Welsh. And such clothing! It was impossible to tell what the original goods were.

Remnants of old bed quilts and blankets served, as overcoats.[7] They were a set of bigots—claimed that they could whip the whole world, and that Johnston's army would not be a breakfast spell for them, as they had the Lord on their side to help fight their battles.[8]

We agreed with them in everything and were very anxious to find what settlement would be the best place for us to stop at and make our home.

Next morning they brought up our ponies and we prepared to start with an escort of seven men, Bill Hickman, their "destroying angel," in charge.

As we started he asked each of us our names. Sherwood and Leach gave their names first. He turned to me.

I said, "They call me Bill Clark."

"Well, I can recollect that, for my name is Bill Hickman," said he. "I suppose you have heard. of me. You heard Doc Hurt speak of me, didn't you?"

I said that I believed I had.

"I reckon he gives me a hard name."

"I didn't hear him say much of anything. Hurt stayed at the soldiers camp and I was with the freighters," said I.

"I'd like to get in reach of him with my old rifle, he wouldn't tell any more tales, and I'll get him yet," said Hickman.

Then he said to me, "Ain't you afraid of me?"

"No," said I, "why should I be afraid of you any more than anybody else[?]"

"Haven't you heard I was a mighty bad man?"

FIG. 11. William Adams ("Bill") Hickman (1815–1883). A Nauvoo Legion lieutenant, Hickman was a trusted Brigham Young "b'hoy" or agent, who was William Clark's captor as well as benefactor. This undated but post–Civil War photo shows Hickman still partially disabled from wounds received during a Salt Lake City gunfight in 1859, the beginning of his slide into alcohol, disfavor, and poverty. Hickman Family photo.

"Saddle Up and Be Quick about It"

I told him that I had heard lots of things I didn't believe.

"Why are you not afraid to go with me?" "Because," said I, "I never was anywhere yet, but that if I behaved myself I was treated like a gentleman, and for that reason expect to be with you, and among the Mormons. If we were very much afraid, we wouldn't have traveled three days to get around the pickets to get in here." I lied a little.

Hickman laughed and said, "Well I guess you will be."

Then I said, "Mr. Hickman, how will you trade horses?"

"I can't spare this one," said he, "I have rode him from Bridger to the City, one hundred and sixteen miles, in fourteen hours."

"He would just suit me, and you would look pretty well on my pony, and I would look lots better on yours."

He laughed and said, "You'd look better on that 'ere little pack mule ahead."

I told him I thought he'd feel bad to have such a good looking prisoner on top of that little mule, and top of that load too. Then I never did like a pack saddle to ride on. He said that he would take me into the City on it.

I said that it would look lots better if he would put me on that big mule he had loose.

"At the next stop you may get on him and ride to Weber Canyon.[9] I'm going to leave him there."

In a few miles we came to a camp and I put my things on him and rode ten miles to Weber Canyon.

We had kept up a lively conversation and Hickman got quite jolly.

It was just noon when we got there, and he asked us into the cookhouse to get dinner with him, saying we need not go hungry while with him, and told us to leave our provisions here, as we did not need any while we were with him.

After dinner I got on my pony, and Hickman said I could ride him a few miles, or till he gave out, then he would pack me on the little pack mule.

I said, "Not much. You don't know the kind of stuff that pony is made of. He's not one that will get his master on a pack saddle." We rode on to Little's camp.[10] This was on top of the mountain, and their last camp before reaching the City. We got here just before dark. There were two of Brigham's sons here, Joseph and Brigham, Jr. These Mormons were a more surly and sarcastic set, full of stinging remarks to us. We kept as cheerful as we could and did not pretend to take their slurs, although hard to bear.

Here they sang several of their Mormon songs. They had board seats to seat the whole camp. They invited us to take seats near the middle with Mormons surrounding us. Then a tall, slim, hatchet faced man by the name of Little knelt in front of us and commenced to pray.

He prayed for a full hour, and asked the Lord to bring death and destruction to the United States officials, to Johnston's whole army and every sympathizer, and every Gentile living. He prayed that they should all be tortured in the most horrible manner.

I think it must have taken the whole combined talent of the heads of the Mormon Church to invent this prayer. It was a hard thing to listen to and keep our nerves quiet and hands off. But to *look crooked* would have been death to us, so we bore it with all the grace we could command. This was a long night to us, after this prayer.

There were about two hundred Mormons in this camp. After breakfast in the morning we gave our wagon cover to the Mormons, as we had no more use for it, and started out. Hickman said I might ride my pony a ways, then he would put me on the pack mule. I told him my pony was all right.

We had a good deal of rough road, and going over the mountain, I would jump off and walk, and rest my pony, every chance I got.

Every little while Hickman would ask if my pony was give out.

I would tell him "No, nor he wasn't going to either." Then he would start off on the jump for a while.

We traveled on till noon, when we came to a station and got dinner and fed our horses well. It being very cold, we rested a good hour, then started on. It began to get warmer, and in a few miles it was muddy. Every little hill that we went over, I would walk and rest my pony. As we turned out of Emigration Canyon there was quite a hill, and I was leading my pony.[11]

"Saddle Up and Be Quick about It"

FIG. 12. Army bull train on the Great Plains. One of the few illustrations accurately portraying a six-yoke string of oxen with the bull whacker walking to the left side to control his twelve cattle. Because of the five-thousand-pound weight of their freight, the oxen in Clark's twenty-six-wagon train probably strained to pull a single vehicle rather than the three-wagon hitch depicted here. ClassStock / Alamy Stock Photo.

Hickman called, "Is the pony give out?" "No," said I.
We were now nine miles from the City.
"Well, come on then," said he, and we went on the jump as fast as my pony could run, clear to the City, without ever letting up for a moment.

SECTION 10

"Difficult for a Man to Escape Their Vengeance"

Life in Salt Lake City

Editorial Notes

During the fall of 1857, the Nauvoo Legion captured scores of U.S. soldiers and civilians falling into differing categories and circumstances: army deserters seeking a safe haven in Latter-day Saint settlements or intent on striking out for the Pacific Coast; discharged (unemployed) teamsters heading for California's goldfields or attempting to return east to the "States"; soldiers and civilians captured while wandering within the sprawling expanse of Camp Scott; hapless travelers uninvolved in the war but who encountered the Legion while oblivious to the risks involved; individuals possessing weapons and ammunition badly needed in Utah; and emigrants displaying cash, jewelry, livestock, vehicles, farm implements, tools, and clothing while passing through Utah's most hard-scrabble communities.

Once they became prisoners, these individuals or groups received widely varying treatment depending upon the timing, location, and other circumstance of their capture as well as their own demeanor, attitudes, behavior, and religious affiliation. Some captives were treated with great kindness and hospitality and quickly sent on their way. Others were welcomed and proselytized as potential Latter-day Saints. Still others were murdered for a variety of reasons and stripped of their possessions. Killing and looting were by no means confined to the victims at Mountain Meadows.

Of all these prisoners, only three are known to have lived and left published accounts of their captivity: Charles W. Becker, a discharged civilian teamster; Henry Feldman, an enlisted hospital steward with the Tenth U.S. Infantry; and unemployed teamster Bill Clark.

"Difficult to Escape Their Vengeance"

In Charlie Becker's case, he struck an immediate rapport in the mountains with Legion major Warren Snow of Manti, Sanpete County, who "stepped out and pledged himself to protect me, a pledge which was faithfully kept, and then some." Becker also had the good fortune to befriend Charles F. Decker, a Brigham Young son-in-law whom the Legion's commanding general permitted to take Becker to his farm near Salt Lake City on condition that he would do chores and promise not to escape. Becker came to view the Deckers as "this most lovable Mormon family" and had occasion to meet Brigham Young at their dinner table during his episodic visits to daughter Lena and her family. Hospital steward Feldman apparently formed no such relationship in captivity, and, in his army debriefing, comes across as a braggart if not liar about the circumstances of his capture on October 30 and supposed attempts to escape. William Clark, like Charlie Becker, had a knack for cultivating an influential protector—Bill Hickman—whose reputation as a killer close to Utah's supreme leader shielded him from rough treatment or worse in Salt Lake City. That Clark seemed young, affable, and respectful to the Latter-day Saints with whom he interacted also helped him to survive, as did his self-described role in the war as merely an "ox teamster" without military prominence or valuable information. That Clark had enough personal possessions to bribe or barter his way out of Utah was also helpful, as was the fact that his assets were not enough to generate destructive envy or prompt an interest in robbing him.

However, once Clark left Salt Lake City and parted company with Bill Hickman, he found a different tone in Utah's southern settlements and along the Old Spanish Trail to California. There, in the immediate wake of the Mountain Meadows Massacre and the very region in which it had been planned and executed, the anxiety that first gripped him when captured by the Nauvoo Legion returned. As this section of Bill Clark's reminiscences conveys, he was again forced to live by his wits and to pay close attention to who seemed trustworthy and who was an existential threat.[1]

I was eight or ten rods behind, doing my best to keep up, when we went down the bench into the suburbs of the City, and every Mormon woman and child was out to see Hickman and his prisoners.

They could tell a Gentile as far as they could see him by their hair and dress. The Mormons all had long hair. Every house we passed, they would rush out to see us. I didn't blame them much for looking at me. I think I would have made a good picture for a comic almanac. I was six feet and an inch and slim. My pony weighed about seven hundred pounds. With my blankets roped around him and rope stirrups, gun slung across my back, my sack of clothing in front of me, and a Scotch cap with a shiny visor on my head, I didn't wonder that they stared at me. But we kept on the jump and when the others reached Main Street they halted till I came up, then we rode down Main Street.

I rode up beside Hickman and said, "You look dry. Can't we get something to warm us up?" I had sized him up.

"No," said he, "they are not allowed to sell a drop in the Territory, but you might inquire at Kimbal[l]'s there." "Hold on, I'll see." I got off and went in and said, "Give me a little good stuff—Valley tan if you have it."[2] They said, "We are not allowed to sell a drop in the Territory."

I laid a five dollar gold piece on the counter and told him to give me a quart in an old tin.

He took the gold piece, put it in the drawer, handed me three dollars, took a two-quart pail, went into the back room, then came back and gave it to me. I took it out and told Hickman, as we were namesakes, we would test it first, and, if it did not kill us, we would give the others some.[3]

I drunk and passed it to him. We concluded that it would not kill us and passed it around.[4] There was a little left, so Hickman and I finished it. Then we went to Townsend's Hotel.

Hickman introduced us to the landlord as "three Gentile prisoners he had captured in the mountains," adding, "They are pretty good boys. Take good care of them, and I will be in in the morning."

I persuaded Hickman to stop and take supper with us. He consented, and the rest of the escort went their way. He got to be very sociable and said he had a "fool Gentile brother" and he would bring him in and introduce him to us, and that he would come tomorrow and take us up to Brigham's and get us a pass to travel where we wished in the Territory, as after a while we would join the Church.[5] We told him we liked it here very much and would try to enjoy ourselves the best we could.

He had begun, by this time, to think we were just about green enough for good Mormon converts, and we were willing that he should.

A great many came in to see the prisoners, among them Hyrum Smith, Kimball, and others at the head of the Church.[6] They asked us all sorts of questions regarding Johnston's army. We were very ignorant, knew but little about it. We were ox teamsters; all we knew about them was that their supplies were short, and they would be on short rations. This pleased the Mormons, and they would say, "The Lord will take care of us and fight our battles," and that Colonel Johnston's army could never come into Salt Lake City.[7]

We agreed with them in every thing that seemed to please them.

Griff Williams, the mail carrier from San Bernadino, was also there that night.

In the evening before going to bed, the office being clear except Williams and us boys, Williams moved over to where we were sitting and said in a whisper, "Be very careful what you say in this house. *These walls have ears.* I know what I am talking about. The man who keeps this house is a villain, an[d] one wrong statement from one of you might put you all out of the way." He said that he had just come in from San Bernardino with the mail. He had hard work to get through, both from Indians and Mormons. A cousin of his, living at Redfield, had hard work to save his life while in her own house. Finally on account of his having the U.S. mail they concluded to let him pass and told his cousin that they would "fix" him on his return. But he had had another man to take the mail back and he was waiting here for Amasy Lyman, one of the twelve apostles, from California, that he was acquainted with, and expected him here in a day or two, and he would go south with him for protection. He said Lyman did not approve of the Mountain Meadows Massacre or any of the murders that had been committed in Utah. He had charge of the San Bernardino Mormons, and, after the Mountain Meadows Massacre, Brigham had ordered him and his flock home to Utah. He had just come into the southern settlements with one train and part of his wives, and was going to send a train from Johnson's Fork

[Fort] back to California for the rest of his family, and help others to come that were not able.[8] Williams was going to California with this train. A Mr. Savage was to take charge of the train.[9] He was a good man, and Williams thought that, if we could reach his place, we might get him to intercede for us. Although, if the Mormons let us pass, the Indians would hardly let us, for the Mormons had them completely under their control, and a wink from a Mormon would settle us.[10] The Mormons had missionaries among them to keep them stirred up all the time. These missionaries claimed that they had to promise the Indians more scalps when Williams came back in order to let him pass.

Williams also said that the Mormons had had the Aikins brothers and comrades—six in all—in prison for two months on one charge or another, and had just sent them out the south route with an escort with Porter Rockwell in charge, and, if we ever heard of them again, we would probably hear that the Indians had killed them.[11]

Porter Rockwell and Bill Hickman were the leading Danites, or "Destroying Angels," and with Porter Rockwell in charge was proof that they would never reach California.

I will state here the condition of the Mormon Church at that time.

Brigham Young and his officials had a death grasp on every man in the Church—or out of it in Utah. He made every Mormon consecrate all of his property to the Church, which was really a deed subject to the dictation of the church. They could not take any property out of the Territory, except with Brigham's Permission.

Brigham also had a revelation that every Mormon must confess all of his sins and crimes to the bishops and high priest of their settlement, and they did so.[12]

He had a set of officers called Danites scattered through the Territory, for the purpose of putting any of their brethren out of the way when they became dissatisfied with the Church, also to take care of any Gentiles they could find.[13] Hence the Mountain Meadows Massacre, the Aikins' murder, the Parrish murder, the Potter murder, and a hundred others.[14]

There were many Mormons who did not sanction these butcheries, but dare not say a word against it for fear that their turn would come next, but they dare not disobey an order said to come from Brigham.

"Difficult to Escape Their Vengeance"

FIG. 13. A ragged, trail-worn bull whacker in Salt Lake City. This self-portrait was by William Henry Jackson, a non-Mormon teamster who retraced William Clark's overland journey in 1866. Jackson, later a prominent western artist and photographer, recorded his end-of-trail wardrobe as so tattered he had to wear two pairs of trousers in Salt Lake to avoid arrest for indecent exposure. Drawing by Jackson, courtesy Scotts Bluff National Monument.

Brigham Young would preach inflammatory sermons, and almost order a murder by saying, "You must make a settlement" with such and such people "or I will turn the Indians loose upon them." The bishops and apostles would do the same. It was difficult for a man not in full sympathy with all of their doings to escape their vengeance. To disobey an order from Brigham was almost certain death, and, in the outer settlements, to disobey an order from a bishop was the same.

But to return to the Townsend Hotel.

About ten o'clock in the morning Bill Hickman came in with his "fool Gentile brother," introduced him to us and was quite jolly. As I found that "medicine" which we had the night before at Kimbal[l]'s did Hickman so much good, I asked him if we hadn't better go and get another dose. He thought we had. So we went to Kimbal[l]'s store and said we would like to go into his back room. He opened the door, handed me a cup, and pointed to a barrel. We went in, drew some, and all drank a little. I paid the bill, and then we went for a walk.

After awhile we went to Kimbal[l]'s again. Then Hickman said that he would take us up to Brigham's, introduce us to him, and see what he could do for us there. We went to Brigham's office, and Hickman introduced us as "three Gentile prisoners," and said, "They are pretty good boys too, and are going to stay with us. They want a pass to travel around to find a good place to stop this winter."

Brigham gave us a pass and we chatted awhile, then went back to Kimbal[l]'s, as we had learned how to treat Hickman's case. Hickman then invited us to come out to his place and stay over night. He told us that, if we couldn't get anything to do to make a living for the winter, he would donate us a fat ox and twenty bushels of wheat and we could get through on that. Then he shook hands, bade us goodbye and rode away.

From Salt Lake to California

The next day a man by the name of Brown came in from the soldiers' camp with a fine horse.

I tried to trade a gold watch that I had for his horse, but, as he lived at Fillmore, one hundred and fifty miles south, he said that he couldn't trade, as he would have no way of getting home.[15] I told him that we intended to go down that way in about a week, and, if I wanted the horse, I would call and see him. He said that I could have him then if I wanted him.

One day we got on our ponies and went out to Hickman's place, eight miles from the City, as we had agreed. He was not at home, but we stayed all night. We came back to the City the next morning.

SECTION 11

"We Started, Badly Scared Inside"

*From Salt Lake through
Utah's Southern Settlements*

Editorial Notes

Not only were the Latter-day Saints encountered by Bill Clark and his remaining "chums" leading a rough life, but the non-Mormons too were constantly in danger from a variety of human and environment threats. Mail conductor J. Griffin ("Griff") Williams and his wagon ran a virtual gauntlet monthly between Los Angeles and Salt Lake City to sustain the crucial overland link that enabled Utahns to send letters to the Atlantic Coast and Europe via Panama. In some cases, Williams himself contributed to the dangers besetting him, as when in 1870 he assaulted a newspaper editor in Gold Hill, Nevada, so viciously that an outraged "Mark Twain" discussed it in his 1872 book Roughing It *and in the pages of Nevada City's* Territorial Enterprise.[1] *Perhaps roughness ran in the family, as Griff was the nephew of legendary trapper-scout William Sherley ("Old Bill") Williams.*

The trader named "Dickey," whom the Clark party encountered with apostle Amasa Lyman, was likely nineteen-year-old Richard Rush Dickey, a non-Mormon resident of San Bernardino whom Cahuilla Indians would murder in 1862 near today's Palm Springs, California.

All this was part of the region's violent tone that added to the news of the recent Mountain Meadows Massacre and the Aiken party killings.

Fortunately for Bill Clark, Edwin Leach, and Martin Sherwood, they fell in with kindly "bishop" Redfield and his wife, who warned them of the dangers ahead from Indians and whites disguised as Native Americans.[2] Whom could they trust? It was an atmosphere and region so dangerous that a month later it prompted James Buchanan to plead with Thomas L. Kane, a friend of the Mormons, to abandon his contemplated mediating mission to Utah as too dangerous. If the president of the United States feared that Kane, Brigham Young's closest non-Mormon friend, might not make it across the desert and Utah's southern settlements to Salt Lake City, what risks awaited William Clark on the same trail?[3]

We started south the next day, saying that we were going to Cottonwood, but we went on south.[4] In the afternoon we fell in company with a young man by the name of Gid Finley from Salt Creek, one hundred and ten miles south of Salt Lake.[5]

He had been out to the Mormon camp with some supplies for the soldiers.

We rode along in company with him for some time, and, as our luggage was burdensome, he said that we might put it in his wagon, which we did. I put my gun in also.

He was quite a nice young man. He wanted my rifle. I told him that I would like to trade my pony and rifle for a larger horse. He said that he had a good horse at home that would suit me.

That night we stayed at American Fork with the bishop. In the morning we started on, intending to go home with Gid Finley and make a trade.[6] We began to place a little confidence in him. When we got to Springville, he told us to stop at Bishop Redfield's for dinner, and he would go to an acquaintance's of his, and if he started before we did, we would find him at Payson at the bishop's that night.[7] We stopped at Bishop Redfield's, and they were very nice people. They got us a fine dinner, and we stayed two hours. We told them that we were going to Johnson's Fort to try to go through to California with Savage's train.[8] The bishop said, "You better not try it. The Indians are very bad."

We said that we would be careful in going from one settlement to another, and that we were in company with Mr. Finley.

He said, "You can trust him. He is a good young man. But he can't keep you from the Indians. They are very bad. I know what I am talking about."

His wife tried to persuade us to stop with them for a while, for it would be impossible for us to get through. But, as our baggage was with Finley, we thought that we would take our chances, and catch up with him.

The bishop said, "From the bottom of my heart I wish you no harm." Then, throwing his head back, "The Indians are mighty bad, and *not altogether the Indians*." As he said this, the tears rolled down his cheeks.

But we saddled up, and he and his wife came out, and, with tears rolling down their cheeks, gave each of us a hearty shake of the hand, saying, "May the Lord bless you."

We started, badly scared inside if we did not show it outside, and rode on to overtake Finley.

As we had lost two hours, we rode to Spanish Fork without coming up with him. Here we inquired about him and learned that he was half an hour ahead. We pushed on out of town and across the creek, then about a mile to the top of a hill which sloped down to the bottom which we had to cross to go to Payson.

At the top of the hill we met a man coming with his horse on the lope [trot]. As he came up to us, he halted and said he had been watching for us all the afternoon, as Jack Brown had told him to be sure to tell us to go through from Spanish Fork in the night, or the Indians would kill us. I asked him who Brown was.

"Why, he is the man that was talking about trading his horse to you for a gold watch."[9]

I said that I remembered him.

"He said that he rode through from Salt Lake to Fillmore in three days, and the Indians had heard that you were coming before he got home, and were on the lookout for you.

"You see that smoke there on the flat near Doc Hurt's old place?"[10]

"Yes."

"Well, fifteen or twenty Indians have just camped there. They described you three and inquired of me if I had seen you. I told them that I had not. They are on the look out for you."

We asked if he had met Finley.

He said that we could just see him. "He can travel anywhere. The Indians never trouble us Mormons. We all can talk their language and go where we please."

I said that Finley had our clothes and my gun.

"Let him go with them," said he, "and you go back to Spanish Fork and stay a day or two, for it is impossible for you to pass that Indian camp."

I asked him if he would go back and get our things.

He said that he would for five dollars. I told him that I would give it.

He said that he would be back to the bishop's by eight o'clock that night, and for us to go there to stay.

We went back and stayed with the bishop that night, but our clothes and gun did not come.

When bed time came they had prayer, and all knelt down but me. When they arose, the bishop took me to task for it, but I told him that I had too much respect for their religion to make a mock of it; that I did not belong to any church, and did not wish to insult them on religious matters.[11] He accepted my apology, but it left Sherwood and Leach in a fix, and he turned to them for an explanation of their actions.

But Sherwood was equal to the occasion, although a little embarrassed. He spoke right up and said that he and Leach were different from Clark as they were both brought up under religious influences and were used to kneeling with church people, and since they came to Utah the Mormons seemed near to them, and they deemed it a privilege to kneel with them in worship.

This explanation satisfied him.

The next day about ten o'clock the man came in with our clothing but no gun. He said that his horse got scared and he dropped the gun and could not find it, and as he had lost the gun, he would not charge us anything for bringing the rest and seemed sorry that the gun was lost.

That day a Mormon claimed Mart Sherwood's horse that he had got in trade from a Mormon soldier, proved that it was his, and took it away.

Now that his horse was gone, Sherwood concluded that he would stay here and join the Church.

He had that day found a Mormon that came from near where he did in Wisconsin. Sherwood joined the Church, and, in the spring *got out*.

I bought his saddle, and in a couple of days, as the Indians had moved their camp about half a mile from the road, Leach and myself determined to go through if possible.

"We Started, Badly Scared Inside"

So we started just at dark and rode to Payson, twelve miles and put up with the bishop.

The next day we reached Salt Creek and stopped with the Finleys. The young man was sorry that I had lost my rifle.

They were clever people and seemed very much alarmed for our safety. That night the sister of the young man's, an old maid, made one of the most pathetic prayers that I ever listened to. She prayed especially for our safety on the trip, asking the Lord to protect us from the Indians or any harm that might come to us, and that we might reach our destination in safety.

Six days before this the Aikins brothers and comrades, who left Salt Lake City the day we arrived under an escort with Porter Rockwell in charge, had, four of them, been killed on the Sevier River, sixteen miles from here, and the other two were wounded and ran back here and went to the bishop's for protection.[12] He kept them four days, then there was an official meeting called, and orders given for them to be taken out to Willow Creek and killed. This creek we crossed four miles from here.

It was at this time reported to us as having been done by the Indians.

In the morning we rode out into the foot hills with Finley to find his pony. We drove him up and I traded with him, giving him twenty dollars to boot.

We got our dinner and it was two o'clock before we started. We learned that Amasa Lyman and Griff Williams, the mail carrier, had passed. We mounted our ponies and started to overtake them.

There was no settlement for thirty miles, and we rode hard, determined to overtake them before camping, which we did about dark on the Sevier River and camped close to where the Aikins boys were killed a week before.

The snow was a foot deep and it was a very cold night. We had no shelter but plenty of wood.

We moved our fire and when the ground got cool enough, we spread our blankets down on the warm place and went to bed and to sleep, but about midnight woke up nearly frozen. We got up shivering and moved our fire again, and soon had another warm bed. But before daylight we froze out again. After this we made our bed on the snow and slept more comfortable.

The next day we arrived at Johnson's Fort where Savage was getting ready to start for California.

Here we stopped, and Griff Williams went on with Lyman to Cedar City.[13] Before going they spoke a good word to Savage for us.

There were two buildings here, and they were forted in with a high adobe wall for protection against Indians. This was five miles south of Fillmore and fourteen south of Corn Creek Reservation where there was quite a tribe of Indians.[14]

Savage went to Fillmore to complete getting ready to start, and Leach and myself went with him. Here I met Jack Brown, the man who sent word for us to come through in the night. He told us that we would have to be very careful, as the Indians were very anxious about us. He said he would do all that he could for us, and thought Savage could keep them off.

When we got back to the Fort that night, there were a dozen or more Indians there. Mrs. Johnson told us they were planning to steal our horses and saddles. She had overheard their plans. They had picked out our horses and saddles and looked them over, and, unless we guarded them closely, they would have them.

She told Savage about it, and he called the Indians and told them that he had bought our horses and saddles. He gave them a big talk in their own language and they went off.

In the morning we made a bargain with Mr. Savage to take us through. We gave him our horses and saddles and twenty dollars apiece, besides driving and taking care of a four mule team, and he was to do the best that he could to get us through to San Bernardino—a good one hundred and twenty-five dollars apiece besides our work, for our grub and his influence.

We now started for California. There was another Gentile by the name of Dickey that had come in from California with Amasa Lyman with goods to sell in the Territory. He went with us.

Lyman had gone ahead to Santa Clara, the southern settlement, and made arrangements as he went along to have all the Indians on the

"We Started, Badly Scared Inside"

FIG. 14. The Center Plaza, Pueblo of Los Angeles, 1857. Probably the first photograph of Los Angeles, then almost entirely composed of single-story sunbaked adobe structures with tile roofs and a few fired-brick buildings. The town's new brick water reservoir is in the plaza's center left. This is the scene William Clark would have experienced upon arriving in southern California in January 1858, the only significant settlement he had seen other than Salt Lake City since leaving the Missouri River in 1857. Photo by Charles C. Pierce.

route from Johnson's Fort to Santa Clara pacified to let us pass, and sent word for all of the Indians to come into Santa Clara the day that we were there.[15] He also sent for Ira Hatch, their best Indian interpreter.[16]

We got to Fillmore the first day. Here a train joined us. Our train was made up of teams from each settlement along the road to Cedar City. When we arrived at Cedar City we were joined by Lyman and Griff Williams.

SECTION 12

"Enough to Make a Man's Blood Run Cold"

Crossing Mountain Meadows and Beyond

Editorial Notes

In 1857 Mountain Meadows was a lush, spring-fed oasis in southern Utah near the Old Spanish Trail southwest of Cedar City. There, local settlers grazed their livestock, and California-bound emigrants paused to rest and "recruit" their animals before pushing across the territory's deserts. Ahead, along the Santa Clara River, Muddy Creek, and at the springs of Las Vegas in New Mexico Territory lay a few tiny missions established by the Latter-day Saints as well as Native American vegetable farms.

In early September 1857, the large Baker-Fancher party arrived at Mountain Meadows after running a gauntlet of hostility in the isolated southern settlements. This friction came from awareness of the Utah Expedition's approach from Nebraska Territory and rumors of federal reinforcements from Texas and California. Adding to the volatility of what some historians have called a general "war hysteria" in the region were a series of local disputes over the Baker-Fancher party's insensitive use of Mormon pastures to graze its large herds as well as rumors of bad behavior by a few of the emigrants that soon tainted the image of the entire party. Overlying all this were four other crucial factors: the provocative rhetoric used by apostle George A. Smith during his August trip to the southern settlements to urge vigilance and war preparations; Brigham Young's related prohibition on selling provisions to emigrants; awareness of apostle Parley P. Pratt's assassination in Arkansas during May 1857; and the so-called oath of vengeance, a commitment made by many Latter-day Saint males to avenge the assassination of founder Joseph Smith Jr. and his older brother Hyrum in Illinois during 1844.

On September 7, following a decision by local church and Nauvoo Legion leaders to eliminate the Baker-Fancher party, the group was attacked without warning by a band of southern Paiutes assembled and instigated by Maj. John D. Lee, a church leader in Harmony and Legion battalion commander, as well as a religiously adopted son of Brigham Young. The emigrants mounted an effective defense, which resulted in Legion troops from the Cedar City area, some painted as Indians, entering the fray as reinforcements for what became a long siege with casualties on both sides. Finally, on September 11, short of water and despairing of any other course of action, the Baker-Fancher party was inveigled to surrender its weapons and entrust members to the safe-conduct assurances of its besiegers. A mixed group of Paiutes and settlers then shot and bludgeoned the entire party except for seventeen children considered too young to tell the story. After looting all their possessions, including animals, rolling stock, and personal possessions (cash, jewelry, household goods, and even blood-soaked clothing), the perpetrators hastily buried the victims in shallow graves, an arrangement that soon brought wolves to the scene. The victims did not receive a proper burial until a party of U.S. troops provided one in 1859 while also erecting a rock cairn and cross as a monument.

There followed nearly a century and a half of obfuscation and acrimonious finger-pointing over virtually every aspect of the massacre, its victims, and their killers as well as the ownership of the massacre site, the marking of its graves, and even road signage. Chief among the controversies during this long period was the question of Brigham Young's role, if any, in ordering the massacre. In the interim, a group of Latter-day Saints from southern Utah were indicted for murder, but only one, John D. Lee, stood trial. After a hung jury in 1875, Lee was retried and convicted in 1876; twenty years after the massacre, he was executed by firing squad at Mountain Meadows.

Prolonged drought and erosion during the 1860s changed the meadows into an arid, ravaged place believed by locals to be cursed. Plagued by this folklore and the federal search for massacre participants, that part of Utah underwent something of a diaspora as suspects fled to other parts of the territory or surrounding venues. Following a rapprochement in the late 1990s between the Church of Jesus Christ of Latter-day Saints and descendants of victims in Arkansas, the church acquired and re-landscaped Mountain Meadows, marking the principal burial site with an appropriate cairn to replace the one erected by the army and subsequently destroyed by settlers.

This monument was dedicated by church president and prophet Gordon B. Hinckley during 1999. At the same site in 2007, apostle Henry B. Eyring read a statement from the Church's First Presidency expressing regret that the Paiute people had wrongly borne the brunt of blame.

Controversies linger, especially among southern Paiutes who believe their tribe has been wrongly demonized for its relatively minor role in the massacre, but the intensity of accusatory rhetoric is substantially less than at the turn of the twentieth century, which is when William Clark likely wrote of the tragedy.

Who were the members of the Baker-Fancher party, from where did they travel, and how many were massacred? Here too controversy has muddied the historiography of the incident. Simply put, there is widespread agreement that overwhelmingly the emigrants were from northwest Arkansas. Nevertheless, almost immediately after the massacre folklore sprang up that en route the party had been joined by a group of young, single, aggressive men dubbed "Missouri Wildcats," some of whom supposedly claimed to have taken part in Latter-day Saint persecution in Missouri during the 1830s. Other rumors had the party containing residents of Illinois who boasted of having participated in the murder of the Smith brothers at Carthage, Illinois. The association of the Baker-Fanchers with Arkansas, scene of apostle Parley Pratt's recent murder, added volatility to such perceptions, which led to assertions that, in effect, the victims at Mountain Meadows brought on their own deaths because of Latter-day Saint persecution in their home states and bad behavior while crossing Utah. In one extreme case, John D. Lee demeaned the victims by arguing they deserved their fate because of bad character evidenced by syphilis, a stunning assertion based on his supposed examination of their bones.

Unlike modern ships and airliners, there was no manifest stating who started out for California with the Baker-Fancher party, and, even if there had been one, the composition of the group changed constantly on the trail as emigrants left or joined the group for a variety of reasons. Absent such a list, it has been impossible to determine with certainty how many people were killed and who they were. Only the fact that there were seventeen young survivors is undisputed.

"Make a Man's Blood Run Cold"

During the first decade of this century, historians Will Bagley, Ronald W. Walker, Richard E. Turley Jr., Glen M. Leonard, and Barbara Jones Brown tried mightily to compile the names of victims but succeeded only partially. The consensus then estimated the death toll at one hundred twenty people, an approximation long used by many historians. Such a loss would constitute the nation's greatest organized murder of unarmed civilians until the 1995 Oklahoma City bombing. However, in 2023 Turley and Brown published their second book on Mountain Meadows and concluded the number of victims was between one hundred one and one hundred fourteen.[1]

From his narrative, it is clear William Clark wrote about Mountain Meadows after John D. Lee's execution in 1877 and probably decades later. The extent to which he was influenced by what he had seen at the massacre site in 1857 and by subsequent national sentiment about the tragedy is an interesting question. In many respects, Clark's treatment of the massacre is one of the principal reasons historians have used his reminiscences since 1922. In most cases they keyed to Clark's provocative assertion, "We were the first train that ever passed over this ground after that wholesale murder," while missing the important qualifier a few paragraphs later that his party had been preceded two weeks before by what he identified as the Crooks, Cooper, and Collins train.

Although historian Juanita Brooks quoted substantial excerpts from the early part of William Clark's reminiscences, she had reservations about the accuracy of the small later portion dealing with Mountain Meadows. In 1950, in The Mountain Meadows Massacre, she commented, "His account of the massacre might have been gathered from the group [of his friends] as they traveled or pieced together from subsequent information; like others, he claimed to be one of the first company to pass over the ground after the tragedy."[2] In his 2002 book Blood of the Prophets, Will Bagley confined his discussion of Clark's narrative to a single paragraph in which he quoted Clark's passage through Mountain Meadows without challenge. Six years later Walker, Turley, and Leonard's book made no reference to William Clark, as was also the case in 2023 with Turley and Brown's Vengeance Is Mine.[3]

The reality is that "A Trip Across the Plains in 1857" contains only a meager three sentences about Clark's passage through the meadows based on his firsthand, personal observations. The rest of his comments about Mountain Meadows, although directionally accurate, were based on trailside speculation and later newspaper coverage connected to the Lee trials or the books flowing from them. Clark's assertion that there were precisely one hundred thirty-two victims came not from his own count in 1857 but some source highly inaccurate and unidentified.

If William Clark and his companions were not the first to cross Mountain Meadows after the massacre, who was? In 1950 Juanita Brooks identified five such individuals or groups that passed through the area soon after September 11 and before Clark's passage in late December. Within a week of the massacre, Indian farmer Jacob Hamblin inspected the gruesome scene unaccompanied; his small ranch virtually bordered the meadows and was then serving as the initial refuge for the seventeen surviving children. The day after the massacre, a train of about twenty commercial freighters, led by Latter-day Saints William Matthews and Sidney Tanner, crossed the meadows en route to San Bernardino; this group was accompanied for safety by three wagons of non-Mormon emigrants led by George Powers. Because of the presence of these gentiles, what has come to be called the Matthews-Tanner train deliberately rolled through the killing field at night, leaving no firsthand account of the scene. Shortly thereafter in September, a large party of emigrants dubbed the Turner-Dukes train (called Crooks, Cooper, and Collins by Clark) passed through the area but bypassed Mountain Meadows and was therefore unable to describe the victims on a firsthand basis. Once the Turner-Dukes group reached southern California, it left multiple accounts of clashes with Indians before reaching Mountain Meadows and of theft of its large cattle herd afterward along the Muddy by Indians in concert with the party's guides. Following the Turner-Dukes party, in early October, emigrant John Aiken passed through with mail carrier John Hunt and later generated an affidavit describing unburied, unclothed victims and feasting wolves. Bagley describes Aiken as "the first non-Mormon to get a good look at the field."[4]

In mid-November, eight or ten weeks after the massacre, a large party of gentile merchants expelled by Brigham Young from Salt Lake City crossed the meadows with their views largely obstructed on orders from their Latter-day Saint guides. Traveling with this group was John I. Ginn, a young former civilian drover with the Utah Expedition, who described in vivid detail what he was able to see of the victims. Working from memory and field notes, Ginn wrote his long dramatic account in the early twentieth century while working as a newspaper reporter in El Paso, Texas. He drafted multiple versions and clearly was aiming to produce a book on a commercial basis; it never found a publisher. Ginn's description of the condition of the massacre victims at what he said was "about three weeks after the slaughter" was so melodramatic and unrealistic, Juanita Brooks viewed it as "clearly written for effect." She ridiculed Ginn's claim to have viewed the bodies at the end of September or early October: "This, on the face of it, is the sheerest nonsense." Brooks's overall assessment of his manuscript was that "Ginn's story reads like a Wild West thriller."[5]

Thus, although William Clark was not first on the spot at Mountain Meadows after September 11, 1857, when his sparse account of the carnage appeared in the Iowa Journal of History and Politics, it was the first credible contemporary account by an eyewitness to surface in published form with national reach.

Clark ended this segment of his reminiscences with his arrival in San Bernardino. Other than to record the weather and his relief at escaping Mormonism, he left no account of the town itself. Had he done so, he would have described a rancho of single-story adobes abandoned by the Latter-day Saints and slowly "melting" under the winter rains as the tile roofs gave way. Three months later, a reporter for the San Francisco *Daily Alta California* visited San Bernardino and filed this dreary dispatch: "In town the first four doors I passed were open to the street; in each I saw a table surrounded by [non-Mormon] men playing cards for drinks, as they do in other towns. Under the old regime it was not so in this town. . . . I looked about for some one of the saints, whom I had once known, and who might still be lingering here, and mourning for the loss of this Zion. I soon found one. . . . I asked my friend what had become of the 2,000 souls who had left their homes and comforts, and passed out through the Cajon [Pass] upon the desert in winter? This subject was his weakness, and as he repeated the names of many persons with whom I have had pleasant intercourse, I could not help feeling respect and admiration for such strong faith, even in Mormonism. . . . They don't believe the charges brought against the Mormons *of tampering with Indians, murdering and robbing emigrants, impeding justice, &c. – that those charges are proved to the satisfaction of the whole world is no proof to them. There is no treason among them; they are still loyal citizens! As the first rays of morning dawned, through a thick mist, we whirled away on our homeward ride, leaving in dim obscurity the vacant lots and tenantless dwellings."*[6]

We took the Mountain Meadows route and camped by a spring, four miles from the Meadows. Next day we went over the ground of the Mountain Meadows Massacre, the most brutal and barbarous massacre ever committed on the American continent—and this plotted and planned by Mormon officials. Bishop Higbee and President Haight of Cedar City, and John D. Lee of Harmony were leaders of this massacre. There were one hundred and thirty-two emigrants killed, and they saved seventeen children. This was said to be the richest train that had ever crossed the plains.

The Mormons and Indians got $80,000, over three hundred head of stock, and the outfits from this massacre, the Indians getting but a small share. Joel [W.] White, one of the Mountain Meadows police, was with our train. We were the first train that ever passed over this ground after that wholesale murder, and we Gentiles were ordered to stay close to our wagons and not be looking around, as it would not be safe for us if we did. But I counted eighteen skeletons close to the road, mostly of women and children with the hair still on their skulls. It was enough to make a man's blood run cold, and to know that some of the perpetrators of that deed were in our train! It will be remembered by the readers of the trial of John D. Lee, a few years later, that Joel White, though not actively engaged in the killing of any, was on police duty, and reported the progress of the massacre to the settlements, it being nearly a week after they were attacked before they surrendered and the massacre took place.[7]

That night we camped near Hamlin's ranch, just over the divide. It was quite cold here.[8]

The next day we rolled down to the Santa Clara [River]. Here it was

"Make a Man's Blood Run Cold"

FIG. 15. Carnage following Mountain Meadows Massacre of September 11, 1857. Clark passed through the meadows in late December about three months after the massacre. This sensational, unattributed drawing appeared twenty months later and was the first to reach a national audience. It appeared on the front page of *Harper's Weekly*'s August 13, 1859, issue to illustrate an unsigned essay titled "The Massacre at Mountain Meadows, Utah Territory," written by the Utah Expedition's assist. surg. Charles Brewer, who witnessed the first decent interment and memorialization for the massacre victims earlier in 1859. Availability of this material could have influenced Clark's reminiscences.

warm summer weather. We had come from cold winter, in one day, into a fine warm climate.[9] We stayed here the next day, and the Indians came in from some distance around to meet the great apostle, Amasa Lyman and receive instructions from him.

He preached to them for some time and Ira Hatch, the interpreter, repeated his sermon to them. Lyman instructed them to let this train and us four Gentiles pass through their country unharmed, and requested the chief of this tribe to send a messenger from one tribe to another for our protection.[10]

This chief sent an under chief to the next tribe on the Rio Virgin, and from there the chief sent a messenger to the Muddy [River] where the big camp of the [Paiutes] was. Here the Mormons had two missionaries,

McConnel and Liston.¹¹ This was the place where they had the Indians worked up to kill Griff Williams on his way down. But after Dickey had gone through with Lyman's train, they thought best to let Williams pass and they would be sure of them both when they came back [heading for San Bernardino].

So they had hard work to get him through this time. The under chief got in here half a day in advance of us and had the Indians quieted down before we arrived. They seemed quite friendly, although some of them acted rather surly.

After dinner, as I was seated on my wagon seat mending some clothing and Williams sitting beside me, McConnell, one of the missionaries, came up to the forward wheel of the wagon and began to tell Williams what hard work he had to keep the Indians from killing him when he went through before. After he had explained how hard he had worked to save his life, a big young buck stepped up to the wagon, climbed up, put his arm around Williams' neck, and said, "Poshupe, McConnel lies. McConnel say *Poshupe Americuts, cots wino* (bad) and to kill *Poshupe*." As he said this he stuck his finger into McConnel's face.

"Poshupe always give Piute *tobac* (tobacco) and *shotcup* (food). Piute like *Poshupe* but McConnel say Poshupe was Americuts, c-o-ts w in o Americuts, and to kill *Poshupe*."¹²

McConnel did not know what to say, and did not say a word, but went away.¹³

Poshupe was the name that the Indians gave Williams on account of his long heavy eyebrows.

Here we left the Muddy and went up a long ravine nine miles, out on the descent to the Vegas Springs about sixty miles.

About two weeks before, a large train from the States had passed through Utah, the first train after the Mountain Meadows Massacre. This was Crooks, Cooper, and Collins's train.¹⁴ They had been very careful not to arouse the Mormons, and had hired Ira Hatch and another interpreter, the two best in Utah, to guide them through and pacify the Indians. They piloted this train through by way of Old Harmony, instead of over the massacre ground.

While that train was moving up this ravine the Indians charged down on them and drove off all of their loose stock, about one hundred head. The men were going to protect themselves, and their property, and there were enough to have done so, there being sixty in the train, but the interpreters ordered them not to or they would all be killed; but let the Indians have their stock and not get into a fight with them, and they would go and get the stock back. They took their advice and Hatch and the other man went off after the cattle, but never returned. The Company paid the interpreters one hundred dollars apiece in advance, and now they had lost their stock in the bargain.

We went on to the Vegas Springs without any trouble. This desert is covered in many places with desert brush, and along the road was a great variety of cactus.

The bayonet cactus grows out of the ground like a mass of bayonets to the height of four feet. The cactus tree, which was plentiful, grows to be twenty feet high, and the trunks of some were a foot through. The top branches were covered with bayonet like leaves. The body was a mass of wiry fibers woven through and through, filled in with a light punky substance. When dead, a man could carry quite a large tree. These dead trees made a beautiful fire, and in the night, when crossing this desert, we would set fire to them as we went along, just to see them burn.[15]

We were nearly two days and one night in crossing this desert to the Vegas. Here was a nice camping place.[16]

We arrived at the Vegas Springs on January first, 1858.

Three or four of us took a bath in this spring on New Year's Day. Although out of the bathing season, we enjoyed it very much.[17]

There was quite a party of Indians here, but they appeared friendly.

Our next camping place was at Cottonwood Springs, a nice place to camp. There was some cottonwood timber here . . .[18]

Our next camp was at Mountain Spring. There were some Indians here, but we had no trouble with them. All of the Indians, after leaving the Mormon settlements, are Piutes. They are not very strong. Scarcely any of these little tribes could muster over fifty warriors. They never had any horses.[19] If they get one, they kill it for food. They are a sort

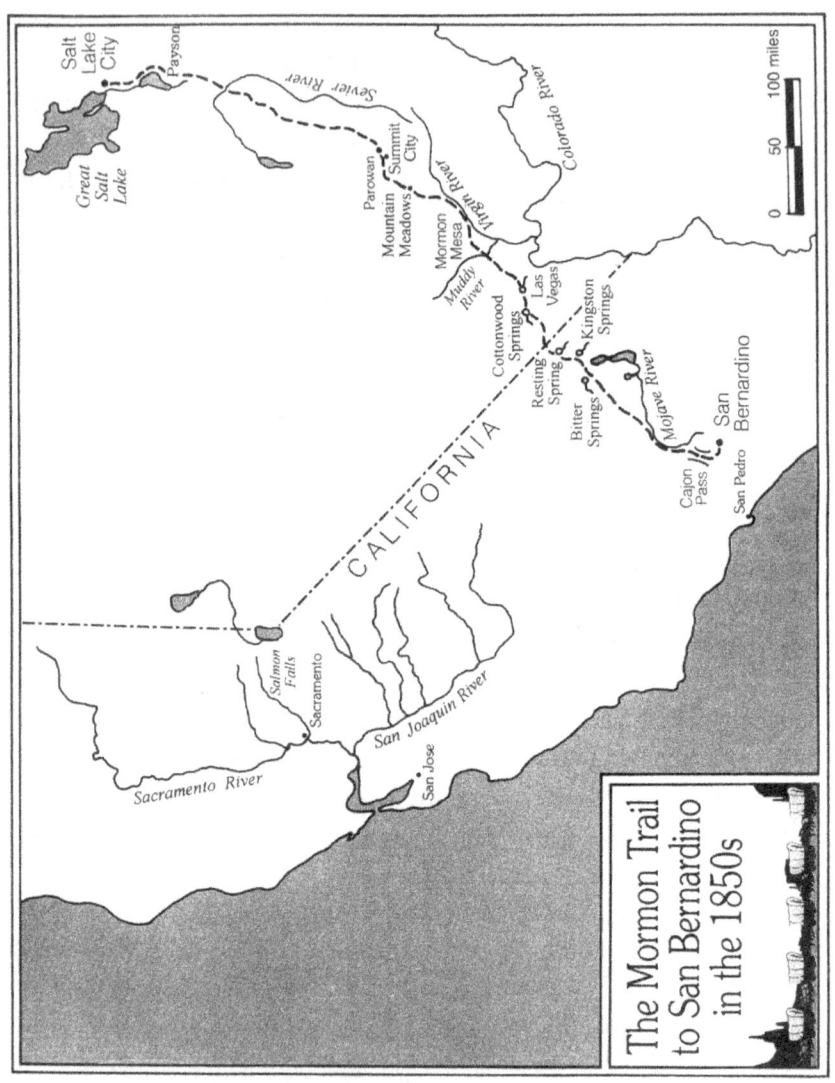

FIG. 16. Map of Clark's travels, Salt Lake City to San Bernardino, November 1857–January 1858. This chart marks William Clark's life-threatening passage through Utah's southern settlements, across Mountain Meadows, and over the Old Spanish Trail and Mojave Desert to the safety of southern California. There he traded bull whacking for gold mining and a wide range of other jobs throughout the West until 1868. Courtesy Leo Lyman, *San Bernardino: The Rise and Fall of a California Community*. Reprinted with permission of Signature Books, Salt Lake City.

of Digger Indian, living mostly on roots and lizards, and in the season when there is no travel they get very poor. In the winter, when there is considerable travel, they fat up like pigs. Everyone that crosses expects to feed them and they seldom attack a train, but often pick off a man if they can catch him away from camp. They will hide in the brush and shoot down a horse or mule in a team, then they get it for food. They never have been known to attack much of a train, unless helped by the Mormons.

From here we went to Kingston [formerly Resting] Spring, forty-five miles. . . . We left the Kingston Spring and crossed the next desert of forty-five miles to Bitter Springs. At these two desert springs the water is very poor, having a bitter taste, but travelers have to put up with it. We seldom saw Indians here.

Our next drive brought us to the foot of the Mojave [River]. Here we found better water and very good grass.

This stream sinks out of sight and there is no water along it, except in holes, for thirty miles.

At the end of the next day's drive we camped at the head of this stream.

From here we drove into San Bernardino, arriving there on the thirteenth day of January, 1858. It was warm and delightful weather and the grass was green.[20]

Here we found Crooks, Cooper, and Collins. When they found out what Mr. Savage charged us to let us work our passage through, they were determined that he should give us back our horses and saddles. But we told them that the ship that landed us safely out of *Utah*, no matter what the cost, was welcome to all it got, for now we could breathe easy.

SECTION 13

"Back to Wisconsin"

The Fate of Sherwood and Tuttle

Editorial Notes

How William Clark learned the postwar fate of chums Martin L. Sherwood and George B. Tuttle as well as former dragoon private Ira O. Tuttle is unknown. Presumably he heard the story from someone in Spanish Fork, Utah, when he revisited the town in 1862 since he later commented he had lost touch with all his chums after the Utah War. What is significant is that Clark recorded the facts of when and how the three returned east inaccurately, and neglected even to mention the later life of two other companions, Edwin Leach and Albert Frank. Leach had gone on to California with Clark at the end of 1857 and Frank had dropped out of the group at Fort Bridger in November; thereafter both men appeared to become nonpersons to Clark. In fairness to them all, this study's epilogue presents as best we can information about their later lives.

To William Clark's twenty-first-century editors, it seems unusual that he ended his reminiscences with a reference to "Mart" Sherwood's unclaimed Latter-day Saint girl in Spanish Fork. We had hoped for at least a tip of the author's hat to his own Cora Jean Clark, the Wisconsin farm lass who waited so patiently for his letters over eleven years. Alas, such was not the case, but at least from our own research we now know what the Bill-Cora story was and that it had a happy ending. The Clarks' married life in Iowa was long and apparently quiet, interrupted occasionally in its later years by William's labors to record his memories of western adventures and tragedies along the overland trails.

"Back to Wisconsin"

I will go back to my friends—Tuttle, whom I left at Bridger to get his brother out of the army, and Sherwood at Spanish Fork among the Mormons.

Sherwood, I afterward learned, joined the Church, and worked around and got enough money to make a payment on a house and lot.[1] He gained the good graces of a prominent Mormon's daughter, and got Brigham's consent to marry her. Then he got an outfit to go back to the States after a threshing machine, and, when spring opened so that he could cross the mountains, Brigham gave him a pass to go after his machine, and he started.

When two days out, he met a man with a few wagons loaded with merchandise. This man had come out and wintered at Bridger, and was going into the city to sell his goods. Tuttle, having succeeded in getting his brother out of the army, was with him.

This man feared that Brigham would not allow him to sell them in the Territory and offered Sherwood and Tuttle a good commission if Sherwood would get a permit from Brigham and help sell them.

Sherwood went back to Salt Lake City and told Brigham that this man was owing him, and his only show to get his pay was out of these goods.

Brigham gave him a permit and he went back, and they bought the goods, and sold them at a big commission, making quite a little stake out of it.

Then Sherwood with Tuttle and his brother went back to Wisconsin.

In 1862 I was in Spanish Fork, but Sherwood had not got back with his threshing machine, nor to claim his Mormon girl.[2]

Appendix A
The Pomeroy and Kingston Story

This short tale is essentially a digression by Clark that does not involve him. Accordingly, the editors have moved it from its original location in his manuscript's section 12 to this appendix.

In summary, it is a story of desert adventure William Clark heard upon reaching California in early 1858 from C. L. Kingston, an early mail carrier on the Old Spanish Trail between Los Angeles and Utah's southern settlements. Kingston's surname became attached to a variety of geographical features (springs, mountains, and trails) in what is now southwestern Nevada near the California border. Clark dates his association with Kingston to the period 1858–1864, which helps to determine the rough outline of his stay on the Pacific Coast before returning to Paoli, Wisconsin, via Spanish Fork, Utah, to marry Cora Clark in 1869. The "Pomroy" to whom Clark refers was one of two brothers, either Ebenezer or Thaddeus Pomeroy, who were Missouri merchants and freighters doing business as the Pomeroy Freighting Company.

After disposing of a load of freight in Salt Lake City during the summer of 1849, the Pomeroys pushed on toward Los Angeles with more than twenty wagons over the southern route constituting the western end of the Old Spanish Trail. In November 1849 (not Clark's early 1850s), the Pomeroy caravan came to grief near Cottonwood Springs (east of the Mojave Desert) from a combination of factors: daunting trail conditions, jaded and dying oxen, overloaded wagons, dwindling provisions, and a near-mutiny by a cadre of bull whackers desperate to reach the California gold fields and willing to abandon their obligations to the Pomeroys.

Leo Lyman, the leading authority on freighting across this route during the pre–Civil War era, accepts the Kingston-Clark story of hardship and avarice in toto as he did William Clark's account of danger in Utah's southern settlements in the immediate wake of the Mountain Meadows massacre.[1]

There is a little history connected with this camp. Early in the fifties a man by the name of Pomroy crossed the plains to Utah with a train of merchandise, eight or ten loads. He went to Salt Lake City, sold his goods, and started across to California.

After he had got out on the desert, he found that his men were planning to steal his money, and he feared they would kill him to get it. So, when within a day's travel of Cottonwood Springs, Pomroy took a mule and some provisions, and started for San Bernardino, leaving his train and money in charge of his wagon boss. The night that he reached San Bernardino he dreamed that he saw his saddle bags, containing his money, move from his wagon into a bank about twenty rods from camp.

He got up wild with excitement over his dream, as he had over $10,000. He hunted up a man by the name of C. L. Kingston who had carried the mail across to Utah, told him of his trouble, and hired him to go back with him to hunt his money. They each packed a pack mule and started. It was two hundred and fifty miles to Cottonwood, where he dreamed that his money was.

They went out to the Mojave and met the train. His wagon boss told him that the money was stolen the night they camped at Cottonwood. Pomroy and Kingston pushed on. When they got to Mountain Spring, twenty-five miles from Cottonwood, they camped for the night.[2] In the morning Pomroy said that he had had another dream. He saw his money move out of the bank where it was hid and out of sight. He was discouraged now and wanted to turn back, but Kingston would not now, and said they would go on to the place.

He had hard work to get Pomroy to go. Pomroy said it was useless, as the money was gone. But, as Kingston insisted, they rode on to the place, and Pomroy pointing to a bank, said, "It was right over there in the side of that bank, but it is not there now."

Kingston got off of his horse, went to the place, and found fresh dirt. He looked around and found a string. Then he called Pomroy, who said that it was the string which fastened his saddle bags. It was greasy, having been covered up with bacon in the mess wagon.

Appendix A

They went down the "wash," as they could see that the gravel had been disturbed. They followed the wash about twenty rods and came upon his money, all spilled out on the gravel, and picked up every dollar, $10,300.

The wolves had smelled the greasy saddle bag, dug it out, dragged it along by one corner, and spilled the money out in a pile.

I knew this man Kingston from '58 to '64, and have heard him tell this story several times, and believe it to be true.

[From here we went to Kingston (formerly Resting) Spring, forty-five miles.] This spring was discovered by C. L. Kingston and Pomroy on their return, after finding Pomroy's money, who gave it this name.

Before that the route had been by the Resting Springs. [We left the Kingston Spring and crossed the next desert of forty-five miles to Bitter Springs.]

Appendix B

William and Cora Clark's Later Years

The editors have scoured the Internet and checked myriad archives, newspapers, and publications seeking information about the lives of William and Cora Clark. We have been disappointed in finding only a single photograph of one of them. Although William was the mayor of Ames, Iowa, for two terms and served an additional three terms as a city councilman, few records or details are available, but we are pleased to share two interesting newspaper articles from their later years here.

The Clarks loved living in Ames, Iowa. After spending a year and a half in the Dakotas, Cora told a newspaper reporter upon their return, "'There is no place like home' and that Ames is the best place on earth."[1] Prior to celebrating their golden wedding anniversary in the fall of 1917, Bill and Cora sat down with a reporter from the *Ames Weekly Tribune*. The unnamed reporter—who categorized them as "greatly esteemed people" whose "lives have been such that they have always done good"—clearly enjoyed the time spent with them. The resulting article is delightful and helps to fill in some of the gaps about their lives:

> "MARRIAGE LEAPS THRU MANY YEARS"
>
> On September 29, 1868, William Clark, and Miss Cora J. Clark were united in marriage at the home of the bride's parents in Paloi, Wisconsin, and since the following year they have made their home in Ames.
>
> Forty-nine years is some extension of time when you come to think about it, but they are of that hardy pioneer stock that means long and clean lives, and a happiness that does not come to all people.
>
> Mr. Clark drifted up into Wisconsin after traveling all about the country and went to work at the Clark home. It was not long

Appendix B

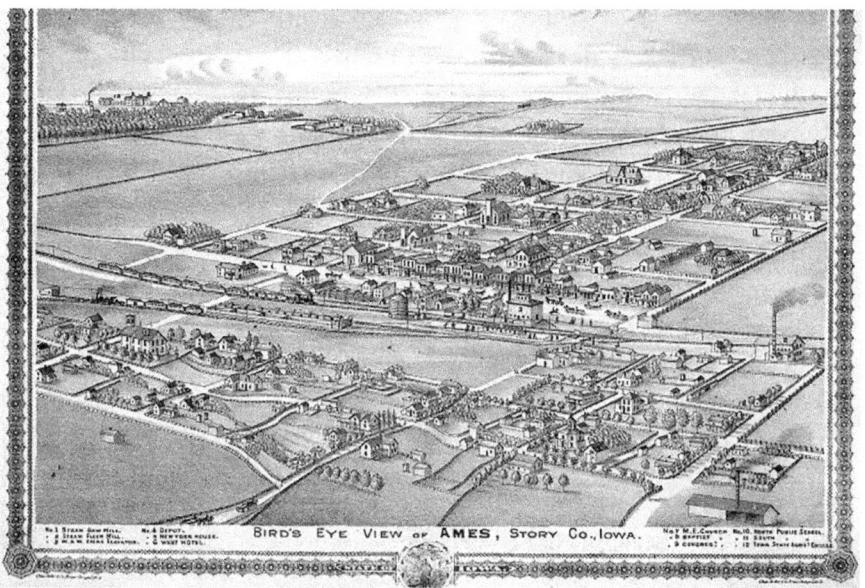

FIG. 17. Bird's-eye view of Ames, Story County, Iowa, 1875. Charles Shober made this lithograph six years after the Clarks' arrival and in the same year William began his first term as Ames's mayor. The town's population then totaled about eight hundred. The cluster of buildings on the horizon (left) was the embryo of Iowa State University. Courtesy Ames History Museum.

until there appeared a Dan Cupid with his bow and arrow and the wedding was the result. But a change came in the plans and Mr. Clark went to California and for thirteen years he traveled the places where there were no trails, herded thousands of head of sheep to the markets, built the largest fence which has ever been built around a vineyard in California, made the plains in a covered wagon and drifted back and forward from one western state to another always doing something that bro[ugh]t a betterment to the wilderness and assisting in the erection of thousands of the frontier cabins.

During this interval of time Miss Clark had remained in Wisconsin. It was along [sic], long time between mails, but the waiting was patient and finally Mr. Clark came back. A marriage ceremony was performed and they started to Ames. Mrs. Clark with a twinkle in her eye, says. "I never found a name that suited me better than Clark." She has been active in much of the charitable work which has been done in Ames and when it is considered she has been here since the rest of us have been born, it can be conceived of the welcome of the youngsters and the older people who have arrived in the city.

Mr. Clark conducted a store in Ames for eleven years. He was mayor of the city for two terms and served on the council for three terms. He was compelled to give up the store game and went to purchasing horses for shipment that he might be in the out door air.

They are a greatly esteemed people. Their lives have been such that they have always done good and the memories that those who have left the city have carried with them have always been of an humble people with every endeavor for the betterment of all the people.

Mr. Clark is now 83 years of age, while Mrs. Clark is 71. They have a neat little home down in the south part of the city, are taking life easy, have the fullest confidence of a large circle of friends and are passing the time happily in the tho[ugh]t that they will celebrate their golden wedding anniversary in one year, and that is not a long time to people who have lived to their age and so long and pleasantly together.[2]

A front page article in the *Ames Tri-Weekly Tribune* in February the following year shared details of the Clark's anniversary celebration.

GOLDEN SHADOWS CAST THEIR GLEAM ACROSS LIFE'S PATH

MR. AND MRS. WILLIAM CLARK CELEBRATE GOLDEN WED[D]ING ANNIVERSARY

ARE LONG TIME RESIDENTS

They Have Been in Ames Greater Part of
Their Married and Happy Life

Appendix B

Fifty years ago yesterday at Paoli, Wis., Miss Cora Clark and William Clark stood before a minister and they both responded to the question as propounded to them "I do."

There has never been any regret on the part of either that the words were spoken in which they both gave their full consent to "live together as man and wife until death do us part." In view of the happy event occur[r]ing on Sunday of this year, Saturday was given over to a day when they received their friends, and when there was the utmost happiness on the part of the people to assemble at their home and add wishes for further honors, further peace, further pleasantries for the couple, who are now creeping down the sunny slope of life, where the shadows have lengthened into long and endless shadows and at the end there appears to the honored old people, the great sign board of life on which is written, "Well done, My good and faithful servant." It was an endless stream of people who made their way to the humble home on Sherman Avenue, and every person carried with them a hand shake of warmth and their hearts expressed, thru words, the feeling that each heart contained and the friendly grasp of the hand, and words of cheer, the words of comfort fell upon ears, failing with age 'tis true, but primed for just the right word that was said and leaving an impression that carried with it the full meaning of the words that meant so much to hearts made light for the day and which will linger thru all the balance of their days.

The review of the lives of Mr. and Mrs. Clark has been made in the public prints before, but when an occasion such as this creeps into their being, it but adds another chapter to the long line of notable and worthy things that have been done by them and which has come to them. Fifty years is a long, long time for folks to live together. With Mrs. Clark, whose maiden name was Clark, there is the twinkling in the eye as she mildly tells "she has never found a name that suited her better than Clark."

They were married in the little Wisconsin town and a year later they entered a covered wagon and "started west." They had no idea at that time where their future home would be. They were but travelers on the broad prairies and some place in the golden west they were to establish themselves and make a home—a home of their own. It was merely a chance that they happened to stop in Ames. But once having arrived, having become acquainted with the very first day as did the people of those early times, they concluded the end of the journey had been reached and it was here they would carve out a niche in the rock of time. This was home to them then and has remained so to this day.

Mr. Clark engaged in farming, and after a few years they removed to the city, then a scattering burg of but a few houses and many dangerous mud holes. He engaged in the general merchandise line and purchased horses on the side. He was elected mayor of the city for two terms, after having served three terms as a member of the town council. He was active in the things that were for the good of the town even in that early day and has carried that same feeling thru to this time. While he was engaged in the activities of the business life, Mrs. Clark was carrying on her part of the busy life of the pioneer. She was active in all the good that is the direct result of her being a resident of Ames and having her part in building the community, in establishing churches and assisting in every way that comes ever day to one with as cheerful and as willing a nature as that of the bride of fifty years ago.

Mr. and Mrs. Clark have not only been attentive to the needs of the people of this vicinity, but they have always be[e]n attractive to the residents of Ames and whether it is among the old or the young, they are known as the most lovable and adorable of the pioneers and their lives are set forth as examples for the coming generation. It is better to have lived among people for a long time and have the esteem of that community than it is to have accumulated great wealth.

Blessed with no children of their own, Mr. and Mrs. Clark raised Mrs. C. E. Sargent, of Boone and started her on the way to the happiest kind of a life. Two brothers of Mrs. Clark arrived in the city Saturday and were here for all the genuine congratulations that were extended. These brothers are A. M. Clark, of Baldwin City, Kans., and Frank L. Clark, of Manchester.

At the end of the rose strewn path that has lead them to such a celebration, there can be but the words of good cheer and all luck and pleasure for them in the future years.

A family reunion was held yesterday at which time many from distant towns were guests for the day and added to the delight of the worthy couple.[3]

Appendix C
William Clark's Obituaries

William Clark's death was front page news for the *Daily Tribune and Evening Times* in Ames, Iowa. A second obituary appeared nearly two weeks later. Both articles are reprinted here.

WM. CLARK, ONCE MAYOR HERE, DIES
Pioneer Citizen and Third Executive of Ames Passes Away at Home of Relatives in Ogden: Former Business Man to Be Buried Here Thursday

Special to the Tribune

OGDEN. Ia, Feb 17—William Clark, of Ames, died here at 2:50 o'clock yesterday afternoon. He, with his wife, was spending the winter here with relatives. He had been ill for some time and but little hope for his recovery was held out Thursday night, February 12, he quite suddenly passed into a comatose state from which he did not recover. The body will be taken to Ames Thursday where funeral services will be held and where interment will be made.

The body of William Clark will arrive in Ames Thursday noon. Funeral services will be held at the Methodist Episcopal church at 3:00 o'clock Thursday afternoon, followed by interment in Oakwood cemetery. One of the early settlers of Ames he was twice honored by being elected mayor of Ames, being Ames' third and sixth mayor. Always taking an active interest in civic affairs, he did much to promote the early growth of the city.

For years he was engaged in the grocery business here, later taking up the buying and shipping of horses. He was probably eighty-five years old and was well known over Story county. Mr. Clark is survived by his wife and one daughter, Mrs Charles Sergant [sic] of Boone.[1]

Appendix C

FIG. 18. Grave marker for William Clark, Ames, Iowa. Following William's death at age eighty-five on February 16, 1920, he was buried in the Ames Municipal Cemetery. As the inscription here indicates, the expectation was that wife Cora would join him in this plot, but she returned to family in the Paoli, Wisconsin, area and was buried there near her parents following her death at age seventy-five in 1922. BillionGraves.com.

WILLIAM CLARK

(Contributed.)

William Clark was born in Java, Wyoming county, New York, April 26, 1834, and died at the home of his sister-in-law, Mrs. Arthur Clark, of Og[d]en, February 16, 1920.

One year ago Mr. Clark was taken ill with paralysis. Since that time he had been in a state of declining health. On September 26, 1867, he was united in marriage to Miss Cora J. Clark of Tably, Wisconsin. Mr. and Mrs. Clark lived a long and happy life together. They celebrated their golden wedding anniversary two years ago in Ames. The past year this couple made their home with Mrs. Arthur Clark of Ogden, where they enjoyed comfort and splendid attention in their feeble condition.

The deceased had a very active business career. At the time of the Civil War, he was engaged in government duties on the western coast. He lived in Ames for fifty years. Part of this time he engaged in horse buying and selling business; for eleven years he ran a mercantile business and for three years was mayor of the city of Ames. He leaves to mourn his loss his wife, Mrs. Cora Clark; adopted daughter, Mrs. C. E. Sargeant, Boone; two brothers, Dr. Orson Clark, Ogden, and James A. Clark of Ravenna, Nebraska, and a number of nephews and nieces and many friends.

Deceased was a true exponent of the Golden Rule, and while he never belonged to the organized church was one of the most liberal men that ever lived. No one ever came to him in distress or need but that his purse was opened, and he has scattered sunshine all along the vista of years that he walked in our midst. His religion was the deep and lasting one, the one that so many of the older generation lived and died by, and one that smacks not of hypocricy and deceit. His life was an open book, and the lonely widow who sits in the shadow and mourns for the companion of her youth can garner consolation for the brief parting in the knowledge that his life has not been in vain, and that he has simply gone on before to prepare the home in the other world where the rough places experienced here below are unknown, and that he is standing on the shores of the black river with extended arms waiting to enfold his loved ones in the life eternal.[2]

Appendix D

Status Differences among Teamsters

Ten years after William Clark worked his way west with a bull train owned by Russell, Majors and Waddell, John Hanson Beadle did the same as a mule-skinner for the firm of Naishit and Hindley, Mormon merchants of Salt Lake City. Most of Beadle's fellow teamsters were Latter-day-Saint lads working in the old way as their coreligionists labored under Brigham Young's direction to build the last sections of the Union Pacific Railroad across Wyoming during the summer of 1868. Even with modernity literality at their heels and the death knell of freighting by ox and mule trains sounding, Beadle and his companions experienced most of the same hardships Clark endured. With the Civil War behind them, though, Beadle's peers were free from the sectional animosities that plagued Clark's. What persisted was the ingrained hierarchy and rivalry between those rough-hewn youngsters who punched oxen and those who lashed mules. Even while enjoying the superior status of a mule-skinner, Beadle recorded the campfire doggerel of the lowly bull whackers.

"The Bull-Whacker's Epic"

Oh! I'm a jolly driver on the Salt Lake City line,
And I can lick the rascal that yokes an ox of mine;
He'd better turn him out, or you bet your life I'll try
To sprawl him with an ox-bow – "Root, hog, or die."

Oh! I'll tell you how it is when you first get on the road:
You've got an awkward team and a very heavy load;
You've got to whip and hollow [holler], (if you swear it's on the sly,) –
Punch your teams along boys – "Root, hog, or die."

Clark's Edited Reminiscences

Oh! It's every day at noon there is something to do.
If there's nothing else, there will be an ox to shoe;
First with ropes you throw him, and there you make him lie
While you tack on the shoes, boys – "Root, hog, or die."

Perhaps you'd like to know what it is we have to eat,
A little bit of bread, and a dirty piece of meat;
A little old molasses, and sugar on the sly,
Potatoes if you've got 'em – "Root, hog, or die."

Oh! There's many strange sights to be seen along the road,
The antelopes and deer and the great sandy toad,
The buffalo and elk, the rabbits jump so high,
And with all the bloody Injuns – "Root, hog, or die."

The prairie dogs in Dog-town, and the prickly pears,
And the buffalo bones that are scattered everywheres;
Now and then dead oxen from vile Alkali,
Are very thick in places, where it's "Root, hog, or die."

Oh! you've got to take things on the plains as you can,
They'll never try to please you, "or any other man;"
You go it late and early, and also wet or dry,
And eat when you can get it – "Root, hog, or die."

Oh, times on Bitter Creek, they never can be beat,
"Root, hog, or die" is on every wagon sheet;
The sand within your throat, the dust within your eye,
Bend your back and stand it, to "Root, hog, or die."

When we arrived in Salt Lake, the 25th of June,
The people were surprised to see us come so soon;
But we are bold bull-whackers on whom you can rely,
We're tough, and we can stand it, to "Root, hog, and die."[1]

In some cases, the invidious comparisons between classes of teamster ran as much to the organizations in which they worked as to their individual behavior, appearance, and the type of draught animals they worked. Percival G. Lowe, a first sergeant of dragoons in the early 1850s and then a civilian wagon master and master of transportation for army quartermasters during the Utah War, was partial to working with mule teams and their teamsters: "Many of these [worthless characters] found employment in ox trains belonging to Government contractors, and were the cause of strikes, mutinies and loss to their employers. . . . The Government [army] trains had more discipline than the contractor's trains transporting Government supplies. The Government train had a sprinkling of discharged soldiers, and the man in charge had himself been amenable to discipline and could not hope to hold a responsible position without maintaining it. He must be a law unto himself or fail. The great contracting firms that transport Government supplies sent numerous ox trains to various military posts, and while they had a good business system, and often accomplished work much better than the Government would have done, yet the immensity of the business left room for many leaks and much defective management."[2]

PART 3

Meaning

FIG. 19. "Bull Whacker" by Charles M. Russell (1864–1926). Note Russell's rough sketch of ox train below portrait, a touch he added to many of his letters and postcards. Courtesy Granger Historical Picture Archive, New York.

Editors' Epilogue

What, then, became of William Clark and the people he mentioned in "A Trip Across the Plains in 1857"? To describe the later life of all of them is neither practical nor necessary, but some brief understanding of thirteen of them provides context for the circumstances under which Clark himself traveled and survived.

The Chums

Edwin Leach

Of William Clark's four "chums," Edwin Leach was the youngest, having just turned eighteen when he encountered Sherwood, Tuttle, and Clark in St. Louis during the summer of 1857. He must have been either a large or mature lad, as Clark remembered him looking around twenty-one. He had been born in Sherman, Fairfield County, Connecticut, in 1839; at an early age the family removed to Illinois. Clark believed that Leach had joined the Utah Expedition from Peoria, but the 1860 census, taken less than two years after he reached San Bernardino with Clark, enumerated him as living with his widowed mother and engaged in farming near Hoyleton, Illinois, in Washington County. Whether Leach had returned east from California overland or via the sea route to Panama and then across to the Caribbean is unknown. Either way, there would have been adventure, but, as with his trek to Utah during 1857, Edwin Leach left no known record of his experiences. In 1870 he was still farming but had moved to Carlyle, Clinton County, Illinois, perhaps in connection with marrying Celia Amelia Barrett, a young widow, living in the same county, at the end of 1869. She had been born in New Fane, Niagara County, New York, near Lockport, and had lived on Michigan's Lower Peninsula before moving to Illinois.

In 1880 the Leach family moved from Illinois to Nebraska with their six children, and worked a succession of farms in Blaine, Buffalo, and Loup Counties. Edwin died in North Loup at the home of a daughter in

1919 at age eighty. He was described as "a very quiet, retiring man, one whose best qualities of mind and heart were known only to those who knew him best. He was an affectionate father and a kind neighbor."[1] It will be recalled that William Clark remembered him as "a bright young man" in 1857.

As with Clark and Albert Frank, there is no sign that Edwin Leach served in uniform during the Civil War.

George Tuttle

Whether George Tuttle was aware his younger brother Ira was serving with the Second U.S. Dragoons before Chat Rennick's bull train reached Fort Bridger is unknown but possible. Ira Tuttle had run away from home, lied about his age, stated his occupation as "pastrie cook," and enlisted for a five-year army hitch at Fort Leavenworth on July 13, 1857. This was about the same time that older brother George became a teamster with Russell, Majors and Waddell at the same post. George's train swung onto the Oregon Trail during the third week of July, while Ira started west with the Second Dragoons from Fort Leavenworth on September 17. Due to this late start as well as snowstorms and subzero temperatures encountered west of Fort Laramie, the dragoons became the Utah Expedition's de facto rear guard. They staggered into Fort Bridger on November 19 after losing half the regiment's horses to starvation, exposure, and exhaustion and one private to lockjaw. What Ira Tuttle and his new comrades endured was among the most arduous winter marches in American military history, one that the troops compared to Napoleon's retreat from Moscow nearly a half-century earlier.[2]

Irrespective of when the Tuttle brothers became aware of each other's presence at the Utah Expedition's winter quarters, it is clear that by the time Sherwood, Leach, and Clark decided to continue on to California, George and Ira had communicated, with George deciding to remain behind to extract his brother from the army. All parties concerned ran enormous risks, not the least of which was the prospect that desertion by Ira could carry a brutal penalty of fifty lashes, if not execution.

For the Tuttles, quick action was essential because in late November 1857 Albert Sidney Johnston ordered the Second Dragoons to leave

Editors' Epilogue

Bridger to herd his command's surviving livestock to better winter grazing along Henrys Fork of the Green River.[3] As the regiment prepared for its relocation, the brothers seized the moment, fleeing east under cover of a snowstorm along the road to Fort Laramie. On November 29 an army patrol apprehended the brothers.

Eight months of legal wrangling followed. At Camp Scott/Fort Bridger, Ira stood trial before a military court martial for desertion and was convicted on January 7, 1858. Notwithstanding this verdict, the court released him from confinement without further punishment and restored him to duty to serve out the four-and-one-half year balance of his enlistment. Ira's army record was blemished as a deserter, but at least he was out of the guard tent and once again a fully functioning member of Company A. This leniency reflected the realities of the Utah Expedition's manpower shortages and recruiting challenges, the lack of secure prison facilities, and a need to resolve quickly mounting administrative and disciplinary problems.[4]

Disposition of George Tuttle's case was more complex because of his ambiguous status and his possession of the Sharps carbine the army had issued to Ira. The Utah Expedition was prepared to defend itself from raiding legionnaires, but subversion from within by a protective older brother and camp follower was unique. Was George Tuttle simply a civilian, or a civilian-thief accompanying an army in the field and subject to the Articles of War? In December 1857, described as a "laborer," he appeared before a grand jury of civilians empaneled by the U.S. district court for Green River County at nearby "Eckelsville," a new makeshift community of tents, dugouts, wagon boxes, and a few log cabins the U.S. government considered the temporary seat of Utah Territory's government.[5]

To defend himself while continuing to press his assertion that Private Tuttle had been enlisted improperly as a minor, George engaged the services of lawyer Charles Maurice Smith, a non-Mormon native of Port Royal, Virginia, who had worked in Washington DC as an attorney and newspaper publisher. How and why such a grandee was at Camp Scott/Fort Bridger is still a mystery. There, in the wilderness of northeastern Utah, he conducted a pickup law practice defending an eclectic mixture of people in trouble: episodic cases with Indians as clients; several Nauvoo Legionnaires captured by the army and indicted for treason; multiple thieves; and now George B. Tuttle, unemployed teamster. Smith never had Thomas L. Kane as a legal client during his brief sojourn at Eckelsville, but there are documentary hints that in March 1858 Kane attempted to acquire Smith's services as a "second" in his putative duel with Albert Sidney Johnston. With Smith, Tuttle chose a counselor struggling with alcohol whom the Nauvoo Legion's adjutant general later describe to Brigham Young as part of the devil's "particularly choice flock" as well as a "puppy, scrub, and vagabond."[6]

On December 19 John M. Hockaday, the U.S. attorney for Utah, presented George's case to the grand jury, and he was indicted for inducing Ira to desert and then hiding him. On December 20, a trial jury found George not guilty. Notwithstanding this verdict, the federal prosecutor, Hockaday, again brought the case before the grand jury, obtained another indictment, and set the date for its disposition at a new trial on January 4, 1858. Tuttle and his attorney responded by arguing that he had already been tried and acquitted under an identical indictment, pleading, in effect, his constitutional protection against double jeopardy. On January 4 Hockaday responded by arguing that the second indictment was separate and distinct from the first, a position seemingly untenable based on the available documentation. There is no evidence that George Tuttle stood trial a second time, perhaps because Judge Eckles intervened to quash the proceedings or because the case simply was dropped in the confusion associated with Hockaday's departure for Washington DC on January 5 in a campaign to exchange his role as Utah's U.S. attorney for that of the federal mail contractor servicing the important St. Joseph to Salt Lake City mail route.

The next chapter in this legal marathon unfolded at Camp Floyd, Utah, in the later part of July 1858, a month after the Utah Expedition entered the Salt Lake Valley and marched through Salt Lake City. Apparently, George Tuttle was still trying to void his brother's enlistment, and was told by Albert Sidney Johnston's adjutant that, although brother Ira had demonstrably been a minor when enlisted, army regulations permitted his discharge only by order of Secretary of War Floyd. An appeal to

Editors' Epilogue

FIG. 20. The Utah Expedition's march through Salt Lake City, June 26, 1858. This image, contrived fifteen years after the event, was the first and most enduring depiction of the army's passage through a city deserted and ready for the torch after Clark had reached California. Engraving (1873) from T.B.H. Stenhouse's book *Rocky Mountain Saints*.

Floyd by the chain of command at the distant post named in his honor was clearly not in the cards, although, unknown to Tuttle, later in the summer the family of dragoon private John J. Healy was able to obtain an order directing his discharge as an underage enlistee by appealing directly to Secretary Floyd. Having delivered this discouraging news to George Tuttle and his lawyer, General Johnston's adjutant, Maj. Fitz John Porter, suggested another approach—having Tuttle seek to extricate his brother from the army by seeking a writ of habeas corpus with the U.S. district court then sitting in Salt Lake City. Once Porter sent a letter to Tuttle and Charles Maurice Smith stating that the army had dropped any remaining vestiges of court-martial proceedings hanging over Private Tuttle's head and had no objection to the filing of such a writ, the supplicants approached Judge Eckels for the last step in this gambit. On July 30, 1858, Judge Eckels approved the writ and issued an order discharging Ira from the U.S. Army. The brothers Tuttle were at long last free to leave Utah.

Meaning

Major Porter's suggestion that attorney Smith seek Private Tuttle's release through a writ of habeas corpus had an unintended consequence that rippled through Utah's already-complex legal scene. Within weeks, this successful legal gambit was replicated in Salt Lake City in the context of another case brought by two other eastern-trained lawyers, Albert G. Browne Jr. of Boston and Washington J. McCormick of Indiana. Both lawyers had previously clerked at Fort Bridger for Judge Delana R. Eckels, a U.S. district court judge for Utah and chief justice of the territory's supreme court. They brought the case in question on behalf of Henry F. Polydore, an English plaintiff seeking repatriation of his twelve-year-old daughter, Henrietta.

As the result of a marital dispute between her parents, the girl had been taken by her mother and aunt from England in 1854 and sequestered under an alias in the polygamous Salt Lake City home of a Latter-day Saint elder of whom the aunt was his fourth wife. Fearing that his young daughter might soon be forced into a polygamous marriage herself, Henry Polydore initiated a chain of diplomatic and legal pleadings in March 1858. These papers passed from the British foreign minister in London to the British ambassador in Washington, the U.S. secretary of state, the secretary of war, the Utah Expedition's commanding general at Camp Floyd, his adjutant, the U.S. attorney for Utah, and finally to the chief judge of the territory's federal legal establishment.

When Judge Eckels ruled in favor of Mr. Polydore's writ of habeas corpus in August 1858, young Henrietta, like Private Tuttle, began the trek home from Utah. For her, it was an eight-thousand-mile transAtlantic odyssey to Gloucestershire rather than a return to the world of William Clark's "chum" amid the lumberjacks and farmers of Wisconsin.[7]

Martin Sherwood

Notwithstanding the absence of documentary support and the fact that it came to Clark secondhand, there is no reason to doubt his account of Martin Sherwood's wintering-over in Spanish Fork. Clark's portrayal of Sherwood's machinations to survive and even prosper a bit in a hostile, isolated community during wartime rings true. We surmise that he did so in such an unwelcoming environment by befriending an influential local settler to serve as his protector. Bill Clark survived by bonding in some fashion with Bill Hickman, William I. Ginn claimed to have done so with Porter Rockwell, and captive teamster Charlie Becker rapidly forged a rapport first with Capt. Warren Snow of the Nauvoo Legion and then farmer Charles Decker, Brigham Young's son-in-law. In Martin Sherwood's case, it appears that he fell in with John W. Mott, one of Spanish Fork's earliest settlers since 1851. Both men had ties to Wisconsin, a commonality that may have run to Sherwood's advantage in gaining Mott's confidence.

If our surmise is correct, what Martin Sherwood accomplished in Spanish Fork during the winter of 1857–1858 was impressive. The town was a hotbed of support for Brigham Young's prosecution of the Utah War and the hostility to non-Mormons that went with it. In the American South of the period, such locals were dubbed "fire-eaters." The Baker-Fancher party and other travelers to Utah that fall discovered how severe these attitudes could be.

As context for the environment in which Sherwood spent the winter, one might consider the letter his new friend, John Mott, wrote to skeptical relatives and friends in Johnstown, Wisconsin, on the eve of the Utah Expedition's arrival in the Salt Lake Valley. After a long, emotional recitation of the Latter-day Saints' persecution and abuse elsewhere, including the murder of Joseph and Hyrum Smith and apostle Parley Pratt, Mott tried to extol the merits and virtues of the Spanish Fork area, but repeatedly he returned to the subject of violence, a need for blood atonement on a large scale, and a willingness to execute Brigham Young's scorched earth strategy in the event of army misconduct. Literally as Mott wrote, another resident of Spanish Fork, Margret Webster Adams, gave birth to her second child. Within a week she wrote to her Presbyterian brother in Scotland to describe her new life in Utah and to emphasize her defiance and willingness to sacrifice everything if Brigham Young touched a match to his Sebastopol strategy: "We have a good house with 3 rooms & a sellar [sic] and we felt first rate about burning it up & all our property and leaving [t]he desolation to our Enemies to Inherit." As Mrs. Adams wrote, Spanish Fork was awash with refugees from northern Utah, part of the thirty thousand people put on the road in late March 1858 for the Move South, perhaps to Mexican Sonora.[8]

Notwithstanding these views by many of Spanish Fork's Latter-day Saints, when John Mott decided in the late summer to embark on a long visit to relatives in Wisconsin, he chose to travel across the plains with Martin Sherwood and the Tuttle brothers, apparently finding them as congenial as William Clark had in 1857. A Latter-day Saint newspaper in Crescent City, Iowa, reported their arrival on October 15: "This morning a company of six men direct from Utah with seven animals and one wagon. Messrs. J. W. Mott, G. W. Sevy, M. L. Sherwood, J. F. Young, G. B. Tuttle and Ira O. Tuttle composed the party. They left Salt Lake City the latter part [20th] of August and have take[n] time for hunting and other sport along the road [killing five buffalo]."[9] Mott, of course, pressed on to Johnstown and later returned home to Spanish Fork. George and Ira Tuttle, perhaps continuing to travel with Mott from Iowa to Wisconsin, returned to their parents' farm in Ripon, Wisconsin, and that there is some indication that during the Civil War Ira may have joined a volunteer regiment (First Wisconsin Cavalry) and distinguished himself as a cavalryman and scout.[10] Martin Sherwood's ultimate destination remains unknown as does his hometown.

Albert Frank

In late November 1857, Albert P. Frank declined to join Clark, Leach, and Sherwood in their plan to circumvent General Johnston's prohibition on westward movement toward Salt Lake City. He also had no appetite for lingering at Fort Bridger as an unemployed vagrant or accomplice in George Tuttle's attempt to extricate his brother from the Second Dragoons. Frank's remaining options were either to enlist in the volunteer infantry battalion being recruited by Johnston, or, in the dead of winter, to return twelve hundred miles on foot to the Kansas-Missouri frontier. With Johnston willing to supply army rations for only about two weeks, the second alternative struck most people as a death sentence. Another discharged teamster told a New York reporter how he viewed this dilemma: "Oh, my name is 'Zekiel Thompson. I came out a drivin' a bull train for Russell & Waddell, and now that they've turned

FIG. 21. Spanish Fork, Utah County, Utah Territory, Martin L. Sherwood's refuge (winter 1858) and William Clark's stopover (1862). This isolated town on the road south to the Old Spanish Trail was hostile to non-Mormon outsiders. Sherwood's ability to winter-over, begin to prosper, and start a local romance reflected his survival skills, if not charm. Photo ca. 1890 by George Edward Anderson, courtesy Utah Historical Society, Salt Lake City.

us out, we can't get anything to eat, and so we're a goin' up to volunteer. I s'pose there's no choice 'cept between volunteerin' and starvin'."[11] But Albert Frank had seen enough of army life and discipline; he chose to run the risks of trekking east and did so successfully.

From Fort Leavenworth Frank presumably returned to Wisconsin; in 1860 he was unmarried and working as a "sawyer" in the woods near his parents' home at Omro, Winnebago County, Wisconsin.

There is no sign that Frank served in the Civil War. In 1865 he resumed his travels, going to Washington in March to witness President Lincoln's second inauguration. Later that year he gravitated to the Keweenau Peninsula of Michigan's remote Upper Peninsula and found work among the lumberjacks and hard rock miners in the copper fields. There, in November he married Helen McQueen Thomson. By 1870 the couple had returned to Omro; in 1882 they moved to Warren, Marshall County, Minnesota, where Albert farmed for the rest of his life. With a wife and five children, he became a pillar of the local and regional Presbyterian church. Although the Franks continued to consider Warren their home, around the end of World War I the infirmities of old age prompted them to begin an extended visit to a daughter and her family living in Longmont, Boulder County, Colorado. Albert died there unexpectedly at the end of 1921, just before his eighty-seventh birthday.

While retired in Warren, Frank was known to his neighbors for the western adventures of his youth. The author of his obituary in that town's newspaper noted, "In 1857, he crossed the plains with the government freight to Fort Kearney, Nebraska, and to Utah with government supplies. He was familiar with the great West and during his lifetime had seen the settlement frontier advance farther and farther west—from the western boundary of New York clear across the continent. And he had himself done pioneering in the different localities where he had lived and had suffered many of the hardships incident to pioneer life."

Once ensconced in Colorado, Albert continued to reminisce, and it is clear his Utah War adventures were the high point of his life. In 1918 "Mr. Frank tells us that sixty-one years ago he made a trip through this part of Nebraska, being employed in a government freighting train which was conveying building material from Ft. Leavenworth, Kans., to Salt Lake City. The train met with disaster, being burned by the Mormons in the Green river valley of Utah, and Mr. Frank, with others of the party, walked back to Leavenworth—two thousand miles."[12]

The Wagon Masters and Freighters

Chatham Rennick

By the end of "A Trip Across the Plains in 1857," Bill Clark seems to have come to view Chat Rennick, his RM&W wagon master, as almost a benefactor. Rennick never became one of Clark's "chums," as an Ames newspaper reporter mistakenly described him after interviewing Clark in the early twentieth century, but the former teamster clearly appreciated Rennick's attempts to help when he fell ill on the plains, became a target for the Southern-oriented hard cases with whom he worked, and needed advice on how best to reach California from Fort Bridger. Intriguing to the editors is whether Clark ever understood what Rennick had done (and with whom) during the Civil War, and, if so, why Clark chose not to signal this complexity to his prospective twentieth-century readers as he alerted them to Bill Hickman's blemished reputation. The same question applies to Professor Stambaugh as he edited William Clark's manuscript posthumously in 1922.

Some Civil War enthusiasts and even professional historians have chosen to portray Confederate guerrillas like Rennick as a type of Robin Hood on horseback—troopers avenging past grievances, rectifying recent Union Army atrocities, and fighting on behalf of Bobby Lee and the Lost Cause. The truth is that in joining William Clarke Quantrill's Confederate partisans, Rennick was part of a band that rode roughshod over the civilians of the Kansas-Missouri borderlands with a ferocity that drove William Tecumseh Sherman's brother-in-law to order the evacuation (depopulation) of four counties of western Missouri.[13] It was a draconian, retaliatory measure perhaps exceeding what Sherman himself was to do later in Georgia and South Carolina, turning more people into refugees than had Brigham Young's Move South in Utah Territory only five years earlier. Riding with Quantrill as his lieutenant, Chat Rennick was part of a band that included other civilian and military veterans of the Utah War. In a broader sense, he had also joined a rough crowd of irregulars that, like "Bloody Bill" Anderson, savaged isolated farms, small towns, and Union Army detachments with human ears dangling as trophies from their horses' bridles.

Chat Rennick—hero or not—met his fate southwest of Lexington in war-ravaged Kentucky on January 29, 1865. Quantrill and his raiders were masquerading as Union soldiers when they rode into the small Kentucky hamlet of Hustonville on a very cold Sunday morning. After stealing horses and killing a Union lieutenant, they rode to nearby Danville, where some of them "helped themselves to boots at one of the shoe stores and left money in part pay for what they took." After dinner they rode toward Harrodsburg where Union guerilla hunters surrounded them. Rennick was killed by rifle fire as he rode to reconnoiter their

Meaning

FIG. 22. Lieutenant "Chat" Rennick of William C. Quantrill's Confederate guerrilla unit, August 1864. This image was made five months before he was killed by Union Army forces in Harrodsburg, Kentucky. Courtesy Emory Cantey, www.canteymyerscollection.com.

situation.[14] His death was as sordid as that of Dave Wagner, the Russell, Majors and Waddell wagon master dry-gulched in Echo Canyon by an aggrieved teamster during the summer of 1858.

Frank McCarthy

In 1879 Frank McCarthy, assistant wagon master for Rennick's train, was in the public eye when William Frederick ("Buffalo Bill") Cody featured him in the first of his autobiographies. In this book Buffalo Bill first asserted that he accompanied the Utah Expedition west in 1857 as a plucky eleven-year-old courier for Russell, Majors and Waddell, spending the winter of 1858 at Fort Bridger after surviving a Sioux attack on the plains thanks to the leadership of a fearless, quick-thinking Frank McCarthy. The whole story of Cody's supposed Utah War involvement was bogus, but the public loved it, and it remained a permanent part of the burgeoning Buffalo Bill legend. And so Frank McCarthy, Bill Clark's assistant wagon master, entered the history books more as a "prop" in the Cody family's myth-making than for his legitimate role as a competent field leader for Russell, Majors and Waddell. What Bill Clark understood of all this is unknown, since he did not mention it.

Russell, Majors and Waddell

What of the firm that employed Rennick, McCarthy, the five chums, and a vast workforce of other teamsters larger than the Utah Expedition itself? Russell, Majors and Waddell enjoyed a size and reach broader than perhaps any enterprise of its time in the United States except the Pennsylvania Railroad and E. I. Du Pont; its fate was both spectacular and disastrous.

Among Brigham Young's first public comments about the Utah War during the summer of 1857 was that President Buchanan had launched the campaign to enrich Russell, Majors and Waddell rather than to restore federal authority in the territory. This view was soon widely shared by other Latter-day Saints as well as non-Mormons, becoming one of the persistent conspiracy theories about the Utah War's origins.[15] Although the firm did indeed receive multi-million-dollar payments from the U.S. government, its Utah War expenses were so large relative to its revenues, the timing of its reimbursements by the Treasury so erratic, and its 1860 establishment of the short-lived Pony Express so costly, its Utah War operations sowed the seeds of overextension and bankruptcy in 1862 rather than creating a financial windfall for the firm.

One partner, the flamboyant William H. Russell with whom William Clark negotiated his employment terms at Fort Leavenworth, was indicted for conspiracy to "cheat, defraud, and impoverish the United

States." Russell's offense was inducing a relative of Secretary of War Floyd to misappropriate $870,000 in government-held bonds from the Department of the Interior to forestall disclosure of Floyd's own irregular Utah War financing arrangements with Russell. Litigation by financial firms over the collectability of Floyd's unauthorized Utah War–related promissory notes (acceptances) continued for decades. This scandal, in turn, prompted Floyd's resignation and indictment for malfeasance during the secession crisis of 1860–1861. Another of the firm's partners, the upright Alexander Majors became destitute but was quietly supported until his death in 1900 by a grateful former employee, Frederick William Cody. Buffalo Bill for his part, engaged in persistent public misrepresentations about his involvement in the Utah War, supposedly as an eleven-year-old boy working with the likes of Bill Clark and Frank McCarthy for Russell, Majors and Waddell.[16]

Latter-day Saints
Bill Hickman

Of all the people about whom Clark wrote in "A Trip Across the Plains in 1857," none other than Brigham Young had a more publicized postwar life than self-confessed killer Bill Hickman, a man who was "notorious" even before the Utah War started. As Clark left Utah in December 1857 the controversy over Lieutenant Hickman's role in the fatal bludgeoning of ammunition trader Richard E. Yates in Echo Canyon (October) and the assassination of the cash-ladened Aiken party on the trail near Cedar City (November) was just beginning. The accusations, reputational controversies, and related legal proceedings would last for decades, again attracting the attention of New York newspaper reporters and eventually involving the U.S. Supreme Court. It was coast-to-coast press coverage heightened by completion of a national telegraph line in 1861 and the transcontinental railroad during 1869—both done in Utah. Fascination with Hickman's alleged misdeeds may have fueled William Clark's growing need in Ames, Iowa, to write about life and death in Utah Territory during 1857.

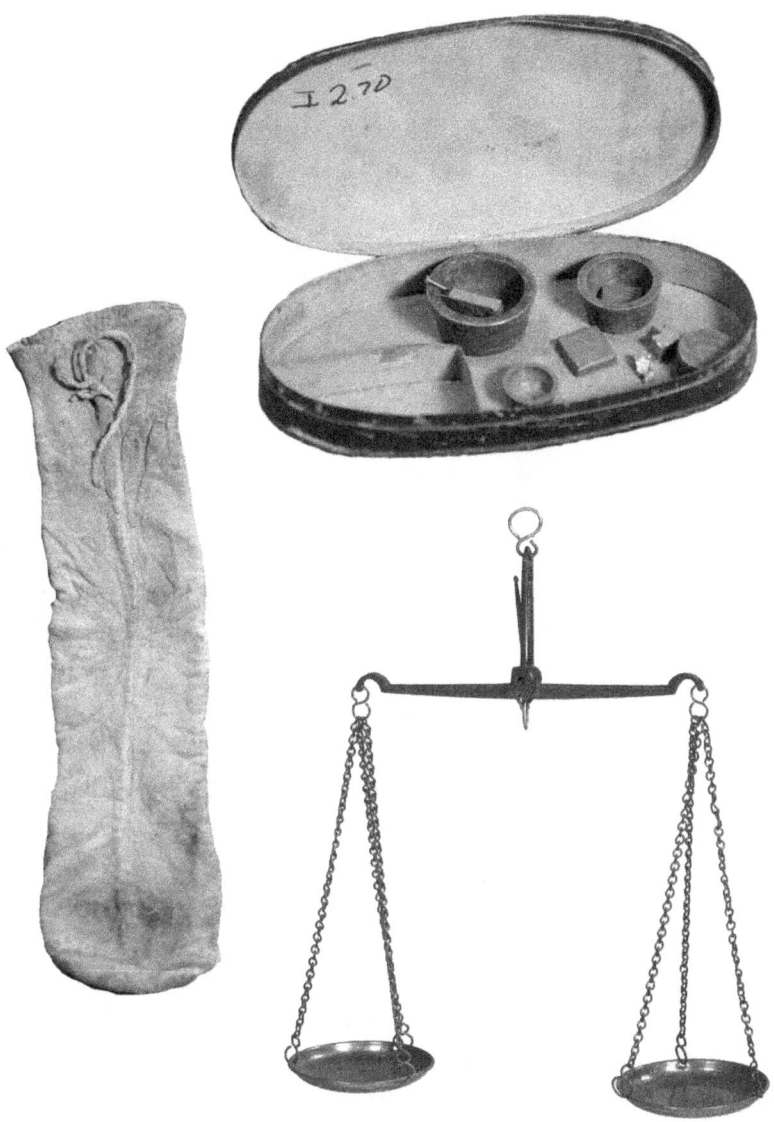

FIG. 23. Clark's mining paraphernalia, taken west 1857. Gold dust scales, weights, and poke used by William Clark along California's streams. After his death in 1920, widow Cora sold these items to Ames's D. A. R. chapter for about five dollars. The chapter then donated these items to the State Historical Society of Iowa. Courtesy SHSI Museum, Des Moines.

With multiple books now available about Hickman and an internet website devoted to him and multiple branches of the Hickman family, suffice it to say here that we now know his postwar story was driven in large part by the arc of his relationship with Brigham Young. At the time William Clark was Hickman's prisoner of war, he was a frequent visitor in Brigham Young's office as one of the "b'hoys" in good standing with special access; Young assumed Hickman's financial debts and even petitioned President Buchanan to appoint him Utah's U.S. attorney. All this began to change in 1859, when Hickman was seriously wounded and somewhat crippled in a sordid nocturnal shoot-out in a Salt Lake City alley. Publicity about this affair and Bill Hickman's growing alcoholism began to cloud his relationship with Brigham Young, who increasingly turned to other operatives like Orrin Porter Rockwell, a Hickman rival. During the Civil War, General Patrick Edward Connor, the new U.S. Army commander in Utah and Brigham Young's arch enemy, hired Hickman as a guide. With perceptions that Hickman's allegiances were no longer reliable and the fact that he had an unmistakable alcohol problem, Bill Hickman's church excommunicated him in 1868. He sank deeper into poverty, disability, and marital discord in his polygamous family.

During Reconstruction, the U.S. government returned to a focus on unprosecuted Utah War violence, especially the Mountain Meadows Massacre and the Yates murder. In 1871 a federal grand jury sitting in Salt Lake City handed down an indictment naming Brigham Young, Daniel H. Wells, Bill Hickman, and several other prominent Latter-day Saints as defendants in the Yates case, deferring for several more years prosecutions for Mountain Meadows. Hickman's codefendants were freed on bail, while he was taken into protective custody at Camp Douglas on the east bench above Salt Lake City, an arrangement that fed speculation he might testify against Brigham Young and others. While at Fort Douglas, Hickman spoke freely with reporters, admitting the Yates murder but arguing that he did it on Brigham Young's orders carried to Echo Canyon by one of Young's sons. One reporter who interviewed Hickman on this subject described his account and the likely content of his book-in-progress as "soup for readers of the most piratical relish."[17]

Editors' Epilogue

In 1872 the U.S. Supreme Court ruled in an unrelated case (Clinton v. Englebrecht, 80 U.S. 434, 1872) that the empaneling of juries in Utah had been procedurally flawed for a number of years, a decision that, in effect, voided the indictments in the Yates case and many others. It was a murder that was never re-prosecuted. During this period, Bill Hickman collaborated with an editor on an autobiography, the title of which spoke volumes about the spectacle that surrounded his postwar life: *Brigham's Destroying Angel: Being the Life, Confession, and Startling Disclosures of the Notorious Bill Hickman, the Danite Chief of Utah*.[18]

Thus freed on a legal technicality, and strapped financially, Hickman moved to the vicinity of Lander, Wyoming, in the Wind River Mountains. He was increasingly immobile and living in a crude, hillside dugout with the only one of his ten wives who stayed with him during his decline. He died there of natural causes in 1883 at age sixty-eight, buried in a plain pine coffin fabricated in a nearby blacksmith's shop. It was a quiet, lonely end for Bill Hickman, one quite different than the death of Porter Rockwell (in an alcoholic haze during 1878 at age sixty-five in Salt Lake City's Colorado Stables) and Lot Smith, of whom Bill Clark also wrote (in Arizona during 1892 at age sixty-two when shot by a Navajo shepherd while engaged in a grazing dispute).[19] William Clark outlived all of these bravos, none of whom survived past their sixties.

Perhaps confusing Hickman's death with the execution of John D. Lee in 1877, Bill Clark offered the opinion in 1912 that "Bill Hickman, when finally placed under arrest, confessed to having been implicated in twenty-nine murders. He was a leading Danite and a vulgar scoundrel, who richly deserved the death that afterward was meted out to him."[20] There is no record of Clark commenting when Brigham Young died of natural causes five months after Lee faced a firing squad at Mountain Meadows.

Brigham Young

William Clark claimed to have had only a single brief interaction with Brigham Young—when he and Bill Hickman visited Young's office in December 1857 to obtain his exit pass from Utah. What happened to Brigham Young thereafter is well known.[21] It is a story so intertwined with the fate of the territory he controlled and led (but technically no longer governed) for the remaining twenty years of his life, it is essentially the complex fate of Utah itself. What Brigham Young experienced before his death from mysterious but natural causes in 1877, after the execution of his adopted son for his role in the Mountain Meadows Massacre, was not part of Bill Clark's postwar life in California, elsewhere in the West, and eventually Ames, Iowa. It would be presumptuous of us, though, to describe Brigham Young as a bit player in "A Trip Across the Plains in 1857." Nonetheless, the fact is that when Clark set out to write about the adventures constituting the high point of his life, he focused on Chat Rennick, Frank McCarthy, Bill Hickman, "bishop" Redfield, David Savage, and a plethora of agitated Indian bands, all of whom seemed to have a more direct impact on his longevity than did Brigham Young.

Before leaving readers with those historians who have recently and ably described in published form President Young's turbulent postwar years, we present excerpts from a private, unpublished document from a gathering of Young's huge polygamous family on Christmas Day 1857. We refer to the blessing for Brigham Young from his older brother, John. In the Latter-day Saint world such blessings were not unusual— then or now. With a restless U.S. Army expedition in winter quarters only one hundred thirteen miles to the east and California ablaze with anti-Mormonism, Young's family was mindful of the burdens that beset even a prophet, seer, and revelator. John Young's blessing recounted his brother's God-given responsibilities, talents, and future rewards. Some of the latter were otherworldly, but some clearly related to the more mundane, immediate challenges of the ongoing Utah War:

> . . . no power shall overcome you; you never shall fall by the hand of an enemy, for that is not the mind of the Spirit, but the mind of the Lord is that you shall escape . . . you shall not only have power over the United States but over the nations of the earth, and you shall do a mighty work . . . Notwithstanding your enemies may hunt you like a Roe [buck] upon the mountains yet you shall

escape as a bird from the hands of the Fowler and not a hair of your head shall fall, but you shall be sustained in all times and places.[22]

And so he was, although the carnage at Mountain Meadows that William Clark saw earlier in December must have weighed heavily on Young's mind. The controversies enveloping Brigham Young's final days were such that his gravesite needed to be guarded around-the-clock for several months following his burial. It was akin to the scene at "Wheatland," President Buchanan's retirement mansion in Lancaster, Pennsylvania, where blame for his failure to avert the nation's slide into the blood bath of disunion prompted his Masonic brothers to guard his house at night during the Civil War.

"Bishop" Redfield

If after the Utah War William Clark retained positive memories about anyone he encountered south of Salt Lake City in November 1857, it was probably Harlow and Alpha Redfield, founders of Provo and proprietors of that town's Provo House hotel. Soon after Clark stayed overnight with Mr. and Mrs. Redfield en route to the Old Spanish Trail and California, the couple sold their hotel, packed up, moved to Salt Lake City, and dropped from historical notice. Why the Redfields decided to relocate is unknown for sure, although a reporter for the New York Herald who stayed in the Provo House at the end of June 1858 reported the following fanciful gossip among the few non-Mormons putting up there: "Old Redfield had departed, taking with him his young and beautifully bewitching wives. He could no longer endure that gallant, manly Gentiles should look upon the fair creatures. He sold out and retired to bury them in some obscure habitation."[23]

It is also tempting to speculate that the Redfields had tired of the violence pervasive in their part of Utah Territory—the atmosphere through which William Clark had to wend his way with great care: the attempted murders along the Santa Clara River called the Ambrose-Betts affair; the Parrish-Potter murders; the assassination of Henry Forbes; the killing of the Aiken party, and, of course, the monumental disaster at Mountain Meadows. It was an often-violent societal tone that spawned an array of code terms (usually verbs) among the local cognoscenti to signify, if not order, killing: to send someone 'cross lots; send them home; push them over the rim [of the Great Basin]; use them up; cut them off; and, most obscure of them all, to "nepo" [open] them.[24]

One way to get a feel for this climate of violence is to understand an obscure incident that took place at the Provo House on June 28, 1858, seven months after Clark stayed there and following the Redfields' sale of the place. In this case it was a knife fight between two hotel guests, both of whom were New York newspaper reporters: James W. Simonton (*Times*); and Lemuel Fillmore (*Herald*). Immediately after the incident, a bystander, Robert Burns, described it in a formal affidavit:

> Robert Burns, Carpenter of Provo, says that he was in Isaac Bullock's Hotel, formerly Redfield's Provo House, 1st Ward Provo, on Monday morning, June 28th, 1858, about half past nine oclock, and heard Mr. Simonton, and Mr. Fillmore discuss on slavery, and high words ensured, when Simonton called Fillmore a damned fool; on which Fillmore said, "You are a wise man—I have received a letter from the East, telling me to beware of you (Simonton) and not associate with you." Simonton said, "You are a damned liar"; and struck Fillmore on the top of the head with his fist, and knocked his hat off. Fillmore then, who was cutting his nails with the small blade of a large pocket knife, then struck Simonton with said knife on the left side, rather towards the back, with a kind of sweeping blow, inflicting a wound about 1 1/2 inches deep. Fillmore then ran to the next room, and he (Burns) followed him; he seized a revolver from the sheath—he (Burns) grasped it from him, and pushed him on the bed, and closed the door on Fillmore. He (Burns) holds the knife in his possession still.[25]

It was a spectacle that titillated apostle George A. Smith as he wrote to a colleague who was a Latter-day Saint working for Fillmore's newspaper in Manhattan: "The reporters of the N. Y. Times & Herald (Symington [sic] & Fillmore) had a fight in the Provo House, Provo, in which the Latter had his hat knocked off & the former received a button hole [slit] in his left side near the short ribs with the Small blade of a large

Jacknife. Our christian friends will, no doubt, rejoice at the advance of civilization in Utah."[26]

David Savage

The line is often a fine one between hard bargaining and taking advantage of, if not abusing, a person at a disadvantage. In the closing pages of "A Trip Across the Plains in 1857" William Clark (and apparently members of the Turner-Dukes train) raised the question about the fairness of the terms David Savage had demanded to "pilot" Clark and his small party from Utah's southern settlements to California. From the safety and comfort of San Bernardino, it was easy to second-guess the economic arrangement between Savage and Clark, especially if one lacks an understanding of the hard scrabble life many such Latter-day Saints led while running appalling risks during wartime amongst the tribes on behalf of unwanted strangers passing through the area with no vested interest in the turmoil left in their wake. After weighing the equities, Clark, the beneficiary of Savage's nerve and skill, concluded that successfully leaving Utah with his life was worth the cash, labor, and outfit his guide extracted from him. It is telling that Clark remembered Savage when he set out to record his western adventures a half-century later.

From this study we now know what happened to Bill Clark after January 1858, but what of Savage? He resumed the life he had led prior to the Utah War, which, as we view it, was a remarkable but underappreciated participation in many of the events on the frontier that helped his church to survive the existential threats of the nineteenth century. He did so while supporting a family that eventually grew to include four wives and nineteen children. Elsewhere, we have likened Maj. Howard Egan of the Nauvoo Legion to Winston Groom's fictive Forrest Gump, a self-effacing character who seemingly went everywhere and saw everything.[27] In a way less dramatic and more anonymous than Egan's, Savage too labored on behalf of his church and religion with a commitment that is difficult for twenty-first-century non-Mormons to appreciate, especially if they have never experienced persecution or extreme poverty.

By 1886, after several years helping to colonize Utah's northernmost settlements in the harsh climate near Bear Lake, Savage had fundamentally worn himself out. His was a life of grueling labor that took him from Upper Canada (Ontario) to New England, Nauvoo, Iowa, and the Great Basin's Wasatch Front, southern Utah, the Old Spanish Trail, and the Utah-Idaho borderlands. Thirty years after David Leonard Savage and William Clark parted company in southern California, Savage died of respiratory complications at age seventy-five at his last pioneering home, northern Arizona Territory's town of Snowflake.[28]

Although Savage did not take part in the Mountain Meadows Massacre, he (like Clark) saw its immediate aftermath firsthand and knew many of the killers. There is no mention of the tragedy in his autobiographical writings, and his descendants have not speculated on his proximity to it.

Our Heroes: Bill and Cora Clark

Colorful as the postwar adventures of Messrs. Rennick, McCarthy, Leach, Tuttle, Sherwood, and Frank were, those of William and Cora Clark surpassed them in many ways.

In closing "A Trip Across the Plains in 1857," Bill Clark left his readers without information about his life after he reached the safety of San Bernardino on January 13, 1858, but during the early twentieth century he twice described his work and travels during the ten years immediately after he fled Utah. In 1905 Clark told the Ames *Intelligencer* that during this period he had been "prospecting, trapping and freighting." In 1917 he expanded this list to say he had traveled to "the places where there were no trails, herded thousands of head of sheep to the markets, built the largest fence which has ever been built around a vineyard in California, made the plains in a covered wagon and drifted back and forward from one western state to another always doing something that brot [sic] a betterment to the wilderness and assisting in the erection of thousands of the frontier cabins."[29] In his reminiscences, Clark stated that in 1862 he returned to Springville, Utah, for an unspecified purpose and period; another newspaper article reported that later in the Civil War he performed some kind of "government duties on the western coast."[30]

Editors' Epilogue

FIG. 24. Corner of Main Street and Clark Avenue, Ames, Iowa. City hall is located at #515 Clark Avenue, named after William Clark, a city councilman and mayor for two nonconsecutive terms during 1875–1877. Photo courtesy of Ames Mayor John Halla and Public Information Officer Susan Gwiasda.

Tempting as it may be to dismiss such a range of jobs as hyperbole, some, if not all, of it is credible. For example, within a few weeks of Clark's arrival in California, a group of German immigrants in San Francisco organized themselves into a residential community dedicated to acquiring a large tract of land forty miles from San Bernardino along southern California's Santa Ana River. Their plan was to develop vineyards and produce wine. This German American group called their site "Anaheim;" it was a place that evolved politically into Orange County and in 1955 morphed into Disneyland. In January 1858 this community hired scores of laborers to dig an extensive web of irrigation canals 450 miles long and build an ingenious fence for the property's perimeter by planting live willow shoots eight feet tall at intervals of two feet.[31] If William Clark gravitated to this venture, he would indeed have taken part in developing what soon became the largest fenced vineyard in the world, a project that could have provided him work for years. Because of the location and timing of Anaheim's establishment vis-à-vis Clark's arrival in nearby San Bernardino, this colony was most likely his and perhaps Edwin Leach's first employment after leaving the Old Spanish Trail.

Historians have virtually no information about Clark's California mining activity, but, as with his fence building, it is possible to speculate about what he did and where. For example, it is known that during 1862 a William Clark and two partners were placer mining for gold in Long Gulch, a claim a half-mile from a place called Hawkeye House (perhaps named by Iowans) in Calaveras County, a district in the Sierra foothills soon famous because of Samuel L. Clemens's celebrated frog story. Whether the trio panning Long Gulch after building a water flume a half-mile in length included a former Utah War teamster is unknown, but a newspaper's description of them as "somewhat troubled for the lack of a Heady supply of water" easily fits what one can imagine "our" William Clark experienced with his scales and gold dust poke at-the-ready.[32]

By 1868 William Clark was back in Kansas to visit his uncle in Lawrence and reclaim the trunk he had left in 1857 en route to his employment with Russell, Majors and Waddell. In the interim, Kansas had morphed from a territory into a state, and the town of Lawrence as well as Bill Clark had also changed. Lawrence had endured a murderous attack in August 1863 by the Confederate guerrilla band led by "captain" William Clarke Quantrill, a former RM&W teamster, camp cook, and card sharp during the Utah War. In 1865 Quantrill and his principal lieutenant, Chat Rennick, were both killed by Union cavalry patrols hunting them in western Kentucky—Rennick was mortally wounded in January and Quantrill in May (dying in June, a few days later). Among the more than one hundred fifty victims of the Quantrill massacre was Lemuel Fillmore, a Lawrence realtor who had briefly worked as a war correspondent in Utah for the New York *Herald* and survived a June 28, 1858, knife fight in the Provo hotel formerly owned by William Clark's benefactor during the previous November, "bishop" Redfield.[33]

Editors' Epilogue

Since 1857 Cora Jane Clark had also changed. With the passage of time, she had become a twenty-two-year-old woman awaiting Bill Clark's letters from the West at her father's Wisconsin farm. Precisely when in 1868 William returned to Paoli to press his suit for Cora's hand is unknown, but return he did, and on September 29, 1868, a local minister married the couple. Through the years, when people remarked on the fact that Cora had married a man with the same surname as hers, she replied, "I never found a name that suited me better than Clark."[34]

In 1869 the couple set out from Wisconsin, heading west as Bill Clark had done twelve years earlier. They stopped and settled for the rest of their lives in what was then the embryonic town of Ames in central Iowa's Story County. A half-century later, a local newspaper ran a romanticized account of their means of travel from Pliny Clark's Paoli farm and their reason for embracing Ames: "They entered a covered wagon and 'started west.' They had no idea at that time where their future home would be. They were but travelers on the broad prairies and some place in the golden west they were to establish themselves and make a home—a home of their own. It was merely a chance that they happened to stop in Ames. But once having arrived, having become acquainted with the very first day as did the people of those early times, they concluded the end of the journey had been reached and it was here they would carve out a niche in the rock of time. This was home to them then and has remained so to this day."[35]

Other than an atmosphere of neighborliness, promising signs for Ames in the late 1860s were the recent construction of a rail line through town, the presence of the new state agricultural college (now Iowa State University), and thousands of acres of rich farmland. Such potential and the infrastructure already under way must have resonated with the Clarks' farm backgrounds as well as William's recent experience with the early agricultural development of southern California. Ames may not have been Anaheim in terms of climate and adventure, but its rail connection and well-watered, easily exploited farm acreage offered advantages not then readily available in California.

After a year or so of farming on the edge of town, the Clarks moved into the center of Ames, and William opened a general store focusing

The New Store!
CHAMBERLAIN & CLARK.

The undersigned having formed a co-partnership in the Stock of Goods and business formerly owned by WILLIAM CLARK, and having made large additions in the way of STAPLE and FANCY GROCERIES, and having removed to the new Store in "THE INTELLIGENCER" building, are now ready to serve the people of Ames and Story county with a fresh and full Stock of

STAPLE AND
Fancy Groceries,
FRESH FRUITS,
CONFECTIONERY,
TOBACCO, CIGARS,
CANNED FRUITS, ETC., ETC.

Under the present arrangement we will be able to sell GOODS CHEAPER than heretofore, and as cheap as any other house in the County. HIGHEST MARKET PRICE paid for

BUTTER AND EGGS.

GROCERIES!
CHEAP CASH STORE!
WILLIAM CLARK,
(Successor to CHAMBERLAIN & CLARK,)
GROCER,
INTELLIGENCER BLOCK,
AMES, - - IOWA.

I Carry a Full Line of
GROCERIES,
CROCKERY AND
GLASSWARE.

The people of Story county are respectfully invited to call and look through my stock, which will always be found full and complete in every department. My goods are selected with great care, and are of the best quality to be found in the market. My prices will always be as low as the same quality of goods can be bought anywhere in Story county, as

I will not be Undersold.
TERMS STRICTLY CASH.

Crockery & Glassware! | **Best Brands Family Flour!**

Fine Teas a Specialty!

on the sale of household goods and vegetables. After eleven years behind the counter, he concluded that he needed to work outside and so traded a mercantile life indoors for a business buying and selling horses, often for shipment to the Minneapolis market. Trading horses and wrangling them into railroad box cars was not the colorful work of a bull whacker on the Oregon Trail, but for the rest of his active days he made his living this way. His early days with Russell, Majors and Waddell and on the Clark family farms of New York and Wisconsin were good preparation for life among large, often unruly animals.

In the mid-1870s Clark entered the world of elected politics as the twenty-year-old Republican Party swept into control of Iowa. During 1875–1877 he served as Ames's sixth mayor; eventually one of the city's major streets was named in his honor and is today the seat of Ames's municipal government.

Cora's life in Ames was what a reporter described in 1918 as "carrying on her part of the busy life of the pioneer. She was active in all the good that is the direct result of her being a resident of Ames and having her part in building the community, in establishing churches and assisting in every way that comes to one with as cheerful and as willing a nature as that of the bride of fifty years ago."[36]

Lacking children of their own, at some point in the late 1870s/early 1880s the Clarks informally adopted a teenage girl from a large family in town (Harriet A. ["Hattie"] Weld) and raised her as their own to become a schoolteacher, wife (Mrs. Charles E. Sargent), and mother. The Ames newspapers of the early twentieth century were filled with social notices of visits exchanged between the Clarks' neighbors and those of William and Cora's siblings and nieces/nephews who had followed them to Iowa. There were also frequent visits with the Sargents, who lived first in Ames and then nearby Ogden, Boone County, Iowa. There are signs that while the Clarks were well-liked in town and economi-

FIG. 25. *opposite*: Newspaper ads for Clark's Ames grocery store, 1879 and 1880. After ten years of farming and municipal politics, William Clark entered the grocery and dry goods business in downtown Ames, Iowa. In the early 1890s, feeling confined by a merchant's indoor life, he became a horse trader for the remainder of his working days. Advertisements from *Ames Intelligencer*.

cally comfortable, they were not people of high net worth. Newspaper writers referred to their home at various times as "little" and "humble," and, upon celebration of their golden wedding anniversary, a reporter gratuitously threw out the bromide that "it is better to have lived among people for a long time and have the esteem of that community than it is to have accumulated great wealth."[37]

As they aged, Cora and William may have grown restless and turned again to thoughts of the West. In 1891 William visited Seattle for five months, presumably alone and traveling by rail. His reason for doing this is unknown, but such a trip at age fifty-seven would be interesting to understand. Even more adventuresome was their eighteen-month sojourn in the Dakotas during 1910–1911 to visit Cora's sister in Redfield, South Dakota, and William's nephew on his ranch near Gladstone, North Dakota. While returning home, Cora traveled by buggy and William drove their automobile, no small feat for a couple their age. Upon arrival, Cora, sounding like Dorothy in L. Frank Baum's 1900 novel *The Wonderful Wizard of Oz*, declared, "There is no place like home and Ames is the best place on earth."[38]

By the end of World War I, the Clarks were ailing and closed up their home at 320 Sherman Avenue in Ames to move in with the widow of William's brother Arthur in Ogden. On February 16, 1920, William passed away there just short of his eighty-sixth birthday. Cora's death followed his two years later, a few months after her late husband's "A Trip Across the Plains in 1857" appeared in the *Iowa Journal of History and Politics*. As discussed above, for unknown reasons Cora received no mention in William's manuscript, but without the chain of events she set in motion with Ames's Daughters of the American Revolution chapter during the summer of 1920, it might never have seen print.

The Manuscript's Provenance

As discussed above, the editors conclude from internal evidence that Clark wrote his reminiscences either in the late 1800s or early in the twentieth century, as newspaperman John I. Ginn concluded in El Paso. Precisely when Clark began to collect his thoughts, assemble notes and start to draft what became "A Trip Across the Plains in 1857" is unknown.

If he was like many westering pioneers, he may well have begun to retail anecdotes of his adventures verbally not long after he and wife Cora arrived in Ames during 1869. As Civil War veterans joined the Grand Army of the Republic and swapped campaign stories amongst themselves, at family gatherings, between friends, and to anyone else who would listen, it would have been natural for Bill Clark to join in with his own tales of derring-do among the tribes, Latter-day Saints, and the hard cases employed by Russell, Majors and Waddell. With the Custer massacre of 1876, the execution of John D. Lee in 1877, the soon-to-follow death of Brigham Young, the appearance of Buffalo Bill Cody's autobiographies and stage extravaganzas, and the so-called closing of the American frontier in 1893, Ames's citizens would have had a high interest in what Clark had to say.

The first documented sign of Clark's eagerness to tell his story came with a long interview that appeared in Ames's *Intelligencer* on June 15, 1905. The interview took place only a few years after the close of the Spanish-American War, the Philippine Insurrection, and the U.S. Senate's controversial foray into the polygamy issue with its marathon investigative hearings about the seating of Utah's senator Reed Smoot. The *Intelligencer* ran the piece on its front page under the heading "A TALE OF ADVENTURE, William Clark, an old Resident of Ames, Recounts His Experiences of an early Day." This article included in summary fashion nearly all of the story elements that appeared seventeen years later in the *Iowa Journal of History and Politics* article; essentially, it was the newspaper reporter's interpretation of Mr. Clark's verbal comments during the interview as well as quotations from some sort of written material provided by Clark. Surprisingly, although Clark casually mentioned the Mountain Meadows Massacre as a fact, he made no claim to having passed through the meadows let alone seeing skeletons of its victims there. In general, what appeared in the 1905 *Intelligencer* piece was jumbled and far less accurate than the polished 1922 journal article, including a characterization of Chat Rennick as one of Clark's traveling "chums" rather than in the role of his overbearing wagon master. In the *Intelligencer* interview Clark presented Bill Hickman without redeeming features and described his role in the torture-murder of an

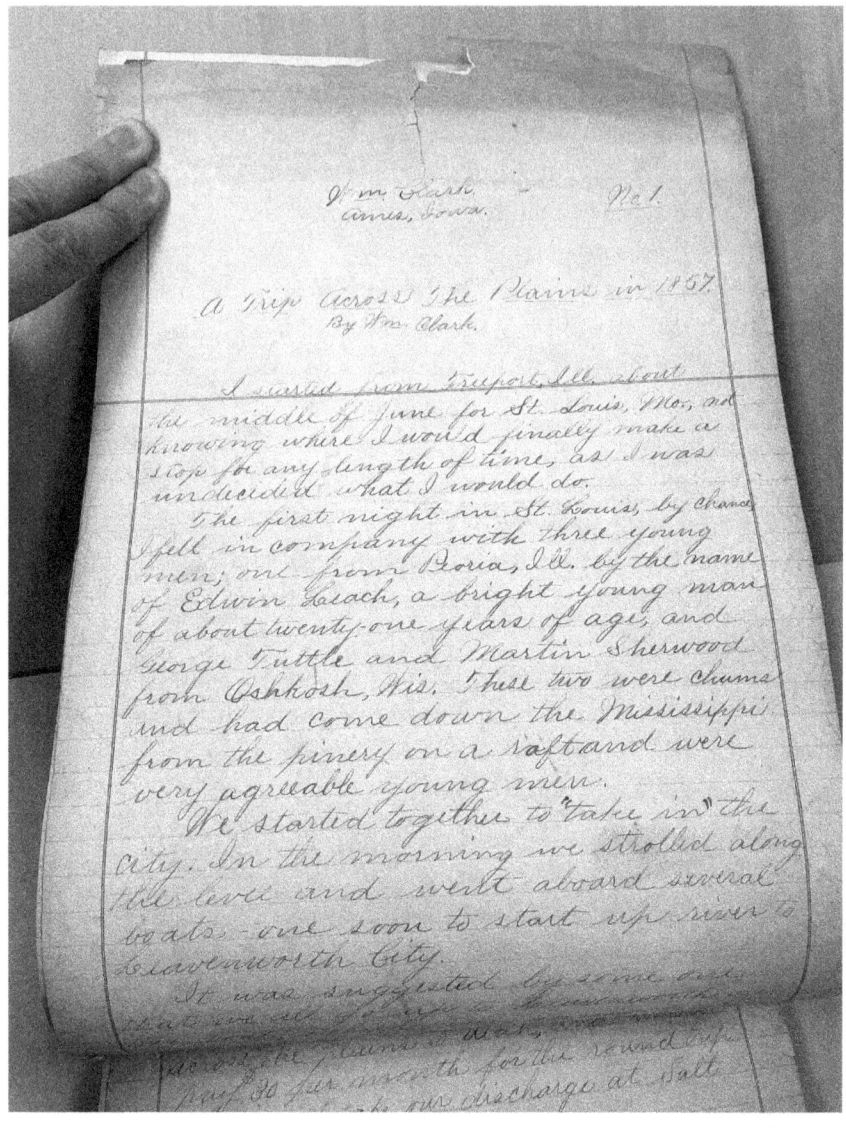

FIG. 26. Holograph manuscript of William Clark's "A Trip Across the Plains in 1857." Following Clark's death in 1920, his widow sold the manuscript for about ten dollars to the local Daughters of the American Revolution chapter, which donated it to the State Historical Society of Iowa. This document was then rapidly edited by Prof. Benjamin Franklin Shambaugh and published in the April 1922 issue of SHSI's quarterly, the *Iowa Journal of History and Politics*. Manuscript photo courtesy SHSI, Iowa City.

overly independent Latter-day Saint that never reappeared in Clark's subsequent written or verbal comments (or anyone else's) about Hickman. As in most of Clark's descriptions of his western adventures, he left his audience with the impression that he was a native of Freeport, Illinois, rather than upstate New York.[39]

Seven years later, on the fifty-fifth anniversary of the Mountain Meadows Massacre, the *Intelligencer* again wrote a front-page article about William Clark, apparently at his initiative. This time much of the piece was couched in the first rather than third person—almost as though Clark was writing a letter to the newspaper's editor rather than engaging in an interview with one of his reporters. Clark's comments, as printed on September 11, 1912, were prompted not by the Mountain Meadows anniversary—the massacre was not even mentioned—but rather as a follow-on to an *Intelligencer* piece run a few days earlier in which a Civil War general casually mentioned the late Albert Sidney Johnston's command of the Utah Expedition. Clark wanted the public to know that he had firsthand experience with General Johnston in this campaign.

After reprising some of his own Utah War experiences, Clark got to his main point—discussion of Johnston's role in one of the then current conspiracy theories about the coming of the Civil War. As Clark phrased it here (but nowhere else subsequently), "A feature of the expedition that impressed itself upon all the soldiers, teamsters and others, was, that the stimulation, while declared to be in the interest of punishing the Mormons, was really a pretext of the Buchanan administration to send General Johnston to Utah to permit him to join the rebel army in the south [in 1861]." Seeing a sensational news item in these comments, the *Intelligencer* grabbed for reader attention with the headline "WENT WITH JOHNSTON ON MILITARY TRIP AGAINST MORMONS . . . Expedition Was for Purpose of Giving Johnston Chance to Join Rebels." While straying into such new territory, Clark made two other comments that also never again appeared in his reminiscences: that he was with scout Jim Bridger in Utah and that his "home" was in New York State.[40]

In any event, it is now clear that Clark had completed "A Trip Across the Plains in 1857" no later than the fall of 1915. At that time he gave the handwritten manuscript to B. H. Read, editor of Ames's *Evening Times*. Whether William Clark wrote this piece with publication in mind or merely for his own amusement and/or family edification is unknown. The newspaper was immediately interested. Editor Read made the substantial commitment to publish it without modification in twelve installments starting on November 10, 1915, and concluding with the issue of December 6. There were no chapter headings or an obvious basis for dividing the manuscript; the length of installments appeared to be geared to the newspaper's normal layout challenges.

The opening piece appeared following a brief editorial explanation filled with teasers to stimulate reader interest: "'A Trip Across the Plains in 1857' by William Clark now of this city, will be the title of a real story we are going to give our readers in installments of the issues of the Times until the narrative is completed. In this article Mr. Clark gives his actual experiences in driving an ox team from Leavenworth, Kansas, in 1857, to Salt Lake, Utah. He then continued the trip to the gold fields of California. Our reason for publishing the written experiences of this adventure is that by many Mr. Clark is personally known. Besides the narrative being of local interest, it will prove to be interesting from other standpoints. The writer tells of how the men who were to be drivers of the ox teams took 'raw' cattle from the field and broke them to the yoke. He gives many thrilling accounts of narrow escapes from the Indians, Buffalos and Mormans [sic]. He was introduced to the then Mormon leader, Brigham Young, and given a pass to go through the Mormon lines and was also given inducements to join the Mormon church."[41]

After the twelfth and concluding installment, there was no additional assessment by editor Read of what had been printed, and there were no reader comments. In the subsequent one hundred nine years, no scholar has taken note of this material.

The next episode in the travels of Clark's manuscript unfolded soon after his death on February 16, 1920, a little more than four years after its first appearance in the Ames *Evening Times*. Oddly, this holograph document's next stop was as part of the deliberations of Ames's chapter of the National Society of the Daughters of the American Revolution.

Editors' Epilogue

Within two weeks of William Clark's death, the Historical Relics Committee of Ames's Sun Dial Chapter of the Daughters of the American Revolution sought and received authorization from its board to purchase the original manuscript of Clark's manuscript, with the understanding that the asking price might be about ten dollars. Discussions with the Clark family ensued for the next six months and were broadened to include disposition of small gold mining paraphernalia Mr. Clark had taken west. Apparently the talks were led by Ms. Pearle Schmidt, wife of Dr. Louis Bernard Schmidt, chairman of the history department at nearby Iowa State University. At the September 6 meeting, with Mrs. Schmidt in the chair as acting regent (presiding officer), the chapter adopted a resolution to "purchase the Manuscript, 'A Trip Across the Plains in '57,' the scales that weighed [out] the gold dust, and the bag that carried the gold, from Mrs. Wm. Clark, for $15.00, the scales and bags to be given to the State Historical Society [Museum] at D. M. [Des Moines] and the manuscript to be given to the State Historical Society at Iowa City."[42] A month later, one of the local newspapers reported this action without mentioning price.[43]

With this donation, Dr. Benjamin Franklin Shambaugh entered the picture. He did so wearing several organizational hats: superintendent (executive director) of the State Historical Society of Iowa (SHSI); founding editor of its flagship quarterly, the *Iowa Journal of History and Politics*; and founding professor/chairman of the department of political science at SHSI's parent organization, the University of Iowa. Emblematic of the intertwined nature of these roles was the fact that, by design, the offices of the two organizations were across the corridor from each other (in Shambaugh Hall) on the university's Iowa City campus.

With Dr. Shambaugh, Clark's reminiscences came to rest in the hands of a distinguished professional with a national reputation. He was a native Iowan who studied at the University of Pennsylvania for his PhD degree in political science and then did postdoctoral work in Germany. He joined the university's faculty in 1896 as chair of the newly established department of political science and added responsibility for SHSI and its publications in 1907. At various times Shambaugh was founder-president of both the American Political Science Association and the Mississippi Valley Historical Association (now Organization of American Historians).[44]

On the surface, Clark's manuscript would seem a natural "fit" for a journal like Dr. Shambaugh's, since one of his prime interests was collecting and publishing documents about Iowa's history. Notwithstanding this background, Shambaugh was an editor without expertise in the history of the American West, Utah, and the Latter-day Saints—the primary focus of William Clark's manuscript. To the extent he may have received editorial help from his Iowa State University friend, Professor Schmidt, Shambaugh would have been relying on a scholar whose field was the economic history of American agriculture. This mismatch of editorial backgrounds and manuscript requirements brings to mind the aphorism coined decades ago by historian Jan Shipps of Indiana-Purdue University. Shipps, a Methodist sometimes described as the consummate outsider-insider of the Latter-day Saint past, commented that the mysteries (challenges) of Mormon history make it (for non-Latter-day Saints) the "hole" in the "doughnut" of research and writing about the American West.[45]

As a result of these limitations and to make Clark's narrative more useful to modern readers, the editors of this book have discarded some of the original Shambaugh footnotes and added a plethora of new ones to explain the otherwise unidentified people, places, and events Clark mentioned. In the process, we have also provided personal background on Clark himself and how his western story took shape during the early twentieth century. The latter was especially important in view of editor Shambaugh's apparent unawareness of the publicity Clark sought for his story through Ames newspapers during 1905, 1912, and 1915.

And so, through this chain of events, "A Trip Across the Plains in 1857" found its way into the pages of the *Iowa Journal of History and Politics* in April 1922. Following this publication—sometime after 1937 but perhaps years later—a holograph variant of the Clark narrative surfaced in the special collections of what is now the Cushing Memorial Library & Archives at Texas A&M University in College Station. Cushing Library's accession records shed minimal light on who donated or sold this document, when, and under what circumstances. This vexing

Editors' Epilogue

ambiguity is not peculiar to Texas; it plagues some of the holdings in a surprising variety of special collections across the country.

Through a serendipitous internet search, the editors of this book became aware of the Texas A&M copy in 2002; twenty years later, in 2021, we sought to examine it for this study with an intent to focus for comparative purposes on its text, handwriting, ink, and paper. Because of its fragile condition, Cushing no longer permits access to this additional document but fortuitously made available to the editors a holograph copy of it written in ball-point ink in what appears to be a secretarial hand by an unknown person at an unknown time. This copy was written on 115 leaves of a lined, spiral-bound notebook perforated by a three-hole punch.

Comparison of this modern holograph copy at Texas A&M with the early twentieth-century holograph "original" (now housed at SHSI) from which the 1922 Iowa article was typeset indicates the texts are virtually identical, although the Texas variant has multiple blank spaces where the copyist was unable to read the "original." As near as we can determine, aside from these gaps of a word or two sprinkled throughout the text, the major difference is a tantalizing and incomplete opening sentence for the Texas A&M variant only. Also two words appear at the end of the Texas A&M text that are not in the conclusion to the Iowa materials: "Good Bye." Accompanying this mysterious 115-sheet copy are five pages of notes written in the same secretarial hand listing the name of each person mentioned by William Clark as well as a comprehensive list (without explanations) of places, landmarks, events, and even foods—all annotated to indicate the pages where each item appears in the copied manuscript. The editors of this book conclude that these lists were the draft of a rudimentary index, and that the copyist was working on the early stages of what was intended to be a republication of "A Trip Across the Plains in 1857" that never came to pass.[46]

What other surprises about William Clark's adventures and reminiscences await discovery? As we have concluded below, there is a need to keep digging. Whatever else Clark wrote during the 1850s and 1860s while roaming the West calls to enterprising researchers.

Editors' Conclusions

What, then, are the conclusions to be drawn from William Clark's reminiscences? The editors believe there are at least seven major takeaways:

Recognize the Gaps

Perhaps most obvious is the fact that what Clark left in his manuscript was far from a complete autobiography. Wholly absent is any mention of his upbringing in upstate New York, his meeting with young Cora Clark in Wisconsin, his long sojourn in California, his and Cora's prolonged, transcontinental courtship, and their more than half-century together after marrying in 1868 and settling in Ames, Iowa. What little we know of these events has come later from census data, a newspaper reporter who interviewed the couple as they prepared to celebrate their golden anniversary in 1917, and Bill Clark's 1920 obituaries. Absent more personal information, Clark's manuscript left his potential readers to their own devices and the erroneous impression that he was a native of Freeport, Illinois.

Still awaiting explanation, then, is the outcome of William Clark's search for gold in California. Was he successful? Did he also mine elsewhere in the West, say near Pike's Peak, Colorado, where other Utah War veterans rushed for gold in 1859–1860? What were the other western states through which he roamed after 1857, and what were the details of his work developing vineyards, herding sheep, and building cabins? What was his "government duty" in California during the Civil War to which his obituary alluded, and why did Clark refer to it so opaquely? Presumably it was not as a soldier, since he generated no military records and had avoided an opportunity for army service as a volunteer at Fort Bridger. What, then, was the character of this activity?

When Bill Clark wrote or spoke of his western rambles during the twentieth century, he always confined himself to the Utah War, while bypassing his other adventures in the region—including the Cora story. Why these limits?

Meaning

Along with these significant gaps in what William Clark provided about his own life, he also stepped over the origins and post-1857 fate of others: his four closest friends during the Utah War (Messrs. Leach, Tuttle, Sherwood, and Frank); as well as the teamsters, wagon masters, killers-in-waiting, and helpful settlers he encountered. With the passage of time, perhaps a fading memory, and limited access to search resources, Clark lost track of these men and women and said so early in the twentieth century. This left him (and readers) unaware of what these people did during and after the Civil War. As reflected by this study's epilogue, there was gold of another kind in the later adventures of who Howard Lamar called the heroes and villains with whom Bill Clark worked his way west.

The principal significance of these gaps is their limiting impact on one's ability to understand and appreciate what William Clark experienced and through whom. He told his neighbors in Ames and left for his posterity only what he wanted them to know, and no more. The good news is that our modern awareness of what remains missing can stimulate and guide a continued search for Clark's complete story.

Beware the Bogus

If, in writing "A Trip Across the Plains in 1857," Clark left future readers hanging because of missing information, some of the material he provided is problematic. To call the latter bogus is too harsh, but it is fair to describe some of Clark's narrative as inaccurate or unverifiable, as we have indicated above.[1] As we see it, the questionable parts of Clark's reminiscences are probably the result of how and when (at what age) he wrote them rather than a deliberate effort to mislead readers.

Clark's original editor, Benjamin F. Shambaugh, alerted readers that Clark composed his polished narrative using contemporary rough notes and then destroyed them. It was a creative process often used by western travelers writing in old age like John I. Ginn, but one posing difficulties for historians trying to assess the surviving text. Editor Shambaugh did nothing to help us understand when—at what age—Clark wrote "A Trip Across the Plains in 1857," information that could shed light on the accuracy of portions of the narrative, especially those written from memory. Although Professor Schambaugh did not comment on them, there are events, landmarks, and people mentioned in Clark's manuscript as well as slang indicating he probably wrote near the turn of the twentieth century—at age seventy or older. It was a stage of life unlikely to improve a former teamster's powers of recall. As one aging first sergeant of dragoons confessed to a son pressing him for details about his youthful Utah War experiences, "It was 50 odd years ago and you would have to have a pretty good memory to remember all those things, you know.... I have forgotten now. It is so hard for me to remember.... I cannot think of any more now, I am getting tired and want to stop."[2]

All these circumstances point to the need for researchers to exercise critical judgment in using Clark's narrative as a source. Notwithstanding the near-iconic status of "A Trip Across the Plains in 1857," caution is warranted. The history of the American West is full of fascinating, exciting true tales. It is also encumbered with more than a few tainted ones.[3] Some books and stories are a blend of both types of material. The challenge is to recognize that such mixtures exist even among the classics, and then determine what stories are to be avoided as unsupportable and how much of such works is reliable.

The more famous the author, perhaps the greater the need for reader vigilance. If there is reason to take care in using Bill Cody's autobiography or even Lt. Eugene F. Ware's *The Indian War of 1864*, it is also in order to approach William Clark's reminiscences judiciously. Hence this study's plethora of amplifying footnotes.[4]

Find and Keep the Nuggets

While casting a gimlet eye on seductively appealing research sources like these, it is equally important not to lose sight of the high-grade nuggets mixed with questionable material. For all its shortcomings, like some of the details of the Mountain Meadows Massacre, Clark's narrative is loaded with other vignettes, names, and incidents that are valuable, demonstrably accurate, and unavailable elsewhere. Either the subsequently destroyed notes from which he worked were detailed and comprehensive or his memory was extraordinary. Clark's reminiscences, especially the later segments we have editorially divided into sections

11 and 12, are replete with names, nicknames, and encounters—many obscure—about which he could not possibly have known other than by firsthand interactions. There were then no published accounts from which Clark could have appropriated such accounts. The large number and verifiability of such details, even his trailside repartee, do much to establish William Clark's overall credibility.

For example, when Bill Hickman described the enmity between him and Dr. Garland Hurt, he told Clark, "I'd like to get in reach of him with my old rifle[;] he wouldn't tell any more tales, and I'll get him yet."[5] It was phrasing about Hurt's peril very similar to that used in their contemporary diaries and letters by Hickman's fellow legionnaires simultaneously hunting three other detested non-Mormons: William M. F. Magraw, David H. Burr, and Hiram F. Morrell.[6] Similarly, it is only through "A Trip Across the Plains in 1857" that we learn of George B. Tuttle's intent to free his brother Ira from his onerous five-year enlistment with the Utah Expedition's Second U.S. Dragoons. Private Tuttle's desertion from Camp Scott and his flight toward Fort Laramie with brother George was a dramatic but obscure incident. The case was not publicized, and, although the army provost marshal's records for 1858 describe what happened, they were inaccessible to the public for more than a century. Only Bill Clark, who was present when George Tuttle hatched his plan to "rescue" Ira Tuttle in late 1857, could have known what was to unfold and alluded to it in his reminiscences near the turn of the twentieth century.

Just because one cannot verify Clark's story of visiting Brigham Young's office with Bill Hickman to obtain a travel pass in the fall of 1857, it would be a mistake to dismiss it. The incident rings true.

Such a document was indeed necessary for non-Mormons to enter, cross, and leave Utah after Young proclaimed martial law on September 15, 1857. The governor's records are filled with retained copies of such passes. Whether Bill Clark obtained one from Brigham Young directly is open to challenge; that he indeed had a pass, as he said he did, is highly likely, especially in light of the penalties associated with traveling without such written authorization. The fate of the victims at Mountain Meadows is proof positive that there were indeed serious risks awaiting non-Mormons moving through southern Utah during the fall of 1857.[7]

In many respects, the best validation of William Clark's overall credibility is the mesh of "A Trip Across the Plains in 1857" with the unpublished reminiscences of three other Utah War teamsters or drovers who shared many of Clark's experiences: John I. Ginn, Lodowick W. Morgan, and Samuel Ackerman. None of these travelers had access to the others' accounts when they, in turn, wrote about their own experiences, but the consistency among them lends general credence to Clark's manuscript. Sometimes, in their details, the other three mirror Clark's account with uncanny similarity. Ideally, to obtain a more complete picture of what William Clark experienced, one should read his reminiscences with those of Ginn, Morgan, and Ackerman at hand, but they are not accessible in a way "A Trip Across the Plains in 1857" now is.[8]

In weighing the complexities and occasional inaccuracies as well as ambiguities of William Clark's reminiscences, then, it is worth remembering the old admonition about not throwing out the baby with the bath water.

Clark's Narrative and Later Life One of "Westering"

Perhaps an obvious one, but a take-away worth considering is that "A Trip Across the Plains in 1857" and Bill Clark's later life were a continuing story of "westering." In 1893, in their own ways, the U.S. Census Bureau and Professor Frederick Jackson Turner had pronounced the American frontier "closed." What followed was a national and even European stampede to have a last look at what the historians Goetzmann have called "The West of the Imagination," fueled as it was in Bill Clark's era by Theodore Roosevelt's accounts of ranching and hunting in North Dakota, Owen Wister's famous novel about Wyoming, and the hype of Buffalo Bill Cody's autobiographies and stage extravaganzas. And so, after spending more than ten years in Utah, California, and surrounding territories, we see Bill Clark and his bride Cora setting off from her father's Wisconsin farm in 1869 in a covered wagon for a western destination then unknown to them. They never looked back, or at least not in an easterly direction. The West was in William Clark's blood, and Cora seemed to share his enthusiasm for the region. To us it is extraordinary to see them pick up stakes and travel by buggy and automobile from Ames to the Dakotas for eighteen months during 1910–1911 when he was seventy-six years old. This odyssey came after his five-month trip in 1891, presumably by rail, to see the wonders of Seattle. When the Clarks were setting out for their trek to the Dakotas, a newspaper reporter interviewed them to find out what they were doing and why. He wrote, "They desire to have the best time of their lives."[9] And so they did.

A Need to Get the Story Out

When one considers the provenance of William Clark's story and its permutations—at least those we know about—during 1905, 1912, 1915, and 1922—it is clear that he had a strong need to have his experiences as a teamster in the Utah War known to the public, or at least that part of it in Ames, Iowa. Perhaps he was motivated by awareness that at about the same time William I. Ginn, a former drover with the Utah Expedition's Tenth U.S. Infantry, had published a serialized newspaper account of his very similar experiences in an El Paso newspaper and was also attempting to publish them in book form. Perhaps he wanted to trade the West of the Imagination for the monotony of selling crockery and potatoes to Ames housewives or wrangling his stock of horses into box cars at the Ames depot for rail shipment to Minneapolis. Whatever Clark's motivation was, it was a strong one. Posterity is the better for his persistence and perspective.

The Power of Serendipity and Linkages

Among the lessons learned in our pursuit of Clark's story was a renewed appreciation of serendipity as a research process and the productive linkages that often flow from it. It is a phenomenon crucial to our discoveries, yet for some reason it is rarely discussed in university history departments.

By serendipity we mean an active process linking a prepared, receptive mind to a sense of curiosity energized to spot promising leads and fruitful connections in the spirit of the hunt. In his final novel (2010),

Robert B. Parker had his detective-hero, Spenser, describe the process of investigative discovery in similar but more prosaic terms: "It's like what I do. I look into something and I get a name and I look into the name and it leads to another name, and I keep finding out whatever I can about whatever comes my way, and sometimes you find something that helps."[10] With an active, receptive mind properly tuned, connections click, things happen—documents surface and insights emerge from the obscurity of the past in a way that would not happen otherwise. These are the springs from which "Eureka!" moments bubble up.

Serendipity is a simple but powerful force for discovery even for sophisticated historians. We ought to recognize it as such and develop a knack for building the friendships and sensitivities that make serendipitous discoveries possible. It is a process far different from its passive, distant cousin with which it is often confused—dumb luck. Such behavior is not just a matter of hanging around in hopes of something interesting turning up. Rather it is a matter of making one's own discoveries happen through preparedness and, above all else, receptivity.

Typically, the author Jack London put it more energetically in advising aspiring writers: "Don't loaf and invite inspiration: light out after it with a club; and if you don't get it you will nonetheless get something that looks remarkably like it."[11] Baseball executive Branch Rickey covered the same bases in more philosophical fashion than did Jack London: "Things worthwhile generally just don't happen. Luck is a fact but shouldn't be a factor. Good luck is what is left over after intelligence and effort have combined at their best. . . . Luck is the residue of design."[12]

In the case of William Clark's original manuscript and his gold mining equipment, we came to know of their existence, provenance, and current location through a serendipitous chain of events that led from California to the pages of a 1920 Iowa newspaper which, in turn, took us to the 104-year-old meeting minutes of a local Daughters of the American Revolution chapter (now stored in the back closet of an Ames club woman's home), and eventually to the collections of the State Historical Society split between buildings in Iowa City and Des Moines. With this information in hand, we then picked up the scent of a variant holograph copy of Clark's reminiscences lodged in a manuscript library at Texas A&M University in College Station, Texas—a find as fortuitous, unexpected, and convoluted as all the others. A similar chain of events brought us to an awareness of assistant wagon master Frank McCarthy's trial for homicide during the fall of 1857 near Fort Bridger. It was a heretofore unknown event bearing directly on William Clark's credibility in independently describing McCarthy as a tough, overbearing boss during the early months of their trek west. In much the same, fortuitous way our chance interaction with Ames, Iowa's current mayor, Hon. John A. Haila, led us (and him) to the realization that the town's city hall is located on a street named for William Clark, his predecessor during the mayoral terms of 1875–1877.

The wonderful connectedness of these research discoveries evokes Ezekiel's biblical visit to the Valley of the Dry Bones (Ezek 37:1–14), or at least the old Black spiritual's description of the prophet's encounter with anatomical linkages and "dem bones, dem bones, dem dry bones."

Keep Digging: New Discoveries Ahead

In 2022 Richard E. Turley Jr., today's leading authority on the Utah War's worst atrocity, commented, "There comes a time in the professional life of most historians when, after years of research and hunting, they begin to feel that the primary sources of their areas of focus have largely been discovered, with little new remaining to find. . . . Yet each time I reach the brink of that seductive conclusion, something new and surprising [about Mountain Meadows] surfaces, usually serendipitously."[13]

We believe the same phenomenon applies to study of the war taken broadly. For that reason, in 2008 one of us predicted that over the next half-century there would be "the discovery of new primary source materials, the stuff from which new knowledge and interpretations will come . . . with new openness and sustained creativity producing astonishing discoveries."[14] Surely, based on the fifteen years that have followed, this is precisely what is happening with the study of the American West, the history of the Latter-day Saints, and their long, turbulent relationship with the federal government during the nineteenth century.

Yet there is more to come in this still-evolving story, as our odyssey with William Clark's reminiscences has taught us. Where are the let-

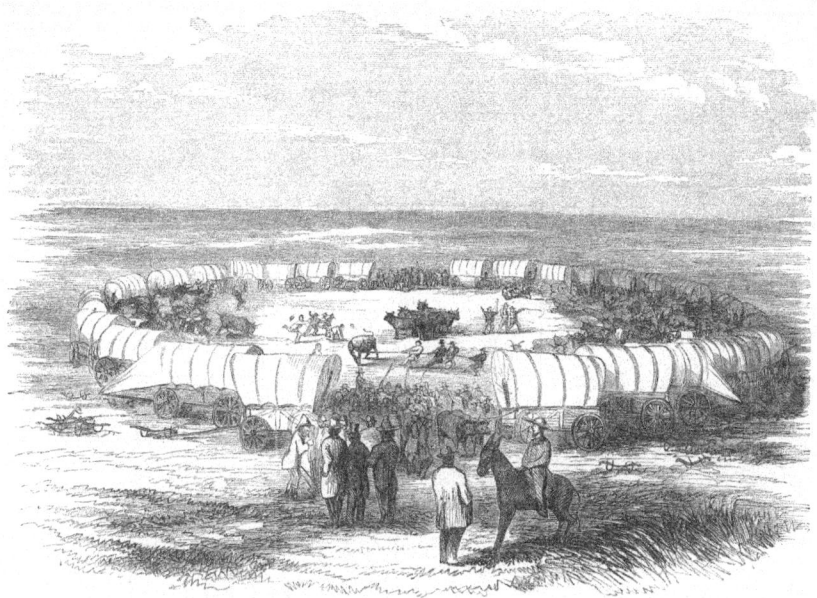

FIG. 27. Yoking oxen corralled by Utah Expedition supply wagons on the Great Plains, 1858. Based on a sketch by a newspaper reporter accompanying the Utah Expedition. *Frank Leslie's Illustrated Newspaper*, January 8, 1859.

ters exchanged by Cora and William Clark from which we might learn more about their remarkable courtship, the Utah War, and his ten years of roaming the region? How did Cora spend her time in Paoli while waiting for Bill's return after an absence of more than a decade? Who has the elusive photographs of this couple with their power to provide a glimpse of what are still-muted personalities?

As Arthur Conan Doyle's Sherlock Holmes put it in 1887 while pursuing his first case—several murders that spilled from Utah Territory into the fog of Victorian London—"quick Watson, the game is afoot!" And so it is.

Notes

Acknowledgments

1. As yet there is no full-length biography of Howard R. Lamar (1923–2023), although autobiographical comments appear in his "Introduction" written for William P. MacKinnon, *A Sixty-Year Hitch with the Utah War: Writing "At Sword's Point"* (South Jordan UT: Bear Hollow Books, 2018), vii–x. There are several short sketches of his life and work, the most recent of which was undertaken in anticipation of his one hundredth birthday: Andrea Thompson Peed, "A Man of Uncommon Qualities," *Yale Today Newsletter*, December 20, 2022, https://news.yale.edu/2022/12/20/man-uncommon-qualities. Soon after Professor Lamar's death at age ninety-nine, several prominent historians of the American West who had been his graduate students published a brief reprise in Mark Alden Branch, "The Westerner," *Yale Alumni Magazine* 86, no. 5 (May/June 2023): 36–41. See also George Miles, William Cronon, and Jay Gitlin, eds., *Under an Open Sky: Rethinking America's Western Past* (New York: W. W. Norton, 1992); and Lewis L. Gould, "Howard Roberts Lamar," in *Clio's Favorites: Leading Historians of the United States, 1945–2000*, ed. Robert Allen Rutland (Columbia: University of Missouri Press, 2000), 84–97. Other assessments of Lamar's work by his peers took the form of multi-paper panels devoted to this subject at the 2003 and 2005 annual conferences of the Western History Association (which he cofounded) and Organization of American Historians, respectively. Howard Lamar's most recent book was *Charlie Siringo's West: An Interpretative Biography* (Albuquerque: University of New Mexico Press, 2005). Siringo was a long-term interest, about which he had created a film for PBS in the mid-1970s as described in Les Brown, "Professor at Yale Will Make Westerns for Television," *New York Times*, April 6, 1976.

Editors' Introduction

1. Among the best narratives written by soldiers and camp followers who trekked west from Fort Leavenworth to Utah in 1857–1858 are: Percival G. Lowe, *Five Years a Dragoon ('49 to '54) and Other Adventures of the Great Plains* (Kansas City: Franklin Hudson, 1906); Charles R. Morehead, "Morehead's Narrative" (appendix C), in William E. Connelley, *War with Mexico, 1846–1847: Doniphan's Expedition and the Conquest of New Mexico and California* (Topeka KS: Crane, 1907); Richard Thomas Ackley, "Across the Plains in 1858," *Utah Historical*

Quarterly 9 (October 1941): 190–228; Henry S. Hamilton, *Reminiscences of a Veteran* (Concord NH: Republican Press Assoc., 1897); William P. MacKinnon, *"My Life in the Army": Campaigning in the West with the Utah Expedition's Private Theodore Boos, 1857–1862* (South Jordan UT: Bear Hollow Books, 2017); Thaddeus S. Kenderdine, *A California Tramp and Later Footprints* (Newton PA: Globe Press, 1888); Robert Morris Peck, "Rough Riding on the Plains 50 Years Ago," *Washington* [DC] *National Tribune*, April 25, 1901; and Henry Smith Adams, unpublished diary, Ulysses S. Grant Presidential Library, Mississippi State University Libraries, Starkville. Of these troops and teamsters, only Kenderdine went beyond Utah to California as William Clark did in 1858.

2. The value of William Clark's reminiscences is apparent in comparing them to the journal kept by William Gregg McPherson, an Illinois lad who with four friends, a covered wagon, and a team of oxen set out on the Oregon Trail in the spring of 1859 to pan for gold at first Pike's Peak and then in California. Notwithstanding superficial parallels with Clark's story, neither McPherson nor his editors in 1935 and 2010 provided readers with even basic information about this party, its fellow-travelers, and the societal events unfolding around them. Even the McPherson group's decision not to travel on Sundays, a major issue for Clark and his train, passes without comment. See Will Bagley, ed., "In the Midst of a Wild and Picturesque Scenery: William Gregg McPherson's Journal of the Pacific Wagon Road, 1859, Part 1 and 2," *Overland Journal* 28, no. 1 (Spring 2010): 24–33 and 28, no. 3 (Fall 2010): 117–28.

Editorial Decisions

1. An amusing description of the hierarchy for the "Lords of the Lash" appears in Henry Pickering Walker, *The Wagonmasters: High Plains Freighting from the Earliest Days of the Santa Fe Trail to 1880* (Norman: University of Oklahoma Press, 1966), 86–87. For a similar description in verse form, see appendix D.

Background and Context

1. Some material in this book has previously appeared in other publications by the editors. For the most recent scholarship on the war, from which this summary is derived, see William P. MacKinnon, *At Sword's Point, Part 1 and Part 2* (Norman OK: Arthur H. Clark, 2008 and 2016); David L. Bigler and Will Bagley, *The Mormon Rebellion: America's First Civil War, 1857–1858* (Norman: University of Oklahoma Press, 2011); Ronald W. Walker, Richard E. Turley Jr., and Glen M. Leonard, *Massacre at Mountain Meadows* (New York: Oxford University Press, 2008); Norman F. Furniss, *The Mormon Conflict, 1850–1859* (New Haven: Yale University Press, 1960); and William P. MacKinnon and Kenneth L. Alford,

eds., *Fact, Fiction, and Polygamy—A Tale of Utah War Intrigue, 1857–1858: A. G. Browne's "The Ward of the Three Guardians"* (Salt Lake City: Tanner Trust Fund and J. Willard Marriott Library, 2022), 41–44. Other important background and analysis appears in Murray L. Carroll, "The Wyoming Sojourn of the Utah Expedition, 1857–1858," *Annals of Wyoming* 72, no. 1 (Winter 2000): 6–24; and Brent M. Rogers, *Unpopular Sovereignty: Mormons and the Federal Management of Early Utah Territory* (Lincoln: University of Nebraska Press, 2017).

Section 1. "We Had an Eye on California"

1. "William Clark Obituary," *Daily Tribune and Evening Times* [Ames IA], March 1, 1920; U.S. Federal Census, 1850.
2. "Marriage Leaps thru Many Years," *Ames Weekly Tribune*, October 4, 1917.
3. One verse was:

> Say, what was your name in the States?
> Was it Thompson or Johnson or Bates?
> Did you murder your wife and fly for your life?
> Say, what was your name in the States?

Louis A. Garavaglia and Charles G. Worman, *Firearms of the American West, 1802–1865* (Albuquerque: University of New Mexico Press, 1984), 221. So prevalent was the escapism implicit in changing one's name, when Theodore Roosevelt arrived in the tiny frontier town of Medora, North Dakota, to take up cattle ranching during the 1880s, he found three men known as "Bill Jones." David McCullough, *Brave Companions: Portraits in History* (New York: Simon & Schuster, 1992), 61.

4. For other teamsters' accounts of shared experiences and sectional animosities see the narratives listed in note 1 under "Background and Context."
5. William Clark, "A Trip Across the Plains in 1857," *Iowa Journal of History and Politics* 20, no. 2 (April 1922): 163–223.
6. As noted in the "Editorial Decisions" section, we have removed several of the editor's notes that were published in 1922 in the *Iowa Journal of History and Politics* article. Remaining notes are prefaced with "ORIGINAL 1922 NOTE." Notes added by MacKinnon and Alford are not italicized. For additional information about the manuscript's provenance, see the epilogue.
7. Five months later, Utah's chief justice demonized such lads, describing them to a U.S. senator as "w[h]arf rats from St. Lewis [sic] and gamblers. Too many young men were corrupted on the way [to Fort Bridger] I fear. The idea was general among them, that because of the Mormon rebellion there was no law, and larceny, forgery & their kindred vices became frequent." Delana R. Eckels

to Jesse D. Bright, December 13, 1857, U.S. State Department Territorial Papers, Utah Series, 1851–71, Microfilm Publication M12, reel 1 (1853–59), NARA.

8. Leach had just turned eighteen on June 24, 1857. For the hometowns of those three, see page 18.

9. ORIGINAL 1922 NOTE: *The name of this firm is usually written Russell, Majors and Waddell. Alexander Majors began freighting across the plains in 1818. It is said that he never drank nor swore and that he made his employees sign a contract not to drink, gamble, or swear. In 1855 he combined with another freighting firm under the name Majors and Russell, but in 1858 the firm name became Russell, Majors and Waddell. This was the largest of the freighting companies, using in the year 1858 some 3500 wagons, 40,000 oxen, and 1000 mules. Over 4000 men were employed. The business was extended to include passenger and express service and in 1860 at the suggestion of William H. Russell, one of the partners, the Pony Express was established.—Hartman's The California and Oregon Trail, a thesis in the possession of the library of the State University of Iowa; Visscher's The Pony Express, pp. 18, 20, 22; Coman's Economic Beginnings of the Far West, Vol. II, p. 355; Rhodes's History of the United States, 1850–1877, Vol. III, p. 237.*

EDITORS' NOTE: For more complete information on the firm, see Alexander Majors and Prentiss Ingraham, eds., *Seventy Years on the Frontier: Alexander Majors' Memoirs of a Lifetime on the Border* (Columbus OH: Long's College Book, 1950); Raymond W. and Mary Lund Settle, *Empire on Wheels* (Stanford CA: Stanford University Press, 1949).

10. The U.S. Army and War Department knew so little about Utah that when the expedition left Fort Leavenworth it was only clear that one of the posts was to be near Salt Lake City; siting of the others was to be left to the commander's judgment on the ground.

11. ORIGINAL 1922 NOTE: *This was Captain Stewart Van Vliet.—House Executive Documents, 35th Congress, 1st Session, Vol. X, Doc. No. 71, p. 26.*

EDITORS' NOTE: During the Utah War, Van Vliet was a captain and assistant quartermaster based at Fort Leavenworth. For his duties during that conflict and interactions with both Brigham Young and the Buchanan administration, see MacKinnon, *At Sword's Point, Part 1 and Part 2*. During the Civil War, Van Vliet, a close friend of William Tecumseh Sherman, rose to colonel and deputy quartermaster general as well as major general by brevet.

12. ORIGINAL 1922 NOTE: *James Henry Lane was president of the Topeka constitutional convention in 1855, was second in command of the free state forces in the so-called Wakarusa War, and was chosen United States Senator from Kansas in 1856 under the Topeka constitution, but his election was not recognized by the Senate.—Spring's Kansas, pp. 70, 92, 272.*

EDITORS' NOTE: During the Civil War Lane served simultaneously as a U.S. senator from the new state of Kansas as well as a brigadier general of volunteers in the Union Army. Increasingly violent and erratic, he committed suicide in 1866.

13. Most likely a misspelling of "buckaroo"—a cowboy; someone who worked with cattle.
14. Saleratus is a precursor to baking soda, "much used in making bread, to . . . render the bread light." S.v. "saleratus," in Joseph E. Worcester, *Dictionary of the English Language* (Boston: Hickling, Swan, and Brewee, 1860) (Hereafter, *1860 Dictionary*.)
15. Many of the Utah Expedition's civilian teamsters saw their employment as a way of working their way to California's gold fields. That Clark intended to do so is reflected in the fact that his personal gear included a small set of scales and a leather poke for weighing and carrying gold dust.
16. Clark probably swung by his uncle's home in 1868 en route to Wisconsin to marry Cora Clark.
17. The rifles were single shot, .58 caliber percussion muzzle-loaders.
18. For modern readers, Clark is not clear about the all-important animals providing motive power for many of Russell, Majors and Waddell's trains, including his own. What Clark was driving ("whacking") were yokes of oxen. An ox could be any breed or gender of bovines, but most frequently was an English Red Durham or Texas longhorn steer. For such cattle to be considered a true ox, they had to be at least four years old, horned, and "handy," i.e., trained to work under a wooden yoke (frequently made of red elm) in response to commands from the drover that were transmitted by voice, body signals, or use of a whip. The drover walked to the left of the teams as their leader, signaling how he wanted them to pull rather than following the teams, with the animals in charge. The designation "ox," then, was a matter of the animal's horns and training rather than gender or breed. Because of the design of their yokes, all of the work cattle used by Russell, Majors and Waddell were horned, but, as William Clark discovered, the extent of their training may have fallen short of what an experienced drover would consider an ox.

For a concise recent explanation of the origins, training, and use of oxen, see Dixon Ford and Lee Krautzer, "Oxen: Engines of the Overland Emigration," *Overland Journal: Quarterly of the Oregon-California Trails Association* 33, no. 1 (Spring 2015): 5–29. Another useful primer on this subject, including the effective behavior and language of teamsters, was written five years after Clark set out for Utah and is found in Asa G. Sheldon, *Life of Asa G. Sheldon: Wilmington Farmer* (Woburn MA: E. T. Moody, printer, 1862). Sheldon was a

19. Notwithstanding this time-consuming chaos at the beginning of the trip, Alexander Majors claimed that by the time they became seasoned bull whackers, William Clark and each of the other drovers in his train could catch, yoke, and hitch twelve oxen to their wagon in sixteen minutes. Majors, *Seventy Years on the Frontier: Alexander Majors' Memoirs of a Lifetime on the Border*, ed. Col. Prentiss Ingraham (Denver: Western Miner and Financiers, 1893), 104.

lifelong user of oxen for heavy construction and farm work. See Ardis E. Parshall, "How to Handle Your Oxen When You Cross the Plains," *keepapitchinin* (blog), July 22, 2008, https://keepapitchinin.org/2008/07/22/how-to-handle-your-oxen-when-you-cross-the-plains/.

20. Clark's frequent use of the slang phrase "on the jump" appears to indicate that he wrote his reminiscences around the turn of the twentieth century rather than earlier in the 1800s. From this phrase came the title of a popular silent film that debuted in 1918.
21. The girth is the band or strap that passes under the animal's belly to hold the saddle in place.
22. ORIGINAL 1922 NOTE: *The Grasshopper River flows into the Kansas River from the north.*

    EDITORS' NOTE: Since renamed the Delaware River, this stream flows for ninety-four miles in northeastern Kansas before emptying into the Kansas or Kaw River.
23. That Sunday would have been July 5, 1857.
24. To "snake a short drive" means "to wind about." S.v. "snake," *1860 Dictionary*.
25. ORIGINAL 1922 NOTE: *Possibly this is Cape Girardeau, Missouri.*
26. For the troops at Fort Riley, Kansas, frog legs were a welcome addition to an otherwise monotonous diet. The garrison's purveyor of this delicacy in the late 1850s was Lorenzo Wesson, a colorful, eccentric Yale alumnus from Ohio.
27. Not established until 1871, Crete is in Saline County in southeastern Nebraska, near the Kansas state line.
28. A claim shanty is "a cabin built hastily on a land claim to legalize possession of the land." S.v. "claim shanty," *Merriam-Webster Dictionary*, online edition, accessed July 31, 2024.

Section 2. "I Was Starving"

1. The heavy covered freight wagons used by Russell, Majors and Waddell had no front bench or seat for their teamsters. Instead, the bull whackers like Clark walked alongside their oxen, controlling them with a long rawhide whip and a few voice commands, often profane notwithstanding their earlier commitment about bad language to Alexander Majors. For this reason, when unable

to walk, Clark rode on his wagon's wooden tongue, to which the twelve oxen were hitched in six yokes of two.
2. Jangle means "to quarrel; to wrangle; to altercate; to bicker in words." S.v. "jangle," *1860 Dictionary*.
3. Notwithstanding Eads's kindness on the plains to Bill Clark, the war correspondent for the *New-York Daily Tribune* described his conduct during the fall of 1857 as nefarious, noting that Eads chose to forfeit a large bond of $500 rather than appear before a federal grand jury seeking his testimony about what he saw when Legion raiders ran off an army herd of eight hundred beef cattle in Utah's Green River district. [Browne], dispatch, "The Utah Expedition," *New-York Daily Tribune*, May 30, 1858. Later, store clerk Richard Ackley observed Eads in action in Salt Lake City during 1858 as "a noted character in his way in this country, principally for blowing [bragging]." Ackley, *Across the Plains in 1858*, 220.
4. Rock Creek in southeast Nebraska was a popular emigrant camp site, about three miles from the present town of Endicott, Jefferson County. During the year of Clark's brief sojourn there, the place was developed as a way station for stages and later the Pony Express. In 1861 a young James Butler ("Wild Bill") Hickok killed David McCanles there. S.v. "Wild Bill Hickock," *Wikipedia*, accessed August 28, 2022.
5. Albert Preston Frank, Clark's benefactor, would later throw in with this foursome to become their "chum" and messmate. Frank was aged twenty-two, a native of Gowanda, Erie County, New York, and a resident of Omro, Winnebago County, Wisconsin, on the Fox River about ten miles west of Oshkosh and near the enormous pinery along the Wolf River, a tributary of the Fox. All these background factors would have resonated with Clark, Sherwood, Leach, and Tuttle. He is not to be confused with John Frank, a teamster captured by the Nauvoo Legion near Fort Bridger in late November 1857.

Section 3. "They Make the Earth Tremble"

1. Seven years after the first publication of Clark's reminiscences, the classic study of this subject appeared as E. Douglas Branch, *The Hunting of the Buffalo* (New York: D. Appleton, 1929).
2. First Lt. E. G. Marshall to Col. Samuel Cooper, August 2, 1857, House Exec. Doc. 71, Serial 956, 17–18. Clark briefly described the Ash Hollow attack in section 5, but attributed it to unspecified "Indians" rather than Cheyennes.
3. Here Clark spells the name of this Nebraska post correctly, unlike many mid-nineteenth-century travelers and soldiers, as well as later historians and cartographers. It was named after Maj. Gen. Stephen Watts Kearny (not "Kearney") of Mexican-American War fame. Not to be confused with a newer fort in

Wyoming Territory named after a different officer of similar name and same rank, Maj. Gen. Philip Kearny, who died in the Civil War.

4. The four mounted men were the wagon master (Rennick), his assistant (McCarthy), and the two extra teamsters, who, unlike the other twenty-six in the train, had not been assigned to a wagon. All others walked.

5. If Clark expected this largesse in sharing buffalo meat to improve relations with its Southern recipients, they would soon disappoint him.

6. This use of salt as a preservative unwittingly did much to deplete the Utah Expedition's supply of this condiment. Assuming that the expedition would reach Salt Lake City by the fall of 1857, commissary officers at Fort Leavenworth packed only a small amount of salt, while quartermasters provided evaporative pans for the wagons to carry with the expectation that plenty of salt could be obtained from the brine of the Great Salt Lake. The impact of this misplaced optimism became apparent when severe weather forced the expedition into winter quarters in late November near Fort Bridger, Utah, more than one hundred miles short of the lake. The ironic spectacle of the army salt-deprived under these circumstances filled the letters of soldiers, teamsters, and the newspaper reporters accompanying them. It was a flow of complaints that mushroomed into press criticism on a national scale while fueling speeches in Congress about the Buchanan administration's planning ineptness. After curtly declining Brigham Young's embarrassing offer to provide the troops with eight hundred pounds of "Mormon" salt, General Johnston obtained emergency supplies through herculean winter pack trips dispatched east to Fort Laramie and south to New Mexico Territory. Brigham Young and Gen. Daniel H. Wells to Johnston, November 28 and 30, 1857, "Utah Expedition," House Exec. Doc. 71, 110–11; MacKinnon, *At Sword's Point, Part 2*, 234–36.

7. Plum Creek, on the south side of the South Platte, was ninety miles east of Nebraska's Little Blue River. It was a favorite camping spot on the Oregon Trail, and in the early 1860s was important to the Pony Express and transcontinental telegraph line. On August 8, 1864, it was the site of a major raid by Cheyennes on overlanders, with thirteen emigrants killed in a tribal descent on a twelve-wagon train bound for Denver.

Section 4. "Consider Yourselves Discharged"

1. [David A. Burr], "The Utah Army in Winter Quarters," dispatch, December 1, 1857, *New York Times* (reprinted Boston *Semi-Weekly Advertiser*, January 23, 1858).

2. [Lemuel Fillmore], dispatch, June 14, 1858, *Herald* [NY], June 30, 1858. Fillmore himself died a violent death five years later when a former Utah Expedition teamster and card sharp, William C. Quantrill, shot him down in Lawrence, Kansas, during a Confederate raid on the town.
3. Julie Beehrer Colyer, ed., "Freighting Across the Plains: True 1858 Experiences of George W. Beehrer from His Diary and Related to a Friend," *Montana: The Magazine of Western History* 12 (Autumn 1962): 2–17.
4. Julius S. Morton, ed., *Illustrated History of Nebraska: A History of Nebraska from the Earliest Explorations of the Trans-Mississippi Region*, 3 vols. (Lincoln NE: Jacob North, 1907), 1:541–42n1.
5. Russell, Majors and Waddell, *Rules and Regulations for the Government of Outfits*, quoted in Settle and Settle, *Empire on Wheels*, 29–30. Not only was profanity endemic among non-Mormon bull whackers, apparently even Latter-day Saint teamsters on the Overland Trail gave in to such behavior. Moving west toward Oregon with his family in 1862, Randall Hewitt's emigrant train encountered a bull train of freighters bound for Salt Lake City whom he assumed to be Latter-day Saints. Hewitt's description of their profanity and abuse of their oxen was so extreme it strains the credibility of his otherwise valuable book: "A more sinister, brawling, profane gang, who would cut a throat or scuttle a ship, it would be difficult to collect together from the slums and cesspools of the universe. . . . Fouler, viler and more blasphemous talk never in more continuous volume flowed from the[ir] lips . . . The very air seemed polluted and redolent with a nastiness . . . while this foul-mouthed crew of Salt Lake Saints were passing." Randall H. Hewitt, *Across the Plains and Over the Divide: A Mule Train Journey from East to West in 1862, and Incidents Connected Therewith* (New York: Broadway Publishing, 1906), 89–91.
6. For the Sabbath issue, see Winton U. Solberg, "The Sabbath on the Overland Trail to California," *Church History* 59, no. 3 (September 1990): 340–55. The travel dilemma William Clark's party confronted is discussed by name in "No Rest for the Weary," *Christian History* 66 (2000), https://christianhistoryinstitute.org.
7. [Lemuel Fillmore], dispatch, May 23, 1858, *Herald* [NY], June 21, 1858.
8. James H. Mills, diary entries, June 24 and July 8, 1866, quoted in Charles E. Rankin, "Overland with James H. Mills: A Newly Discovered Bozeman Trail Diary," *Overland Journal, Quarterly of the Oregon-California Trails Association* 41, no. 3 (Fall 2023): 98.
9. To "run" bullets was to shape lead bars into ammunition using a mold or small press. S.v. "run," *1860 Dictionary*.

10. This confrontation took place along Plumb Creek, Nebraska Territory, in what became Phelps County.
11. As a measure of length or distance, one rod is equal to 16.5 feet or 5.0292 meters. Clark's repeated use of this term may indicate that he had experience working with surveyors.
12. Quinine was "an alkaline substance of a bitter taste, obtained from different species of Cinchona [a variety of trees native to Peru] . . . forming the base of certain salts used in medicine." S.v. "chichona," "quinine," *1860 Dictionary*.

Section 5. "Grand and Beautiful Scenery"

1. Doubling up meant that the length of train was cut in half by changing formation from twenty-six wagons moving in a single file to thirteen pairs of wagons arranged side-by-side.
2. Clark describes here the most extensive Indian attack on a RM&W train of the whole campaign, a raid by fifteen Cheyenne led by Chief White Crow in August 1857. His secondhand account of the incident (via the buffalo hunters) is accurate, although he misrepresents the role of the train's wagon master, Oliver Perry Goodwin, who in fact saved the day by arming and rallying his teamsters and wounding White Crow. Goodwin was age twenty-seven and had extensive military experience in the Mexican War, the Indian campaigns in Oregon Territory, and as part of William Walker's filibustering expedition to Nicaragua. *Enterprise* [Kansas City MO], August 22, 1857; Walker, *Wagonmasters*, 264.
3. For those who made the descent into Ash Hollow, it was an unforgettable experience filled with the perils of broken wheels, smashed wagons, terrified animals, and an occasional crushed teamster. The hollow was a ravine of daunting steepness encountered by those heading for the North Platte River after leaving the South Platte—one of the major landmark-obstacles on the Oregon Trail in Nebraska. In autumn 1857 dispatches to the *Saint Louis Leader*, William Porter Finlay, the oldest son of a prominent Belfast newspaper publisher, explained that at Ash Hollow the "appearance of the country changes in a remarkable manner . . . and below us all is different. A succession of the boldest bluffs intersected by deep ravines running in every possible direction, with some scattered cedar bushes and rocks, present a really pretty and striking scene. One of its greatest charms is the suddenness with which it opens on you, almost like a scene shifting in a theater." There, along nearby Blue Water Creek, Brevet Brig. Gen. William S. Harney, had led a punitive expedition against a Brule Lakota camp on September 2–3, 1855, in retaliation for the 1854 massacre of an army detachment led by Brevet Second Lt. Joseph L. Grattan.

Army casualties were light, but those of the Sioux, including women and children, were devastating, prompting Harney's enduring nickname "Squaw Killer." It was a label later adopted by the Latter-day Saints while Harney briefly preceded Albert Sidney Johnston as the initial commander of the Utah Expedition during the summer of 1857. R. Eli Paul, *Blue Water Creek and the First Sioux War, 1854–1856* (Norman: University of Oklahoma Press, 2004); Finlay, "Dispatches of 17 July–2 September 1857" in MacKinnon, *At Sword's Point, Part 1*, 203.

4. "Originally called Fort William, Fort Laramie was built in 1834 by fur traders William Sublette and Robert Campbell at the junction of the Laramie and North Platte rivers. . . . In 1849 Fort Laramie was sold to the U.S. government as a military post." Howard R. Lamar, ed., *The New Encyclopedia of the American West* (New Haven, Conn: Yale University Press, 1998), 385. "For westbound travelers, this post was the last significant settlement and military establishment until the civilian trading post of Fort Bridger. Because of the Buchanan administration's late decision-making and the availability of wood, water, and forage at Laramie, Generals Scott and Harney argued unsuccessfully that the Utah Expedition should winter-over there and push on to the Salt Lake Valley in the spring of 1858. Saved from planned deactivation and abandonment by the substantial requirements of the Utah War, Fort Laramie took on new life as a forward support post and played a key role in the great conflicts with the Plains tribes that followed." MacKinnon, *At Sword's Point, Part 1*, 219. See also, Douglas C. McChristian, *Fort Laramie: Military Bastion of the High Plains* (Norman OK: Arthur H. Clark, 2008).

5. Chimney Rock, now a National Historic Site, is four miles south of present-day Bayard, Millard County, Nebraska, towering over the North Platte River Valley close to the Oregon Trail. With a stand-alone stone spire standing 325 feet above its conical base, this rock formation was the most noteworthy sight along the trail. Virtually every emigrant and soldier who described it, shared William Clark's observation about its misleading distance from the trail. At almost the same time Clark camped near this formation, Capt. Jesse A. Gove of the Utah Expedition's Tenth U.S. Infantry wrote his wife to describe Chimney Rock as "a curious freak of nature . . . a spire of rock running up precisely like a chimney, and I cannot give you a better idea of it than to say that it has the appearance of a chimney standing after the house has burned down. In olden times the bases of chimneys were very large, occupying half of the house; this has a perfect appearance of such a standing chimney. I have often seen in the country an exact counterpart." Merrill J. Mattes, "Chimney Rock on the Oregon Trail," *Nebraska History* 36 (1955): 1–26; Gove to Mrs. Gove, August

27 and 28, 1857, *The Utah Expedition, 1857–1858: Letters of Capt. Jesse A. Gove, 10th Inf., U.S.A., of Concord, N.H., to Mrs. Gove, and Special Correspondence of the New York Herald*, ed. Otis G. Hammond (Concord: New Hampshire Historical Society, 1928), 47–48.

6. Scrubby means shabby, stunted, or dense underwood. S.v. "scrub," "scrubby," *1860 Dictionary*.

7. Horse Shoe Creek was a station for Brigham Young's Y. X. Carrying Company. MacKinnon, *At Sword's Point, Part 1*, 224.

8. At this point in the manuscript, Clark begins to call George Tuttle "George Washington." Contemporary court records and newspaper accounts list his middle initial as "B." The editors believe that Clark misremembered the name, probably because so many Americans of the period were named after the country's first president, as in the case of several of the Utah Expedition's soldiers.

9. Encounters with wolf packs, like buffalo herds and mosquitoes, were an experience on which virtually all overlanders commented. For a harrowing account of his pursuit by wolves across the plains during December 1857, only a few months after Clark's encounter, see the reminiscences of Charlie Morehead, William H. Russell's nephew and an agent of Russell, Majors and Waddell. Charles R. Morehead, "Morehead's Narrative" (appendix C) in William E. Connelley, *War with Mexico, 1846–1847: Doniphan's Expedition and the Conquest of New Mexico and California* (Topeka KS: Crane, 1907), 600–22.

10. The army built Fort Fetterman in 1867 on the south bank of the North Platte River to guard the nearby Bozeman Trail to Montana Territory's goldfields. The site is about eleven miles northwest of Douglas, Wyoming, although when constructed it was in what had earlier been organized as Dakota Territory. The fort was named after Captain William J. Fetterman, who together with his eighty-man detachment, was killed the previous year by Lakota (Sioux), Arapaho, and Cheyenne warriors during Red Cloud's War. During the Great Sioux War of the 1870s, a number of army campaigns were staged from Fort Fetterman. The army abandoned (but did not demolish) the post in 1882, which may or may not give a clue as to when Clark wrote, depending upon the interpretation of his phrase "now stands."

Section 6. "A Sage Brush Country"

1. An understanding of the Mormon raid on the army's mule herd at Pacific Springs under Brigham Young's orders has been clouded by the Utah War's mythology. The most verifiable and consistent contemporary accounts of what took place are encompassed in the journal of one of the raiders, twenty-one-year-old Pvt. John Bagley, and the after-action report about the attack written to Young by

Bagley's embarrassed superiors, Cols. James W. Cummings and Robert Taylor Burton. For these documents, see MacKinnon, *At Sword's Point, Part 1*, 331–38.

2. A tributary of the Platte River, the Sweetwater River winds through over two hundred miles of present-day Wyoming. T.B.H. Stenhouse described it as "beautiful to the eye as it rolled over its rocky bed as clear as crystal." T.B.H. Stenhouse, *The Rocky Mountain Saints: A Full and Complete History of the Mormons* (New York: D. Appleton, 1873), 312. According to explorer and U.S. Army captain Howard Stansbury, "The river is about seventy feet wide, from six to eighteen inches in depth, with a uniform and tolerably rapid current." Howard Stansbury, *An Expedition to the Valley of the Great Salt Lake of Utah* (Philadelphia: Lippincott, Grambo, 1852), 64. Travelers on the Mormon Trail crossed the Sweetwater at least four times as they journeyed to Utah. Carol Cornwall Madsen, *Journey to Zion: Voices from the Mormon Trail* (Salt Lake City: Deseret Book, 1997), 589.

3. Independence Rock was one of the best-known landmarks on the emigrant trails so named because travelers sought to pass it prior to the Fourth of July in order to reach their destination before the first snowfall. "It was covered with names of the passing emigrants, some of whom seemed determined, judging from the size of their inscriptions, that they would go down to posterity in all their fair proportions." Stansbury, *Expedition to the Valley of the Great Salt Lake of Utah*, 5.

4. Also called Saleratus Lake. (For a definition of "saleratus," see note 14 under "Section 1: We Had an Eye on California.") Sarah DeArmon Pea Rich, a Latter-day Saint pioneer who crossed the plains in 1847, wrote that it "was a beautifull lake, as white as snow, and was pure saleratus, which we could cut out in large cakes. We gethererred sacks full and brought with us to the Valley, which lasted us a long time to make bread with." In Madsen, *Journey to Zion*, 382.

5. A seine is "a kind of large fishing-net." S.v. "seine," *1860 Dictionary*.

6. "Practically treeless, South Pass is the invisible divide between watercourses bound for the Pacific and the Atlantic or the Gulf of Mexico . . . [its] classically western appearance disappointed the expectations of at least a hundred thousand travelers. . . . South Pass is the only corridor that anything on wheels could use to cross the massive cordillera of the Rocky Mountains without great physical or engineering challenges. Without this natural road, wagons could not have left the Missouri River and reached the Pacific in a single season . . ." Will Bagley, *South Pass: Gateway to a Continent* (Norman: University of Oklahoma Press, 2014), 15.

7. Winding for over seven hundred miles, the Green River—called by the Crows Seedskeedee Agie (Prairie Hen River)—is the largest and longest of the twenty-

five significant tributaries that join the Colorado River. Albert Sidney Johnston briefly considered, then abandoned, plans in March 1858 "to engage Chief Washakie's Shoshones to operate and defend the Green River ferries—an arrangement never disclosed to army headquarters." Frederick Samuel Dellenbaugh, *The Romance of the Colorado River: The Story of Its Discovery in 1540* (New York: Knickerbocker Press, 1909), 67, 107; MacKinnon, *At Sword's Point, Part 2*, 316, 614. Granger, a stagecoach station, was located near the confluence of the Blacks Fork and the Hams Fork rivers. Always small, the town had a population of only 142 in 2020. Data USA, "Granger, WY," accessed July 31, 2024, https://datausa.io/profile/geo/granger-wy/.

Section 7. "The Boss Surrendered"

1. Because of a paucity of his personal papers, there are few biographies of Smith. The most recent is flawed in terms of scholarship and perspective: Carmen R. Smith and Talana S. Hooper, *Lot Smith: Mormon Pioneer and American Frontiersman* (Salt Lake City: Greg Kofford Books, 2018). More thorough but dated in terms of sources is Charles S. Peterson, "A Portrait of Lot Smith Frontiersman," *Western Historical Quarterly* 1 (October 1970): 393–414. For Lot Smith's own account of his operations against the Utah Expedition in the Green River district during the fall of 1857, see "Narrative of Lot Smith," in *Mormon Resistance: A Documentary Account of the Utah Expedition, 1857–1858*, ed. LeRoy R. Hafen and Ann W. Hafen (Lincoln: University of Nebraska Press, 1982), 220–46; "Vaux" [Junius F. Wells], "The Echo Canon War," *Contributor* 3 (1882): 271–74; 4 (1883): 27–29, 47–40, 167–69, and 224–26. A synthesis of sources about this campaign appears in MacKinnon, *At Sword's Point, Part 1*, 347–58.
2. This may be a nickname for an otherwise unidentified wagon master. No wagon boss by this name was among those giving affidavits to Judge Eckles after Lot Smith's raids.

Section 8. "Into Winter Quarters"

1. Capt. John W. Phelps, diary, typed transcription, Hamilton Gardner Papers, Mss B-113, Utah Historical Society, Salt Lake City, from New York Public Library Manuscripts Division; Private Scott, October 20, 1857, "Charles A. Scott's Diary of the Utah Expedition," ed. Robert E. Stowers and John M. Ellis, *Utah Historical Quarterly* 28 (April 1960): 166; Maj. Fitz John Porter to Lt. Col. Irvin McDowell, November 29, 1857, in "Interesting News from the Utah Expedition," *Washington Union*, January 24, 1858; Cooke to Porter, November 21, 1857, House Ex. Doc. no. 71, Serial 956, 99.
2. Although a West Point graduate and twice-breveted veteran of the Mexican

War, Col. Edmund Brooke Alexander (October 6, 1802–January 3, 1888), commander of the U.S. Tenth Infantry, was not viewed by his subordinates as a decisive or competent military officer. He led the Utah Expedition in the field on an acting basis until relieved by Albert Sidney Johnston. Alexander, who was "plagued with uncertainty about how best to move toward Salt Lake City," was described by Capt. Jesse A. Gove as "the most worthless old fogy in the world, frightened to death. He is in his dotage, and I really believe he is a little frightened." MacKinnon, *At Sword's Point, Part 1*, 209; Jesse A. Gove to Mrs. Gove, September 27, 1857, in Gove, *The Utah Expedition, 1857–1858: Letters of Capt. Jesse A. Gove, 10th Inf, U.S.A.*, ed. Otis G. Hammond (Concord: New Hampshire Historical Society, 1928), 66. One of the several embarrassments suffered by the Utah Expedition during its march west was Colonel Alexander's disclosure to his subordinates (and Brigham Young) that he did not know why he was in the field heading for Salt Lake City or to which senior officer he reported. When General Harney, the expedition's initial commander, was relieved by Albert Sidney Johnston at Fort Leavenworth in September 1857, he did not give Johnston a copy of the operational orders he had received in late June, although the two officers conferred at length verbally. Alexander's complaint about the absence of instructions for him, a form of organizational whining, enraged Johnston when he heard about it on the march; he felt that, as the senior officer present, Alexander should have automatically assumed command and pressed on to Salt Lake City until Johnston caught up with him, as happened at Hams Fork near the Green River in early November.

3. Echo Canyon, northeast of the Salt Lake Valley in present Summit County, Utah, was the most direct route to Salt Lake City. Nauvoo Legion militiamen fortified the canyon's natural defenses in advance of an anticipated march by the U.S. Army through the canyon. Latter-day Saint militia private George D. Watt wrote on October 14, 1857, "The defences in Echo Canyon cannot be described on paper, suffice it to say that all that can be done by nature, apparently has been done, and what seemed deficient has been, and is being added by the labor of our boys." Quoted in MacKinnon, *At Sword's Point, Part 1*, 362. Traveling through Soda Springs, in present-day southern Idaho, would have required a more northernly route to the Salt Lake.

4. For the capture, imprisonment, and eventual release of those three teamsters and a soldier, see MacKinnon, *At Sword's Point, Part 2*, 72–75.

5. Clark's accidental, self-inflicted gunshot wound was common among western travelers unused to handling and stowing rifles and shotguns properly. In 1859, when the army assigned Capt. Randolph B. Marcy to write what was, in effect, a manual for military and civilian travelers crossing the Great Plains,

he described in depth how and why such accidental discharges happened and how to prevent them. Marcy attributed most of the accidents to young, inexperienced males who carelessly stored a loaded weapon with the percussion cap still on the nipple. In other common cases, the shooter made the mistake of pointing the weapon in the wrong direction, often wounding himself in the process. Randolph B. Marcy, *The Prairie Traveler: A Hand-Book for Overland Expeditions* (New York: Harper & Brothers, 1859), 142–44.

6. Clark and his train never got as far north as Soda Springs in their cross-country march. They halted and reversed course on October 19, 1857, along Hams Fork, just south of Sublette's Cutoff on the Oregon Trail.

7. Established in 1843, Fort Bridger was a civilian trading post to service emigrant traffic. The area served as a crossroads for many routes, including the Mormon Trail. Fred R. Gowans and Eugene E. Campbell, *Fort Bridger: Island in the Wilderness* (Provo UT: Brigham Young University Press, 1975).

8. Welting is when the "edge of a garment, turned over on itself and sewed together to strengthen the border." S.v. "welt," *1860 Dictionary*.

9. U.S. Army dragoons were "cavalry trained and armed to act either on foot or on horseback, as emergencies may require." S.v. "dragoon," *1860 Dictionary*.

10. The sergeant major of the Utah Expedition's volunteer battalion reported to a newspaper the meat the troops were eating was "the worst possible kind of tough bull, consisting of those misguided oxen who crossed the plains with teams this Summer, worn to the bone almost, and who were foolish enough not to die before they got here." [William Porter Finlay], dispatch, December 21, 1857, undated issue of *Saint Louis Leader*, reprinted in *New York Times*, March 2, 1858, and *New York Herald*, March 7, 1858.

11. Charles R. Morehead was the young but capable nephew of one of the firm's partners, William H. Russell.

12. For the recruitment of four companies of volunteer infantrymen for nine-month service, see MacKinnon, *At Sword's Point, Part 1*, 459–66.

13. For insight into how unappealing the alternative of remaining at Camp Scott/Fort Bridger as unemployed vagabonds for the winter would have been to Clark and friends, see the subsequent complaints of eight discharged teamsters who did so. They aired tales of mistreatment in the Los Angeles *Vineyard* once they made their way to California in June 1858. "Statement of Eight Teamsters," reprinted in San Francisco *Daily Alta California*, June 14, 1858.

14. At this point, the fifth "chum" (Albert Frank) decided to return to the Kansas-Missouri frontier. Some of the structural factors prompting Frank to leave Utah at this point are discussed in this book's epilogue ("The Chums"), but there may have been other more personal reasons such as disgust with regimentation,

money in his pocket, and simple homesickness. Percival G. Lowe, an army wagon master, discovered this in trying unsuccessfully to recruit eastbound men like Albert Frank on the overland trail to return to Utah: "Met Russell, Majors & Waddell's train en route to Nebraska City with discharged men, but I could not hire one of them. With money enough to buy a suit of jeans, pair of boots with a half moon and some stars on the tops, a wool hat and a blanket for an overcoat, and some silver in their pockets, why should they turn their faces to the mountains [again], sure to encounter cold weather and the possibility of not coming back until next year? To him it matters not that he could clear money enough to buy a quarter section of fine Missouri land and capture the girl whose 'heel kep' 'er rockin,' whom he could see afar off in his mind's eye. There were no charms behind [in Utah] that be cared to return to, and he looked across the prairie to the 'cabin on the creek' away over in Missouri." Percival G. Lowe, entry for August 27, 1858, *Five Years a Dragoon*, 317.

15. As Utah governor, Brigham Young declared martial law throughout Utah Territory on September 15, 1857. The proclamation began by declaring "We are invaded by a hostile force who are evidently assailing us to accomplish our overthrow and destruction" and concluded that "martial law is hereby declared to exist in this Territory, from and after the publication, of this Proclamation; and no person shall be allowed to pass or repass into, or through, or from this Territory, without a permit from the proper officer." This proclamation was illegal and was a factor in Young's indictment for treason by a federal grand jury sitting near Fort Bridger in December 1857. MacKinnon, *At Sword's Point, Part 1*, 284.

16. Spanish Fork, about forty-five miles south of Salt Lake City, was the site of the farm established for Native Americans to learn and practice farming. Dr. Garland Hurt reported to Brigham Young as one of Utah's Indian agents starting in 1855. Hurt had little respect for Brigham Young and, in turn, was not respected by Latter-day Saints. In the fall of 1856, Hurt wrote to U.S. congressman John M. Elliott referencing the "autocratical de[s]potism of the man [Brigham Young] himself," derisively calling Young "His Excellency." In a January 1, 1857, letter to Utah's territorial delegate in Congress, John M. Bernhisel, Young called Hurt a dog and skunk. MacKinnon, *At Sword's Point, Part 1*, 59, 67.

17. Here Clark refers to (but almost overlooks) the most arduous winter march in American military history until the fighting withdrawal from North Korea's Chosin reservoir system in 1950–1951. This was the sixteen-hundred-mile trek of Capt. Randolph B. Marcy, Fifth U.S. Infantry, and a small detachment down the trackless spine of the Continental Divide from Fort Bridger to northern

New Mexico Territory and back. Albert Sidney Johnston tasked Marcy with buying thousands of mules, horses, and sheep as well as salt to power and feed the Utah Expedition for its anticipated push into the Salt Lake Valley during the spring of 1858. Upon his return to Fort Bridger in June and subsequently, Marcy wrote multiple descriptions of his experience of varying length and character depending upon his readership. One of the most interesting, but least known, was an article ("Ramblings in the West") Marcy wrote for *Harper's New Monthly Magazine* just before his death in 1887, excerpts from which may be found in MacKinnon, *At Sword's Point, Part 2*, 50–54. In referring to Marcy as "colonel," Clark may have signaled that he wrote before Marcy's permanent promotion to brigadier general in December 1878, but the editors believe it more likely that he lost track of Marcy's complicated promotion history when generating his manuscript closer to the turn of the century.

18. Hobbles were two loops of rope or rawhide connected by a short length of the same material. When the front legs of a horse or mule were placed in the loops, the animal could move but with restricted mobility that permitted it to graze but not wander any significant distance. The principle was like that of handcuffs for humans.

Section 9. "Saddle Up and Be Quick about It"

1. A graphic example of Hickman's work in such a role was his alleged murder of Jesse Thompson Hartley on May 3, 1854, in East Canyon en route from Salt Lake City to Fort Supply. The assassination, supposedly done on Brigham Young's orders transmitted to Hickman by apostle Orson Hyde, was because of Hartley's authorship of an intercepted letter written to then–secretary of war Jefferson Davis discussing Young's malfeasance as territorial governor and urging his replacement. No one was ever charged in Hartley's death. H. Michael Marquardt, *The Coming Storm: The Murder of Jesse Thompson Hartley* (Norman OK: Arthur H. Clark, 2011).

2. William A. Hickman with J. H. Beadle, *Brigham's Destroying Angel: Being the Life, Confession, and Startling Disclosures of the Notorious Bill Hickman, the Danite Chief of Utah* (New York: G. A Corfutt, 1872); Hope A. Hilton, *"Wild Bill" Hickman and the Mormon Frontier* (Salt Lake City: Signature Books, 1988); George A. Smith to John L. Smith, February 5, 1858, Historian's Office, Letterpress Books, CHL. Charlie Becker, a teamster captured and held separate from Clark in first an outlying farm and then an improvised prison cell in Salt Lake City, described a less friendly, stricter Hickman, who he claimed was the city's "Provost-Marshal." Charles W. Becker, "The History of the Expedition

against the Mormons in the Year of 1857," typescript narrative, CHL; excerpts in MacKinnon, *At Sword's Point, Part 1*, 474–77.
3. "The Bear River is the longest continuously flowing river in North America that does not reach the ocean. The Bear River's headwaters are in Utah's Uinta Mountains; the river then flows into Wyoming, back into Utah, back into Wyoming again, into Idaho, and then returns to Utah where it drains into Great Salt Lake. After traveling a several-hundred-mile horseshoe-shaped course, the river ends only about 90 miles from its source." Jim Davis, "Why Does a River Run through It," Utah Geological Survey, accessed July 31, 2024, https://geology.utah.gov/map-pub/survey-notes/glad-you-asked/why-does-a-river-run-through-it/.
4. Nineteenth-century Latter-day Saints sometimes referred to non–church members (even Jews) as "Gentiles."
5. Here Clark attempts to reconstruct one of the endless verses of "Doo-Dah," a song written during the summer of 1857 by Isaac B. Nash, a Nauvoo Legionnaire, as a morale-builder for the Latter-day Saints. For the song's music, Nash borrowed Stephen Foster's "Camptown Races," then a wildly popular song across the country. By the time the Utah Expedition reached Salt Lake City, "Doo-Dah" had become the equivalent of the American Revolution's "Yankee Doodle." Numerous other songs and poems commenting on the U.S. Army's march on Utah were written during the Utah War. See Kenneth L. Alford, "Latter-day Saint Poetry and Songs of the Utah War," *Mormon Historical Studies* 12, no. 1 (Spring 2011): 1–28.
6. Contemporary views on the effectiveness of Echo Canyon's fortifications were wide-ranging, depending upon the viewer's military background and religious affiliation. The Utah Expedition's officers who marched through the canyon in 1858 ridiculed them as easily dealt with, if not useless; their civilian camp followers, like Clark, were more impressed, and the eastern newspaper reporters filled their dispatches with descriptions and sketches of rock walls and dams. The Latter-day Saints were laudatory about their own military engineering work, and the surviving remnants of the canyon's fortifications are still a tourist attraction as well as the object of preservation work by Utah's Boy Scout troops. People who never saw Echo Canyon sometimes expressed concern about its defenses based on the spectacular military setbacks experienced by the British Army in Afghanistan's mountain defiles earlier in the century.
7. Clark accurately describes the wide range of clothing worn by Nauvoo Legionnaires in the field during the Utah War, understating if anything its eclectic character. As territorial militiamen, the Legion's troops would normally be

expected to wear uniforms very similar to those of the U.S. Army, but the hardscrabble realities of Utah's economy and remoteness precluded uniforms for any but the most senior officers. Nonetheless, Lt. Gen. Daniel H. Wells exercised overall command of the Legion from smokey Cache Cave near Echo Canyon resplendent in a uniform that rivaled General Winfield Scott's in New York. Brigham Young took pains to order from St. Louis silver buttons, epaulettes, and other adornment for his senior officers. The rank and file campaigned attired in clothing fashioned from available materials such as Pvt. James Eardley's striped mattress ticking and, in another case, a wife's prized Irish bearskin rug. Private George D. Watt, one of Brigham Young's office clerks, complained to his wife that his boots were so worn that, as he punned, they "are parting soul from the body." Another legionnaire, Jonathan Ellis Layne, wore out his only shirt to the point that he returned home on leave half-naked, sporting only his shirt's intact cuffs. "Interesting from Utah," [William Bell], interview, New York *Herald*, February 23, 1858; Brigham Young to Horace S. Eldredge, June 30, 1857, CHL; Bertha Irvine, "A Pioneer Suit of Clothes (A True Story)," *Young Woman's Journal* 27 (1916): 424. See also "Biography of Jonathan Ellis Layne" and George D. Watt to Alice Watt, October 1, 1857, George D. Watt Papers, both CHL.

8. Heber C. Kimball, a counselor to Brigham Young in the Latter-day Saint Church's First Presidency, once publicly declared, "Send 2500 troops here . . . God Almighty helping me, I will fight until there is not a drop of blood in my veins. Good God! I have wives enough to whip out the United States, for they will whip themselves." "Remarks by Pres. Heber C. Kimball, Bowery, July 26, 1857," *Deseret News*, August 5, 1857. Spelling standardized. Excerpts from Heber C. Kimball's comments were reprinted in eastern newspapers. See, for example, "From Washington," *New York Times*, October 1, 1857. See also Kenneth L. Alford, "'We Have Now the Territory on Wheels': Direct and Collateral Costs of the 1858 Move South," *Journal of Mormon History* 45, no. 2 (2019): 92–114.

9. Weber Canyon (pronounced "WEE ber" not "webb er") in the Wasatch mountain range lies east of Ogden, Utah. The Weber River, which runs through the canyon, "rises in the Uinta Mountains south of Fort Bridger and flows northwest past the mouth of Echo Canyon and into the Great Salt Lake." MacKinnon and Alford, *Fact, Fiction, and Polygamy*, 110.

10. This camp was likely that in Parley's Canyon of Feramorz ("Ferry") Little, a seasoned Latter-day Saint frontiersman who knew the terrain of the Great Plains and Rockies intimately because of his dozens of trips carrying the mail between the Missouri River and Salt Lake City. It was Little, Bill Hickman, and Ephraim K. Hanks who had brought first news of the Utah Expedition's

formation to Brigham Young in late June 1857. Through the complexities of his religion's plural marriage system, Little was both a nephew and brother-in-law to Young, who named one of his sons Feramorz Little Young. Although William Clark did not know it, Little too was a native of upstate New York. Ironically, when Clark would later serve as mayor of Ames, Iowa, in the 1870s, Ferry Little was at the same time mayor of Salt Lake City. James A. Little, *Biographical Sketch of Feramorz Little* (Salt Lake City: Juvenile Instructor Office, 1890).

11. "Emigration Canyon starts in the Wasatch Mountains east of Salt Lake City with its City Creek flowing through the heart of Salt Lake City into the Jordan River and via it to the Great Salt Lake." MacKinnon and Alford, *Fact, Fiction, and Polygamy*, 110.

Section 10. "Difficult to Escape Their Vengeance"

1. Holograph and typescript versions of some or all of Becker's multipart narrative ("The History of the Expedition against the Mormons in the Year of 1857"), prepared for publication but never printed, are in several repositories: Oregon Historical Society (Portland); the library of Utah State University (Logan); and in Salt Lake City, at Utah Historical Society and CHL. A newspaper interview with Feldman at Camp Scott immediately after his return from captivity in Salt Lake City may be found in "Statement of the Soldier Taken Captive by the Mormons," *Pittsfield* [MA] *Sun*, March 25, 1858.

2. "Valley tan" was a slang term for locally distilled hard liquor. After marching through Salt Lake City on June 26, 1858, the U.S. Army established Camp Floyd on the west side of Utah Lake in Utah Territory. There, on November 6, 1858, former St. Louis newspaperman Kirk Anderson published a newspaper catering to soldiers he christened *Valley Tan*. With a seeming wink and a nod to readers who most certainly knew the popular alcoholic meaning of the term, Anderson explained, in the inaugural issue that "this name [Valley Tan] will doubtless excite some curiosity in the 'States,' as to what it signifies and we will therefore make an explanation. Valley Tan was first applied to the leather made in this Territory in contradistinction to the imported article from the States; it gradually began to apply to every article made, or manufactured, or produced in the Territory, and means in its strictest sense, *home manufacturers* until it has entered and become an indispensable word in our Utah vernacular, and it will yet add a new word to the English language." "Our Christening—Valley Tan," *Valley Tan*, November 6, 1858, 2. Notwithstanding church and Nauvoo Legion prohibitions on the sale of such beverages, during the Utah War it was readily available to an extent that Brigham Young wrote Hugh Moon, a prominent distiller, a blunt cease and desist demand. Young to Moon, April

19, 1858, CHL. The army and its provost marshal also had serious problems of drunkenness with which to cope.

3. The Kimball store where Clark purchased his liquor was not connected to Heber C. Kimball but rather was the emporium of John Kimball, a non-Mormon distant relative who a few years earlier had migrated from New Hampshire to enter the mercantile business. John's connection to Heber no doubt helped his store to prosper, and his status as a nonmember of the dominant local church facilitated his use by Brigham Young and other leaders as a sort of go-between or independent conduit between the war's opposing sides. John Kimball's image of impartiality was largely a fiction.

4. Kirk Anderson was correct in predicting the memorability of Valley Tan the drink if not the newspaper, that folded in 1859. Clark remembered the beverage even in old age, as did a former first sergeant of dragoons, Benjamin Wilson Kelsey, when interviewed around the turn of the twentieth century: "They had only one good thing there [in Utah]. Every one had a distillery of their own, made their own whiskey. They called that 'Jolly Tar Whiskey,' made from some corn and rye, I suppose and it was frightful stuff to drink, too, for a person that was not used to it. It would burn all through a Navajo blanket." Interview by Benjamin R. Kelsey with Benjamin Wilson Kelsey, 7, typescript in possession of great-great-granddaughter Tiffany E. Kelsey.

5. "said he had a 'fool Gentile brother'": William Adams Hickman had two brothers in the territory during the Utah War, Thomas Jefferson Hickman and George Washington Hickman, MD, neither of whom was a Latter-day Saint at that time. Their parents had an obvious fondness for presidential names. "and get us a pass": The requirement for non-Mormons (including U.S. Army troops) to obtain written passes to enter, cross, or exit the territory during the Utah War was established by Brigham Young's gubernatorial proclamation of martial law on September 15, 1857. This extraordinary proclamation and the passes it required were illegal and helped to trigger Young's indictment for treason by a federal grand jury sitting under the army's protection at Fort Bridger in December 1857. Copies of the passes and related proclamation are offered occasionally by antiquarian book sellers and command high prices. MacKinnon, "Arise Like Men of God: Proclaiming Martial Law," *At Sword's Point, Part 1*, 285–92.

6. ORIGINAL 1922 NOTE: *Probably Heber C. Kimball, a prominent Mormon leader.*

EDITORS' NOTE: During the Utah War, Kimball was among the three most senior men in the Latter-day Saints' hierarchy, serving as Brigham Young's first counselor in the church's First Presidency. William Clark is confused, though, about Hyrum Smith, who was assassinated by a mob in Illinois with his brother, Joseph Smith, Jr., during June 1844. Possibly Clark meant George A. Smith, who in 1857 was an apostle as well as church historian.

7. "John Jaques, a survivor of the 1856 Willie and Martin handcart company disaster, published a lengthy (and somewhat rambling) poem in the *Deseret News* on February 17, 1858. Titled 'Uncle Sam and his Nephews,' his opening lines echoed Young's threats:

> "If Uncle has determin'd on this very foolish plan,
> "The Lord will fight our battles, and we'll help him all we can,
> "If what you now propose to do should ever come to pass,
> "We'll burn up every inch of wood and every blade of grass.

"Jacques's poem was reprinted in a May 1858 issue of the *New York Times*." Alford, "'We Have Now the Territory on Wheels,'" 97.

8. Apostle Amasa Mason ("Amasy") Lyman was considered one of the founders of the Mormon colony at San Bernardino, California, as a result of his purchase of the enormous Rancho San Bernardino in 1852. As part of Brigham Young's defensive strategy during the Utah War, Latter-day Saints living there (including Lyman's family) were ordered to evacuate to Utah during the fall of 1857. For Lyman's life, conflicts with Young, and eventual excommunication, see Edward Leo Lyman, *Amasa Mason Lyman: Mormon Apostle and Apostate—A Study in Dedication* (Salt Lake City: University of Utah Press, 2009).

9. This was David Leonard Savage, a Canadian convert, who lived in Cedar City and worked as a teamster and mail carrier across the Old Spanish Trail to San Bernardino in December 1857 but made no mention of William Clark and his friends. See "Record of David Leonard Savage, 1810–1886," Family Search database.

10. In April 1857, a month prior to announcing that the army was being sent to accompany Utah's newly appointed territorial governor, the *New York Times* reported that the Mormons had "200,000 spies and agents scattered throughout the country . . . [and they are] in close alliance with 300,000 Indians upon our Western border." Those were clearly amazing claims, considering that in 1857 there were only 55,236 Latter-day Saints in the entire world and the largest proportion of them lived in Great Britain. Notwithstanding the demographics, there was a kernel of accuracy in the newspaper's assertion of such behavior. In the fall of 1857, Young put out the word that if California volunteer troops entered Utah, he would order pre-positioned secret agents to incinerate the principal cities in that state and elsewhere in the Midwest and East. In all likelihood, this threat of arson was one of bluster rather than seriousness as part of Brigham Young's campaign of disinformation, although in October

Young did order the Nauvoo Legion to burn two church-owned settlements in Utah (Forts Bridger and Supply) and to prepare northern Utah and Salt Lake City for the torch as part of his Russian-inspired "Sebastopol strategy." See Kenneth L. Alford, "The Utah War and the *New York Times*," *Proceedings of the South Carolina Historical Association* (2013): 5–18; MacKinnon, At Sword's Point, Part 2, 83–84.

11. "with Porter Rockwell in charge": A captain in Utah's Nauvoo Legion, Orrin Porter Rockwell, "Brigham Young's Sampson-like Bodyguard" and an employee of the Y. X. Carrying Company, is one of the most colorful characters in early Latter-day Saint history. His riding, tracking, and shooting skills were legendary. Rockwell was one of the riders who interrupted Young's festivities in Big Cottonwood Canyon on July 24, 1857, to announce that the U.S. Army had been ordered to march on Utah. In spring 1858 Rockwell, Young, and eighteen others were indicted on a treason charge by the Territory of Utah U.S. District Court—later to be pardoned by President James Buchanan. MacKinnon, *At Sword's Point, Part 1*, 36, 38, 227, 471–74. See also Harold Schindler, *Orrin Porter Rockwell: Man of God, Son of Thunder* (Salt Lake City: University of Utah Press, 1993). The Aiken (not "Aikin") party was a six-man group of Californians arrested by the Nauvoo Legion near what is now Brigham City, Utah, carrying a large sum of cash and sporting silver-studded saddles and other flashy gear. The Legion viewed them as spies for the army, but in all likelihood, they were freebooters intending to set up a gambling operation amid the Utah Expedition's troops, whom they mistakenly believed had reached Salt Lake City instead of being snowed-in at Fort Bridger. It was a fatal miscalculation. This party was detained in Salt Lake City and then set on the southern route to California under the protection of Legion officers (Lieutenant Hickman and Captain Rockwell), who murdered them and looted their possessions. Theft of the Aikens' cash, weapons, watches, animals, horse furniture, and even clothes was part of a pattern of looting during the war in hardscrabble Utah that reached its zenith with the victims of the Mountain Meadows Massacre. David L. Bigler, "The Aiken Party Executions and the Utah War, 1857–1858," *Western Historical Quarterly* 38 (Winter 2007): 451–70.

12. A reference to the "Reformation" that began in Utah during 1856 as a period of religious cleansing and rededication. This thrust soon became enmeshed in controversy, including perceptions by non-Mormons and some Latter-day Saints that church leaders were calling for the "blood atonement" of the most serious sins. Brigham Young, Discourse, February 8, 1857, *Deseret News*, February 18, 1857; Paul Peterson, "The Mormon Reformation of 1856–1857: The Rhetoric and the Reality," *Journal of Mormon History* 15 (1989): 59–87;

Thomas G. Alexander, "Wilford Woodruff and the Mormon Reformation of 1855–57," *Dialogue: A Journal of Mormon Thought* 25 (Summer 1992): 25–40; Will Bagley, *Blood of the Prophets*, 50–52. See also MacKinnon, *At Sword's Point, Part 1*, 54–55.

13. "Danites" or Sons of Dan (a biblical term) were a small, extralegal society of Latter-day Saints formed in Missouri during the 1830s to protect their coreligionists and leaders from violence by anti-Mormon mobs and assassins. Whether this group survived into the Latter-day Saints' turbulent sojourns in Illinois, Iowa, and Utah is questionable and debatable. Those critics and historians inclined to believe the worst of Latter-day Saints as violence-prone argue that Danites (sometimes also called "Destroying Angels") were active up to and throughout the Utah War, while church apologists assert that their continued existence was mythic. Frequently targeted for this label were members of the small, rough-hewn group of Brigham Young intimates and henchmen dubbed "the b'hoys" after the street gangs then plaguing Manhattan. By the time of the Utah War, the term "Danites" was used frequently, casually, and indiscriminately by newspaper reporters and soldiers with whom Clark came into contact, and it was still in use at the time he wrote his reminiscences. So widespread and pejorative was the use of "Danite" in the mid-nineteenth century that when Utah governor Alfred Cumming applied the term to self-confessed killer Orrin Porter Rockwell during an 1861 drinking bout in a Salt Lake City "grocery," Rockwell responded by calling out Cumming in an unsuccessful attempt to inveigle him into a gunfight. George A. Smith to Amasa M. Lyman, March 11, 1861, Historian's Office Letterpress Copybooks, vol. 1966–68, CR100/38, CHL.

14. For studies of violence in the territory during the Utah War era other than the Mountain Meadows Massacre discussed above, see Ardis E. Parshall, "'Pursue, Retake & Punish': The 1857 Santa Clara Ambush," *Utah Historical Quarterly* 73 (Winter 2005): 64–86; Polly Aird, "'You Nasty Apostates, Clear Out': Reasons for Disaffection in the Late 1850s," *Journal of Mormon History* 30 (Fall 2004): 129–207; MacKinnon, "When Your Finger Crooks, We Move: The Ambrose-Betts Affair," in *At Sword's Point, Part 1*, 77–82, and "'Lonely Bones': Leadership and Utah War Violence," *Journal of Mormon History* 33 (Spring 2007): 121–78.

15. Fillmore served as the capital of Utah Territory from 1851 to 1856. The territory's legislature gathered in Fillmore for only one complete legislative session (1855), returning to Salt Lake City the following year.

Section 11. "We Started, Badly Scared Inside"

1. For Williams's assault on newspaper editor and mineral assayer Conrad Wiegand and Samuel L. Clemens's journalistic intervention on Wiegand's behalf,

see Fred N. Holabird, "Conrad Wiegand (1830–1880): A Western Assayer of the Mark Twain Period," essay in auction catalogue ("Treasures from the S. S. New York and Other Important Properties") for Stack's Rarities, LLC sale of July 30, 2009, in Los Angeles. Leo Lyman, the historian who has written most about Griff Williams as a mail conductor, argues that he was a frontier character who operated on both sides of the law, with his activities ranging from participation in Ute horse stealing among the California ranchos in the early 1850s to a later ill-defined connection to the California state prison at San Quentin. MacKinnon, telephone interview with Lyman (Leeds, Utah), April 16, 2023; and Lyman, "Southern Paiute Relations with Their Early Dixie Mormon Neighbors," Twenty-Seventh Annual Juanita Brooks Lecture Series, March 10, 2010, 10, Utah Technological University, St. George.

Whereas Leo Lyman believes Griff Williams's first name was James, historian George D. Smith argues that it was John. Smith gives Williams's dates as 1805–1872 and states that he and wife Mary emigrated from Wales in 1850, settling first in San Bernardino, California, and then Tooele, Utah. George D. Smith, ed., *Brigham Young: Colonizer of the American West* (Salt Lake City: Signature Books, 2021), 2:6n10.

2. This was Harlow Redfield (born 1801), who in 1857 lived in Provo, not further south as Clark described. Redfield had lived in Provo since 1849, was a founder of the town and had served as one of its aldermen as well as a second counselor to Provo's bishop, Elias H. Blackburn. That Redfield's home doubled as a hotel in tiny Provo made it likely that he would have hosted the Clark party as it pushed south from Salt Lake City. If Provo's Harlow Redfield was indeed the person to whom Clark referred, then his unnamed wife was the former Alpha Luranda Foster, whom he had married in 1835.

3. MacKinnon, "Across the Desert in 1858: Thomas L. Kane's Mediating Mission and the Mormon Women Who Made It Possible," *Juanita Brooks Lecture Series* (St. George: Utah Technological University, 2018).

4. Although Clark does not specify, there are two canyons east of Salt Lake City named Cottonwood—Big Cottonwood Canyon and Little Cottonwood Canyon. Brigham Young and many Latter-day Saints were at Silver Lake in Big Cottonwood Canyon on July 24, 1857, when three mail riders from the Y. X. Carrying Company—Orrin Porter Rockwell, Abraham O. Smoot, and Judson Stoddard—interrupted the annual Pioneer Day celebration to announce that the army was marching on Utah. MacKinnon, *At Sword's Point, Part 1*, 224–25. "Cottonwood" (not to be confused with the two canyons east of Salt Lake City) was also the name of a spring and resting place on the Old Spanish Trail southwest of Las Vegas, through which Clark's party passed.

5. Gid [presumably Gideon] Finley's identity is unknown. The Salt Creek settlement is now part of Nephi.
6. American Fork, located in Utah County about thirty miles south of Salt Lake City, sits at the base of majestic Mount Timpanogos (which rises to 11,752 feet). Settled in 1850, in 1852 the city was incorporated as Lake City. The city was built on traditional Ute fishing and hunting grounds, which caused numerous tensions between Latter-day Saint settlers and local Native Americans. The name was changed to American Fork in 1860.
7. Springville, home of one of the editors (Alford), was founded by eight families in 1850, and was incorporated as Hobble Creek in 1853. The town was renamed Springville, after nearby Fort Springville, shortly before Clark traveled through Utah. "Payson": Like American Fork and Springville in Utah County, Payson (twelve miles south of Springville) was settled in 1850. Originally called Peteetneet Creek (which means "our water place" in Timpanogos Paiute), the town was renamed by Brigham Young the following year after Payson, Illinois—a town near Quincy, Illinois, where Young's family had lived in 1839 after being driven from Missouri. Payson was incorporated in January 1853. Edward Sapir, "The Southern Paiute a Shoshonean Language," *Proceedings of the American Academy of Arts and Sciences* 65, no. 1 (1930): 1–296; Brigham Young, Payson Branch, March 9, 1851, Mss History, Diaries, Correspondence, Journals, boxes 11–42, Brigham Young Collection, CHL; Emmeline B. Wells, "Biography of Mary Ann Angell Young," *Juvenile Instructor*, January 15, 1891. With the aggressive Aaron Johnson long-serving as Springville's bishop and Legion brigadier, the town was frequently the center of intrigue during the Utah War era.
8. Present-day Enoch, Utah, was first settled by Joel H. Johnson in 1851. Johnson is known as the author of Latter-day Saint hymns "High on a Mountain Top" and "The Glorious Gospel Light Has Shone." Other settlers arrived in 1853 and built a fort which they named after Johnson. J. Spencer Cornwall, *Stories of Our Mormon Hymns* (Salt Lake City: Deseret Book, 1975), 69–71; "Johnson's Fort," *Utah State History Markers and Monuments Database*, accessed July 31, 2024, https://archive.ph/20120708153854/http://history.utah.gov/apps/markers/detailed_results.php?markerid=1133.
9. It is difficult to determine who Clark's "Jack Brown" from Fillmore was, partly because of the commonality of his name and partly because of Clark's less-than-precise grasp of southern Utah's geography. There is a possibility that he was Homer Brown, a Nauvoo Legionnaire farming in Nephi, who recorded mingling on the road south with several unnamed Utah Expedition teamsters heading for California in November 1857. If so, Bill Clark and his companions were indeed traveling in dangerous company, as Homer Brown, with urging from bishop

Jacob Bigler, had participated in the Aiken party killings during the last week of November in that region. The horse Brown offered to trade to Clark could have been part of the substantial amount of cash and other possessions stripped from the dead Aikens. The fact that Brown was willing to trade such an item during wartime with a "gentile" for a gold watch was suspicious and contrary to Brigham Young's instructions about retention of weapons, accumulation of ammunition, and avoidance of selling grain and provisions to non-Mormons. The following year Horace Brown became a cavalry trooper in Brigham Young's short-lived Army of Israel. Bigler, "Aiken Party Executions," 451–70; Homer Brown, "Journal April 1850–March 1858," entries for October–November 1857, typescript by Keith Franklin Larsen, MS 2181 1, Historian's Office Records, CHL; MacKinnon, At Sword's Point, Part 2, 252.

10. Garland Hurt, MD, was a non-Mormon from St. Louis who was Brigham Young's agent at the large Indian farm at Spanish Fork. His sensational letters to congressmen and others in the East accusing Young of suborning tribal allegiances to the U.S. government in favor of forging alliances with the Latter-day Saints were a significant factor in bringing on the Utah War. In early September 1857, with news of the Utah Expedition's formation and march across the plains, Young sent a Nauvoo Legion detachment to arrest Dr. Hurt, but he managed to escape east into the Wasatch Mountains under the protection of a few loyal Ute warriors. Once Hurt and his tribal guides found the Utah Expedition in October, he wrote a long account of Brigham Young's controversial dealings with Utah's Indians as well as a fairly accurate description of the Mountain Meadows Massacre as obtained from the Utes. From Fort Bridger in January 1858, General Johnston sent Hurt and his Ute protectors south into the Uintah Valley to enlist help from the Indian bands there in thwarting Brigham Young's plans to intercept Captain Marcy's spring return from New Mexico with thousands of animals to remount the Utah Expedition. This mission to the Uintahs, in turn, drew from the Latter-day Saints accusations that Johnston and Hurt were provoking scalp-hunting, with Mormons as targets. David L. Bigler, "Garland Hurt, the American Friend of the Utahs," *Utah Historical Quarterly* 62, no. 2 (Spring 1994): 149–70; [Albert G. Browne Jr.], "Interesting from Utah: The Case of Dr. Garland Hurt," dispatch, July 5, 1858, Salt Lake City, *New-York Daily Tribune*, August 11, 1858; MacKinnon, "To Rely upon the Indians: Protecting Captain Marcy," in *At Sword's Point, Part 2*, 93–95.

11. Clark's religious beliefs in 1857 are unclear. In 1868 he would be married by a Wisconsin minister, and in February 1920 his funeral would be held in Ames's Methodist Episcopal church. An obituary described him as "a true exponent of the Golden Rule, and while he never belonged to the organized church was one

of the most liberal men that ever lived. No one ever came to him in distress or need, but that his purse was opened, and he has scattered sunshine all along the vista of years that he walked in our midst. His religion was the deep and lasting one, the one that so many of the older generation lived and died by, and one that smacks not of hypocrisy and deceit. His life was an open book." "Wm. Clark, Once Mayor Here, Dies," *Daily Tribune and Times* [Ames], February 17, 1920; "Obituary: William Clark," *Daily Tribune and Times*, March 1, 1920.

12. The Sevier is the longest (four hundred miles) river that flows entirely within the state of Utah. Flowing in southwest Utah, the river originates west of Bryce Canyon National Park. John W. Van Cott, *Utah Place Names: A Comprehensive Guide to the Origins of Geographic Names* (Salt Lake City: University of Utah Press, 1990), 335.

13. Cedar City, Utah, is located two hundred fifty miles south of Salt Lake City and one hundred seventy miles north of Las Vegas. Settled in 1851 midway between iron ore and coal deposits, it was the heart of Brigham Young's effort to make Utah self-sufficient in iron products, which were expensive to ship from the East. The site only attempted iron production for seven years. The town was not incorporated until 1868. John Ridge, ed., *Iron Ore Deposits of the Iron Springs District, Southwestern Utah, in Ore deposits of the United States, 1933–1967* (New York: American Institute of Mining, Metallurgical, and Petroleum Engineers, 1968), 992–1019.

14. Established in the mid-1850s a few miles south of Fillmore, Utah, for Pahvant Utes, Corn Creek was one of three farms established in Utah Territory during the 1850s by Brigham Young, superintendent, and Garland Hurt, Indian agent for Utah. The other two farms were by Twelve Mile Creek in Sanpete County and at Spanish Fork in Utah County. In the immediate aftermath of the Mountain Meadows Massacre, Corn Creek became notorious as the place where Latter-day Saints claimed emigrants brought their fate on themselves by alienating Indians by allegedly poisoning a dead beeve and nearby spring.

15. Santa Clara, Utah, was settled by Jacob Hamblin in 1854 at the request of Brigham Young. Hamblin was "soon to become known as the most prominent scout and Indian missionary in nineteenth-century Utah." MacKinnon, *At Sword's Point, Part 2*, 137.

16. Ira Hatch served as a Latter-day Saint missionary among several Native American tribes, including Paiutes and Mojaves, and was well-known for his facility with native languages. Thomas L. Kane "told seventeen-year-old Joseph Fish of his difficulty in communicating with Hatch in English, a language in which the missionary was awkward because of his immersion in tribal dialects" and prolonged isolation from whites. His role in the recent Mountain Meadows

Massacre remains ambiguous and controversial. In March 1858 both Hamblin and Hatch would become part of monitoring the U.S. Army's ascent of the Colorado River in an effort to find an invasion route into southern Utah. MacKinnon, *At Sword's Point, Part 2*, 120, 134–39, 209n48.

Section 12. "Make a Man's Blood Run Cold"

1. The best researched accounts of the massacre, albeit ones with substantially different views of Brigham Young's role, are Juanita Brooks, *The Mountain Meadows Massacre* (Norman: University of Oklahoma Press, 1960); Will Bagley, *Blood of the Prophets: Brigham Young and the Massacre at Mountain Meadows* (Norman: University of Oklahoma Press, 2002); and Ronald W. Walker, Richard E. Turley Jr., and Glen M. Leonard, *Massacre at Mountain Meadows* (New York: Oxford University Press, 2008). With these studies in place, the first volume of MacKinnon's documentary history of the Utah War (*At Sword's Point*) chose not to reprise Mountain Meadows directly but instead provided context by analyzing Utah's climate of violence created by the plethora of other unpunished killings surrounding that tragedy in time and place. The latest analysis of the death toll and the atrocity's legacy is Richard E. Turley Jr. and Barbara Jones Brown, *Vengeance Is Mine: The Mountain Meadows Massacre and Its Aftermath* (New York: Oxford University Press, 2023), 40, 49, and 70; we are indebted to the authors for their willingness to share research while this study was still in-press. Some historians have tried to diminish the appalling scale of Mountain Meadows by pointing out that the numbers killed were greater at the Bear River Massacre of 1863 and Tulsa's race riot of 1921, although in both cases at least some of the victims were armed and fighting to defend themselves unlike the disarmed, defenseless Baker-Fancher party.
2. Brooks, *Mountain Meadows Massacre*, 132–36.
3. Bagley, *Blood of the Prophets*, 184. Whether these other books stepped over Clark's reminiscences because of their inaccuracies, anti-Mormon bias, or for other reasons is unknown.
4. Brooks, *Mountain Meadows Massacre*, 110–126; Bagley, *Blood of the Prophets*, 157.
5. Brooks, *Mountain Meadows Massacre*, 127–29; MacKinnon, "Unquestionably Authentic and Correct in Every Detail," 322–42.
6. [William A.] Wallace, dispatch (Los Angeles), April 22, 1858, *Daily Alta California* [San Francisco], May 3, 1858.
7. In 1857 Joel W. White was a twenty-six-year-old resident of Cedar City, Utah, laboring in support of the local iron works, one of Brigham Young's highest profile efforts to make the territory economically self-sufficient. He was pres-

ent at Mountain Meadows before and during the massacre as a captain and company commander in the battalion of the Iron County Militia (Nauvoo Legion) led by Maj. Isaac C. Haight. In describing White as engaged in "police duty," William Clark meant that he acted as a courier or "expressman" carrying dispatches between Mountain Meadows and the nearby settlements like Pinto and Cedar City involved in the atrocity. Notwithstanding Clark's assurance White did not take part in the killings at Mountain Meadows, the historians most knowledgeable about the primary sources dealing with the massacre have established that White was one of the killers. He testified as a prosecution witness at John D. Lee's two trials, the only person to do so. In 1859 White and his family moved to another part of the territory and continued to relocate until his death in 1914, part of the depopulation of southern Utah following the massacre. White was the brother-in-law of David Savage, the Latter-day Saint on whom William Clark and his companions depended to guide them in their flight from Utah to California. One of the most accurate, brief accounts of Joel W. White's background and role in the Mountain Meadows Massacre is attorney Robert Briggs's "1857 Iron County Militia Project," accessed March 28, 2023, http://www.1857ironcountymilitia.com.

8. Jacob Hamblin (not "Hamlin") was the Indian "farmer" or agent in southern Utah appointed by Brigham Young in his role as U.S. superintendent of Indian affairs for Utah. Technically Hamblin's duties were to teach agriculture to the tribes and look after their well-being, although de facto he also acted as a missionary as well as Young's eyes and ears in the region. Hamblin's rough ranch house was virtually on the edge of Mountain Meadows; to it the killers took the seventeen distraught, blood-spattered young children who survived the massacre immediately after murdering their parents. There they placed the children in the care of Hamblin's dismayed wife, Rachael, since Hamblin himself was absent in Salt Lake City to take a plural wife. Although Hamblin was uninvolved in the planning and execution of the massacre, upon his return he played a key role in its subsequent cover-up and was actively involved in parceling out the surviving children to Latter-day Saint families until federal agents forcibly retrieved them for return by the army to relatives in Arkansas. The most recent and best biography is Todd M. Compton, *A Frontier Life: Jacob Hamblin, Explorer and Missionary* (Salt Lake City: University of Utah Press, 2013).

9. What Clark casually refers to as the "divide" near Hamblin's ranch was a major topographical landmark of the American West, the southern rim of the Great Basin. Between Cedar City and what soon became the settlement of St. George to the south, the terrain's elevation dropped thirty-one hundred feet (53 percent) to twenty-seven hundred feet above sea level. The result was a more salubrious

winter climate in St. George and the deserts to its west that attracted Brigham Young and millions of other Utahns seeking respite over the decades from the harsh climate of the Great Basin.

10. Apostle Lyman's efforts to quiet the Native Americans along the trail to San Bernardino and to permit non-Mormons as well as Latter-day Saints to pass unmolested, worked in terms of avoiding further violence, but not without an economic cost to emigrants. The tribal bands exacted tribute or tolls in the form of cattle and other goods, often through heavy-handed raids. Four years later Griff Williams was still shaken at the risks involved, but he was grateful to Lyman for what he had done. Williams told the son of a Lyman friend, "God bless him forever, if the prayers of a Gentile will avail anything [and] he thinks they will." See Lyman, *Amasa Mason Lyman*, 257.

11. The missionaries were Jehiel McConnell and the improbably named Commodore Perry Liston. Copies of Liston's autobiography and journal for this period, in which he denies any involvement with the Mountain Meadows Massacre, may be found in the collections of the Henry E. Huntington Library (San Marino CA); L. Tom Perry Special Collections, Harold B. Lee Library, Brigham Young University (Provo); and Washington County Library (St. George UT).

12. This exchange is emblematic of a volatile controversy rippling through Utah and across the overland trails that ran to the question of whether the Latter-day Saints, led by Brigham Young, were attempting to "tamper" with the allegiances of the tribes in the region. Because Native Americans frequently used different terminology for Latter-day Saints and non-Mormon Americans, there were widespread perceptions that Indian use of the label "Mericats" for the latter reflected a deliberate attempt by Young to draw distinctions between the two groups in a way that ran to the detriment of the U.S. government while placing emigrants in danger. Young argued that the distinction in tribal perceptions and terminology was a natural one based on observed behavioral differences rather than the result of a prejudice fostered by him. The controversy was aggravated by Young's gift-giving responsibilities as U.S. superintendent of Indian affairs for Utah, a power that critics believed he abused by representing the largesse he and his agents dispensed as coming from the Latter-day Saint Church rather than the federal government. Brent M. Rogers, "A Distinction between Mormons and Americans," *Utah Historical Quarterly* 82, no. 4 (Fall 2014): 250–71.

13. With this byplay between a Native American and two Anglos, one of whom was a Latter-day Saint and the other a non-Mormon, Clark unwittingly sheds light on several of the earliest controversies enveloping the Mountain Meadows Massacre only weeks after its commission: whether or not Brigham Young was encouraging Indian attacks on the lives and property of gentiles crossing

southern Utah; and the effectiveness of communications about this policy, whatever it was, as it flowed between church leaders in Salt Lake City and Cedar City and then on to isolated, impoverished tribal bands. Here, the Paiute warrior Clark encountered is, in effect, saying that missionaries McConnell and Liston were plotting to dry-gulch non-Mormon Griff Williams, a practice from which Brigham Young was careful to distance the church (once controversy arose from the massacre), but which the two missionaries believe was still expected of them. In furtherance of Young's post-massacre wishes to help rather than prey upon emigrants, apostle Lyman on December 19, 1857, spoke at a special meeting of settlers in Cedar City to say explicitly "at some length [about] not encouraging the Indians to shed the blood of strangers and passers by." Nonetheless, when Indian farmer Jacob Hamblin came across McConnell and Liston along Muddy Creek he recorded, "For some cause a plan had been laid and matured in their minds to kill off this [Turner-Dukes] company and take the spoil. I told them the instructions I had from Gov. Young; but they held out the idea to me that there was secret instructions that I knew nothing of—we had much talk upon this subject—I felt vexed at the course that had been taken, and I told them that words were to convey ideas, and that I had written instructions from Brigham Young to take this company through safe, and that I would stand by them to the last." Hamblin came away from his encounters with these two missionaries with the belief that they were being influenced negatively by local Legion commander Isaac C. Haight, and "With Zion standing against the world, and with the Indians as allies, they were prepared to prey upon every passing emigrant company as part of their contribution to the war." Lyman, "Southern Paiute Relations," 9; Brooks, *Mountain Meadows Massacre*, 126–31. Of this encounter in the desert between the unidentified Paiute and Messrs. McConnell and Liston witnessed by William Clark, Leo Lyman argues, "Although no corroboration exists of the details of Clark's account, there is no reason to discount any part of it, negative though it may be toward McConnell." Edward Leo Lyman, *The Overland Journey from Utah to California: Wagon Travel from the City of the Saints to the City of Angels* (Reno: University of Nevada Press, 2004), 144.

14. This was a subgroup of what has more generally been called the Turner-Dukes train, a largely non-Mormon group. As discussed earlier, several small caravans of Latter-day Saints heading to San Bernardino preceded it across the Old Spanish Trail.

15. Such wanton destruction of vegetation, timber, and animals by passing emigrants and settlers infuriated the Native Americans of the region, who depended on these resources for survival in a harsh environment. In August 1858 cutting

of a few cottonwood trees by the Latter-day Saint Rose-Baley party to build rafts at Beale's Crossing of the Colorado River triggered an attack and massacre by a local Mojave band. Dennis G. Casebier, *The Mojave Road* (Norco CA: Tales of the Mojave Road, 1975), 66–67.

16. Oddly, Clark does not mention the springs' proximity to the Latter-day Saint Indian mission, one of the major landmarks along the Old Spanish Trail since its establishment in 1855. In 1857, before Clark passed through Las Vegas, the religious purpose of this way station was supplanted by its transformation into a base for mining and smelting ballistic lead to provide the Nauvoo Legion with ammunition during the soon-to-follow Utah War.

17. While Clark and his companions were celebrating the arrival of 1858 in the hot springs at Las Vegas, New Mexico Territory, the friends they left behind at Camp Scott, Utah, were trying to make the best of the same occasion in freezing weather at an altitude of seven thousand feet above sea level. For a description of how the troops and camp followers of the Utah Expedition fared under these conditions, see MacKinnon and Alford, *Fact, Fiction, and Polygamy*, 80; "A. B. C." [David A. Burr], "Life at Camp Scott—How the Holidays Were Spent," dispatch, January 4, 1858, *New York Times*, April 9, 1858.

18. EDITORS' NOTE: Several extraneous paragraphs that appeared here in the 1922 publication and a few additional sentences two paragraphs later have been moved to appendix A.

19. Piutes, alternately spelled Paiutes or called "Pedes," were generally nonequestrian. They tended to move to reservations and adopt settler ways more easily than other tribes within Utah Territory. See Kenneth L. Alford, "Indian Relations in Utah during the Civil War," in *Civil War Saints*, ed. Alford (Provo UT: BYU Religious Studies Center and Deseret Book, 2012), 203–25.

20. Although William Clark was not mentioned by name, the arrival of his party in San Bernardino was reported in the California newspapers with news that it brought about assassination of the Aiken party in November. *Star* [Los Angeles], January 16, 1858; "Later from the South," *Daily Alta California* [San Francisco], January 25, 1858.

Section 13. "Back to Wisconsin"

1. A search of available church records yields no indication that Sherwood ever became a Latter-day Saint. He was apparently a "Winter Mormon" in the worst sense of the term.

2. In an earlier (1915) version of this material, the final word of Clark's narrative was "wife" rather than "girl." Who made the change, when, and why is an interesting question. See *Evening Times* (Ames IA), December 6, 1915.

Appendix A

1. Lyman, *Overland Journey from Utah to California*, 71–74.
2. ORIGINAL 1922 NOTE: *Mountain Spring is in southern Nevada* [formerly Utah and New Mexico] *southwest of Las Vegas.*

Appendix B

1. "Back to the Best Place on Earth," *Intelligencer* [Ames IA], May 18, 1911.
2. "Marriage Leaps through Many Years," *Weekly Tribune* [Ames IA], October 4, 1917.
3. "Golden Shadows Cast Their Gleam across Life's Path. Mr. and Mrs. William Clark Celebrate Golden Wedding Anniversary," *Tri-Weekly Tribune* [Ames IA], September 30, 1918.

Appendix C

1. "Wm. Clark, Once Mayor Here, Dies," *Daily Tribune and Evening Times* [Ames IA], February 17, 1920.
2. "Obituary. William Clark," *Daily Tribune* [Ames IA], March 1, 1920.

Appendix D

1. Quoted in J. H. Beadle, *Life in Utah: Or, the Mysteries and Crimes of Mormonism* (Philadelphia: National Publishing, 1872), 227–28. Having arrived in Salt Lake City in September 1868, Beadle, unlike Clark, stayed and made a career churning out newspaper articles and books critical of the Latter-day Saints. This sensational material often featured the misdeeds of William Clark's captor during the Utah War, Bill Hickman.
2. Lowe, *Five Years a Dragoon*, 305–6.

Editors' Epilogue

1. U.S. Census for 1850, 1860, and 1870; "Edwin Leach," August 1919, findagrave.com; "Brief Obituary of Mrs. Celia [Barrett] Leach, Former Resident Here," *Ord Journal* [Ord NE], June 9, 1927.
2. Ira Tuttle left no known account of this march, but a bugler in his Company A and a civilian merchant traveling with the regiment did so. See William D. Drown, "Personal Recollections—A Trumpeter's Notes ('52–'58)," in *From Everglade to Canyon with the Second United States Cavalry*, comp. Theophilus F. Rodenbough (New York: D. Van Nostrand, 1875; repr., Norman: University of Oklahoma Press, 2000), 208–18; "Diary of William A. Carter—1857," transcribed by David L. Bigler from original in Carter Papers, Wyoming Archives

and Historical Department, Cheyenne, excerpted in MacKinnon, *At Sword's Point, Part 1*, 401–3 and "Diary of Judge William A. Carter," *Annals of Wyoming* 2 (April 1939): 75–110.

3. So onerous and demeaning was the prospect of herding duty distant from the camaraderie of Fort Bridger, Lt. Col. Philip St. George Cooke, the dragoons' commander, challenged it. First, he made an abrupt plea to Albert Sidney Johnston followed by a letter of protest to Winfield Scott, the general in chief in New York. Officers' letters to relatives written from the Second's new camp on Henrys Fork were filled with descriptions of boredom and isolation as well as concern about the prospect for raiding by the Nauvoo Legion.

4. Private Ira O. Tuttle's legal problems while serving with the Utah Expedition are summarized in part in Roger B. Nielson, *Roll Call at Old Camp Floyd, Utah Territory: Soldiers of Johnston's Army at the Upper Camp 8 July to 8 September 1858* (Springville UT, n.p., 2006), 122n9. See also War Department, Department of Utah, Letters Sent, July 16, 1857–July 15, 1858, microfilm, Utah Historical Society, Salt Lake City, courtesy of the late Curtis R. Allen, Centerville.

5. George Tuttle's legal problems in Utah are documented in People vs. George B. Tuttle, U.S. Third District Court, Utah Territory, case files, 1851–1896, series 9802, microfilm reel 1, Utah State Archives, Salt Lake City.

6. Information about Smith's activities in Utah is scant. First notice of his presence and legal representations there came with [Browne], "Mormon Prisoner—His Trial," dispatch, January 5, 1858, *New-York Daily Tribune*, March 1, 1858. See also Brig. Gen. James Ferguson to Brigham Young, June 21 and 26, 1858, CHL. There are signs of a potentially colorful story here, but thus far historians have ignored Charles Maurice Smith, George Tuttle's Virginia lawyer in the wilderness.

7. For this complex international case, see MacKinnon and Alford, *Fact, Fiction, and Polygamy*. With disposition of the Tuttle and Polydore cases, a third such effort arose, this one initiated by a Danish family seeking return of two daughters, Dorthea and Maria Hastrup, who had emigrated to Utah Territory in 1858 after converting to Mormonism and being turned out of home by their parents. In this case the now-remorseful parents, claiming their daughters had been improperly enticed by Mormon missionaries, engaged Alexander Wilson, a former U.S. attorney for Utah then in Washington to lobby for appointment by President Buchanan as Utah's chief justice. Notwithstanding attorney Wilson's connections and efforts, pursuit of the Hastrup case failed because the facts differed substantially from those in the Polydore suit. The Hastrup sisters were adults, and, when queried, they stated their desire to remain in Utah to practice their new religion. Case closed. Documentation involving the Hastrups may

be found in RG 59, General Records of the Department of State, Miscellaneous Correspondence, 1784–1906 (vol. 49) and Territorial Papers, 1764–1873 (vol. 64), NARA.

8. John W. Mott to Dear friends and relations, June 20 and 22, 1858, MS 5200, CHL; Margaret Webster Adams to brother George, June 26 and 27, 1858, MS 2446, CHL.
9. "Arrival from Salt Lake," *Crescent City* [IA] *Bugle*, October 15, 1858.
10. Kristen M. Taynor, ed., *Military Intelligence during the Civil War: Provost Marshal Records on Spies, Scouts, Guides, and Detectives* (Bethesda MD: LexisNexis, 2009), 74; Wisconsin Adjutant General's Office, *Roster of Wisconsin Volunteers, War of the Rebellion, 1861–1865* (Madison: Democratic Printing Company, 1886), 1:14. It is conjecture that the Ira O. Tuttle listed in this material as a scout during 1864 and the private soldier of same name who served in the First Wisconsin Cavalry was George B. Tuttle's brother, but the combination of name, state affiliation, and affinity for mounted service makes such a connection likely.
11. [A. G. Browne Jr.,] "Later from the Utah Expedition. A Volunteer Battalion Enlisted," dispatch, December 13, 1857, *New-York Daily Tribune*, February 2, 1858.
12. U.S. Census for 1860; "A. P. Frank, Warren Pioneer, Dies in Colorado" and "A. P. Frank, Warren Pioneer," *Sheaf* [Warren, Marshall County, MN], December 14, 1921, and December 21, 1921; "A Pioneer Experience," *Minden* [NE] *News*, November 15, 1918, and *Nebraska History and Record of Pioneer Days* 1, no. 8 (December 1921): 2.
13. Susan Bohl, "A War on Civilians: Order Number 11 and the Evacuation of Western Missouri," *Prologue: The Journal of the National Archives* 36 (Spring 2004): 44–51.
14. Prior to joining Quantrill's raiders and serving as a second lieutenant, Rennick had served as a Confederate sergeant in Company B, Sixth Regiment, Missouri Infantry. "Renick, Chatham E.," National Park Service, Soldier and Sailors Database, accessed July 31, 2024, https://www.nps.gov/civilwar/search-soldiers.htm. See also Thomas Shelby Watson with Perry A. Brantley, *Confederate Guerrilla Sue Mundy: A Biography of Kentucky Soldier Jerome Clarke* (Jefferson NC: McFarland, 2008), 136–39.
15. MacKinnon, "125 Years of Conspiracy Theories: Origins of the Utah Expedition, 1857–58," *Utah Historical Quarterly* 52, no. 3 (Summer 1984): 219–22.
16. Raymond W. and Mary Lund Settle, *War Drums and Wagon Wheels: The Story of Russell, Majors, and Waddell* (Lincoln: University of Nebraska Press, 1966), 143–55.
17. "Brigham Young's Janissary. Interview with Bill Hickman," November 18, 1871, *New York World*, November 25, 1871.

18. William A. Hickman with J. H. Beadle, *Brigham's Destroying Angel: Being the Life, Confession, and Startling Disclosures of the Notorious Bill Hickman, the Danite Chief of Utah* (New York: G. A. Corfutt, 1872). Note that the moniker "Wild Bill" was not yet being used.
19. Hope A. Hilton, *"Wild Bill" Hickman and the Mormon Frontier* (Salt Lake City: Signature Books, 1988). See also MacKinnon, "'Lonely Bones': Violence and Leadership," *At Sword's Point, Part 1*, 295–328 (chap. 12) and "Epilogue to the Utah War: Impact and Legacy," *Journal of Mormon History* 29, no. 2 (Fall 2003): 211.
20. "Went with Johnston on Military Trip against Mormons," *Intelligencer* [Ames IA], September 11, 1912.
21. John G. Turner, *Brigham Young, Pioneer Prophet* (Cambridge MA: Belknap Press of Harvard University Press, 2012); Thomas G. Alexander, *Brigham Young and the Expansion of the Mormon Faith* (Norman: University of Oklahoma Press, 2019); Leonard J. Arrington, *Brigham Young: American Moses* (New York: Alfred A. Knopf, 1985); Newell G. Bringhurst, *Brigham Young and the Expanding American Frontier* (Boston: Little, Brown, 1986).
22. Patriarchal Blessings, vol. 27, 326, CHL.
23. [Lemuel Fillmore], dispatch, June 28, 1858, *Herald* (NY) July 30, 1858, reprinted in Hammond, *Utah Expedition 1857–1858*, 362. Harlow Redfield was not a polygamist, and his wife of twenty-three years was forty-two years old rather than "young." As mentioned above, their new home was in Salt Lake City, the largest settlement between St. Louis and San Francisco.
24. MacKinnon, "Explaining Violence: Gubernatorial Language, Leadership, and Example," *At Sword's Point, Part 1*, 318–28; J. Pulsipher, "A Scrap-book Containing Some of the Phraseology and Selected Instruction—& Abridged Speeches of Inspired Men," Pulsipher Family Papers, L. Tom Perry Special Collections, Lee Library, BYU cited in Marquardt, *Coming Storm*, 8n21.
25. Robert Burns, affidavit, June 28, 1858, CR 1234/1, box 73, folder 26 (reel 86), CHL.
26. George A. Smith to T. B. H. Stenhouse, July 2, 1858, George A. Smith Papers, MS 1322, box 3, fol. 12, CHL.
27. MacKinnon, review of William Hartley biography of Egan, *Utah Historical Quarterly* 87, no. 2 (Spring 2019): 169.
28. "Record of David Leonard Savage, 1810–1886," Family Search database.
29. "A Tale of Adventure," *Intelligencer* [Ames IA], June 15, 1905; "Marriage Leaps thru Many Years," *Weekly Tribune* [Ames], October 4, 1917. See also appendix B to this study.
30. "Obituary. William Clark," *Daily Tribune* [Ames IA], March 1, 1920. As discussed above, it is unlikely this service was in uniform. On February 15, 1862, the Salt

Lake City post office was holding mail for "Wm Clark." Whether this was for Cora J. Clark's roaming correspondent is, of course, unknown. "List of Letters," *Deseret News*, February 19, 1862.

31. "Letter from Santa Anna Valley. The German Vineyard," *Daily Alta California*, January 22, 1858; "Annaheim—The Estate of the Los Angeles Vineyard Company," *Star* [Los Angeles], January 30, 1858; Lucile E. Dickson, "The Founding and Early History of Anaheim, California," *Annual Publication of the Historical Society of Southern California* 11, no. 2 (1919): 26–37; Julius L. Jacobs, "California's Pioneer Wine Families," *California Historical Quarterly* 54, no. 2 (Summer 1975): 139–74.

32. Hal, February 18, 1862, "Letter from Calaveras County," *Independent* [Stockton CA], February 22, 1862. At the request of the editors, the State Historical Society of Iowa staff examined William Clark's poke but did not find any gold residue—leaving unanswered the question of whether Clark found any gold during his California travels.

33. George A. Smith to T.B.H. Stenhouse, July 2, 1858, George A. Smith Papers, MS 1322, box 3, folder 12, CHL; Robert Burns, affidavit, June 28, 1858, CR1234/1, box 73, fol. 26 (microfilm reel 86), CHL.

34. Appendix B.

35. "Golden Shadows Cast Their Gleam across Life's Path. Mr. and Mrs. William Clark Celebrate Golden Wedding Anniversary," *Tri-Weekly Tribune* [Ames IA], September 30, 1918.

36. "Golden Shadows."

37. "Golden Shadows."

38. *Intelligencer* [Ames IA], April 21, 1910, 4/3; "Back to the Best Place on Earth," *Intelligencer*, May 18, 1911.

39. "A Tale of Adventure," *Intelligencer* [Ames IA], June 15, 1905.

40. "Went with Johnston on Military Trip against Mormons," *Intelligencer* [Ames IA], September 11, 1912. For an explanation of this conspiracy theory and several others that still swirl around the Utah War, see MacKinnon, "125 Years of Conspiracy Theories," 212–30.

41. "A Real Story of Local Interest, Man Well Known Here Writes of Experiences in Crossing the Plains," *Evening Times* [Ames IA], November 10, 1915. Subsequent installments ran in the busy Thanksgiving and Christmas holiday issues of November 12; November 15; November 17; November 19; November 22; November 24; November 26; November 29; December 1; December 3; and December 6.

42. Meeting minutes, [Ames IA] Sun Dial Chapter, National Society of the Daughters of the American Revolution, March 1–November 1, 1920, minutes book,

89–102. For access to these records, the editors are indebted to Ms. Susan K. Harris of Ames, their keeper as well as past leader of this group (now named the Sun Dial-Solomon Dean Chapter). Ms. Harris has also been a senior officer of its organizational parent in the national D.A.R. During the discussions about the manuscript with Cora Clark in 1920, the chapter's secretary, Ms. Clarissa K. Snyder, described what was being acquired as a typewritten document, the hand-written original having been destroyed. The editors believe Ms. Snyder misunderstood the paper flow. What ultimately entered the collections at SHSI was Mr. Clark's holograph (not typed) reminiscences; what Clark destroyed were the scraps of paper on which he had jotted his contemporary field notes and perhaps a fragmentary journal.

43. *Daily Tribune and Evening Times* [Ames IA], October 5, 1920.
44. "Benjamin Franklin Shambaugh (January 29, 1871–April 7, 1940)," *The Biographical Dictionary of Iowa*, accessed May 19, 2023, http://uipress.lib.uiowa.edu/bdi/DetailsPage.aspx?id=334.
45. Jan Shipps, *Sojourner in a Promised Land: Forty Years among the Mormons* (Urbana: University of Illinois Press, 2000), 21; David B. Marshall, "The Latter-day Saints, the Doughnut, and Post-Christian Canada," *Journal of Mormon History* 39, no. 2 (Spring 2013): 35–77.
46. All the Texas material discussed is found in the William Clark Manuscript Collection (US-214), Cushing Memorial Library & Archives, Texas A&M University, College Station. It was transmitted to the editors electronically via Anton R. DuPlessis (Curator, Texas Collection, Cushing Library) to MacKinnon, March 25, 2022. Complicating an already Byzantine provenance is the fact that in the fall of 1937, before Texas A&M University acquired this material, it was loaned to the library of the University of Texas at Austin by Mr. C. E. Evans, registrar of the University of Kansas City [MO]. On November 15, 1937, Ms. Winnie Allen, archivist at UT returned the variant Clark manuscript to Mr. Evans with thanks and an offer to make a typescript of it so that the text of the document might be shared between the two universities. Apparently, nothing came of Ms. Allen's offer, and so this material and her letter subsequently gravitated at an unknown time in an unknown way from Kansas City back to Texas, but to College Station rather than Austin.

Editors' Conclusions

1. Aside from errors that found their way into his manuscript, Clark's extemporaneous storytelling and newspaper interviews around Ames grew to contain embellishments such as his claim to have met Porter Rockwell and the Aiken brothers in Utah and his support for the conspiracy theory that President

Buchanan sent Albert Sidney Johnston west with the Utah Expedition as some sort of proto-Confederate plot in advance of the Civil War.

2. Undated twentieth-century interview by Benjamin R. Kelsey with former Utah Expedition first sergeant Benjamin Wilson Kelsey, Company D, Second U.S. Dragoons; typescript in possession and used by courtesy of great-great-granddaughter Tiffany E. Kelsey.

3. Among the more fantastic accounts of a Utah War teamster was the 1889 publication of John V. Nelson's reminiscences, filled with encounters with Porter Rockwell, Brigham Young, an abusive wagon master, and the obligatory description of a skeleton-strewn Mountain Meadows. Harrington O'Reilly, *Fifty Years on the Trail: A True Story of Western Life* (New York: Frederick Warn, 1889).

4. For case studies in approaching "classics" with such caution, see Peter Wild and Neil Carmony, "The Trip Not Taken: John C. Van Dyke, Heroic Doer or Armchair Seer?" *Journal of Arizona History* 34, no. 1 (Spring 1993): 65–80; and John S. Gray, "Fact Versus Fiction in the Kansas Boyhood of Buffalo Bill," *Kansas History: A Journal of the Central Plains* 8 (Spring 1985): 2–20. Also see three articles by MacKinnon: "Trouble in Paradise: Beware the Bogus," in "Loose in the Stacks: A Half-Century with the Utah War and Its Legacy," *Dialogue: A Journal of Mormon Thought* 40 (Spring 2007): 66–67; "'Unquestionably Authentic and Correct in Every Detail': Probing John I. Ginn and His Remarkable Utah War Story," *Utah Historical Quarterly* 72 (Fall 2004): 322–42; and "Ironquill Meets the Mormon Richelieu: Lt. Eugene F. Ware, Apostle George Q. Cannon, and a Cautionary Tale of the Overland Trail, 1864," *Overland Journal: Quarterly of the Oregon-California Trails Association* 39, no. 4 (Winter 2021–22): 145–61.

5. Section 9, page 69.

6. Magraw was the unpopular former contractor on the Independence to Salt Lake City mail route, Burr was Utah's federally appointed surveyor general, and Morrell was the hated postmaster of Salt Lake City. All three men were prominently anti-Mormon, and, like U.S. Indian agent Hurt, they took refuge from Legion death threats with the army at Fort Bridger during the fall of 1857. MacKinnon, *At Sword's Point, Part 1*, 314–15.

7. Thanks to Brigham Young's enthusiasm for record-keeping, it is possible to determine with some accuracy who passed through his well-staffed office and for what purpose, even in the midst of a guerrilla war on the American frontier. (Thus, one can verify the brief courtesy call paid by Samuel L. Clemens and his brother while stopping en route to Nevada Territory in August 1861. It was an encounter Clemens described eleven years later in *Roughing It* in such comedic fashion that it would be easy to assume it was apocryphal had not Young's office diary verified the visit.) That this source does not record an

office visit by Bill Hickman with William Clark in tow during the fall of 1857, does not necessarily mean that one did not happen. The records are voluminous and generally accurate but not exhaustive. See Smith, *Brigham Young*, 2 vols. One reason why there is no record of William Clark's visit to Brigham Young's office may lie with the way in which the required travel passes were written. After teamsters Morgan and Ackerman obtained their exit document in Young's office on February 5, 1858, they described the procedure to a Los Angeles newspaper: "The Governor wrote his name on a [blank] sheet of paper, which was handed to a clerk, who wrote the form of passport over the signature. Thus, the passports bear Brigham Young's signature, although he does not sign them." Accordingly, some applicants, like perhaps Clark, may have visited the office but not interacted with Brigham Young in person to obtain a pass. Supporting this supposition is the fact that, although a member of the Morgan and Ackerman party verifiably called at the office for an exit document, the visit was not recorded in Young's office diary. The text of the Morgan-Ackerman pass may be found in "Salt Lake News," *Star* [Los Angeles], March 6, 1858; the identically phrased retained copy is in Brigham Young Gubernatorial Letterbook, 698, CR 1234/1, box 50 (reel 63), CHL. The copy these former teamsters showed the *Star* was signed, while the retained copy understandably was not.

8. These four men traveled the Fort Leavenworth to Fort Bridger leg of the trail at approximately the same time, although they did so separately as employees of three different organizations: Russell, Majors and Waddell (Clark); quartermaster of the Tenth U.S. Infantry (Ginn); and Second U.S. Dragoons sutler C. A. Perry & Co. (Morgan and Ackerman). The experiences of the four in and around Salt Lake City were quite different, and they traveled from southern Utah to San Bernardino at different times: Ginn in early November 1857; Clark a few weeks later in November-December; and Morgan and Ackerman two months after him in early 1858. Ginn, an experienced newspaperman, wrote multiple versions of what he saw in the early twentieth century and hoped for commercial book publication but unsuccessfully so; while the story of Ackerman's and Morgan's adventures, including excerpts from their contemporary diary, appeared only in a single 1858 issue of a short-lived Los Angeles newspaper, the *Star*.
9. *Intelligencer* [Ames IA], April 21, 1910.
10. Robert B. Parker, *Painted Ladies* (New York: G. P. Putnam's Sons, 2010), 61.
11. Dale L. Walker and Jeanne Campbell Reesman, eds., *No Mentor But Myself: Jack London on Writing and Writers* (Stanford CA: Stanford University Press, 1999), 57.

12. Branch Rickey, quoted in column by Arthur Daley, *New York Times*, November 17, 1965, in Paul Dickson, *Baseball's Greatest Quotations: An Illustrated Treasury of Baseball and Historical Lore* (New York: HarperCollins, 2008), 444.
13. Richard E. Turley Jr., foreword in MacKinnon and Alford, *Fact, Fiction, and Polygamy*, 13.
14. MacKinnon, "Predicting the Past: The Utah War's Twenty-First Century Future," *Leonard J. Arrington Mormon History Lecture Series*, no. 14 (Logan: Utah State University, 2009).

About the Editors

WILLIAM P. MACKINNON, an independent historian residing in Montecito, Santa Barbara County, California, has written extensively about territorial Utah and the American West since 1963. His one hundred thirty articles, chapters, essays, and book reviews have appeared in more than fifty journals, monographs, and encyclopedias. The Arthur H. Clark imprint of the University of Oklahoma Press published the two award-winning volumes of his documentary history of the Utah War of 1857–1858, *At Sword's Point*; MacKinnon has written a total of five books. He is a Fellow and Honorary Life Member of the Utah Historical Society and member of the Utah Crossroads Chapter of the Oregon-California Trails Association. MacKinnon has been presiding officer of such diverse organizations as the Mormon History Association, Santa Barbara Corral of the Westerners, Yale Library Associates, and Children's Hospital of Michigan. In his parallel business career, he has been a vice president of General Motors Corporation and is president of MacKinnon Associates, a management consulting firm. He is an alumnus or veteran of Yale College (BA, Magna Cum Laude and Phi Beta Kappa), the Harvard Graduate School of Business Administration (MBA), and U.S. Air Force. MacKinnon and his wife Pat, also a native of New York State, have five children and nine grandchildren.

KENNETH L. ALFORD is a professor of church history and doctrine at Brigham Young University. After serving almost thirty years on active duty in the United States Army, he retired as a colonel in 2008. While on active military duty, Ken served in numerous assignments, including the Pentagon, eight years teaching computer science at the United States Military Academy at West Point, and four years as a professor and department chair teaching strategic leadership at the National Defense University in Washington DC. He has served as the Religious Education Teaching Fellow and the H. Ephraim Hatch Teaching and Learning Faculty Fellow at Brigham Young University. He is an Honorary Life Member of the Utah Historical Society and member of the Utah Crossroads Chapter of the Oregon-California Trails Association. His twelve books include *Utah and the American Civil War: The Written Record*; *Saints at War: The Gulf War, Afghanistan, and Iraq*; *Civil War Saints*; *Latter-day Saints in Washington DC*; and *Fact, Fiction, and Polygamy—A Tale of Utah War Intrigue, 1857–1858: A. G. Browne's "Ward of the Three Guardians."* Ken and his late wife, Sherilee, have four children and twenty grandchildren.

Index

Abbreviation "WC" stands for William Clark. Page numbers in italics indicate illustrations. Two-letter State abbreviations (e.g. UT) may designate either a State or a Territory.

Ackerman, Samuel, 161, 207n7, 208n8
Ackley, Richard, 173n2:3
Adams, Margret Webster, 127–28
Aiken, John, 92, 206n1
Aiken party killings (1857), 67, 81, 134, 139–40, 190n11, 193n9, 200n20
alcohol/drunkenness, 37, 70, 136, 137. *See also* "Valley tan" (liquor)
Alexander, Edmund Brooke, 180n2
Alford, Sherilee Bond, v, xv, 211
Allen, Winnie, 206n46
Ambrose, John G., 139
American Fork UT, 82, 193n7
Ames *Daily Tribune*, 112
Ames *Evening Times*, 9, 112, 152
Ames IA: Clark Avenue named in memory of WC, xiv, 143, 147, 164; lithograph of, *107*; WC and Cora's arrival and their life in, 106–11, 145–47, 157; WC and Cora's children and family, 147–48; WC and Cora's travels and departure from, 148; WC as mayor and councilman, 4, 19, 106, 186n10; WC's death and obituary, 4, 19, 112–14, 194n11; WC's grocery store, 145–46
Ames *Intelligencer*, 142, 146, 149, 152
Ames *Weekly Tribune*, 106

Anaheim CA, 143–44
Anderson, "Bloody Bill," 131
Anderson, Kirk, 187n2, 188n4
Antonio (teamster), 38
Arapaho Indians, 178n10
Army of Israel, 67, 193n9
Ash Hollow, 32, 47–48, 52, 173n2, 176n3
Ash Hollow Massacre (1855), 47, 176n3

Bagley, John, 178n1
Bagley, Will, 91, 92
Baker-Fancher party, murder of. *See* Mountain Meadows Massacre (1857)
Battle of Ash Hollow (1855), 47, 176n3
Battle of Little Big Horn (1876), 32
Beadle, John Hanson, 115–17
Bear River Massacre (1863), 196n1
Bear River-Soda Springs, 60, 62, 68, 181n3, 182n6, 185n3
Becker, Charles W. "Charlie," 74–75, 95, 127, 184n2
Beehrer, George W., 38
Bernhisel, John M., 193n16
Betts, Thomas W., 139
"b'hoy" (slang term): Hickman as trusted, 70, 136; meaning of, 191n13; as moniker for Young's operatives, 4, 67

213

Big Blue River (NE), 26
Bigler, Jacob, 193n8, 193n9
Blackburn, Elias H. (bishop), 191n1, 192n2
Blacks Fork, 8, 13, 57, 179n7. *See also* Green River
"Bleeding Kansas," 13, 21
blood atonement, 127, 190n12
Blood of the Prophets (Bagley), 91
Blue Water Creek, 47, 176n3
Book of Mormon, 7
Bozeman Trail, 178n10
Brewer, Charles, 94, 95
Bridger, Jim, *xi*, 151
Brigham's Destroying Angel (Hickman), 137
Brooks, Juanita, 91, 92, 93
Brown, Barbara Jones, 91
Brown, Horace, 193n9
Brown, Jack, 80, 83, 86, 193n9
Browne, Albert G., Jr., 126, 173n2:3, 202n6
Buchanan, James: background on the Utah issue, 11–13, 81–82; conspiracy theory about Expedition, 133–34, 151, 206n1; interactions with Young, 136; pardoning Young for treason, 190n11; planning the Utah Expedition, 57, 174n6, 177n4; post-presidency home ("Wheatland"), 139
buffalo, WC encounters with, 33–36, 44
Bullock, Isaac, 140
bull trains: construction of freight wagons, 172n1; "doubling up," 44, 48, 176n1; encounters with Indians, 47–49, 51, 173n2, 176n2; illustrations of, 1, 73; oxen, trained to the yoke, 171n18; oxen, "yoking up" the, 15, 22, 24–25, 41, 165; oxen and wagons, numbers required, 20; river crossings, challenges of, 44–46; RM&W "Rules and Regulations," 39–40, 175n5; wagon masters, 23, 38–40
bull whacker. *See* teamster
"The Bull-Whacker's Epic" (poem), 134
Burns, Robert, 140
Burr, David H., 207n6
Burton, Robert Taylor, 178n1

Campbell, Robert, 177n4
Camp Floyd, 124–25, 126
Camp Scott, 13–14, 37, 74, 123, 160, 182n13, 200n17
"Camptown Races" (Foster, song), 185n5
Cedar City UT, 86–89, 94, 134, 189n9, 195n13, 196n7, 197n9, 198n13
"The Celebrated Jumping Frog of Calaveras County" (Twain), 144
Charlie Siringo's West (Lamar), 167n1
Cheyenne Indians, 32–33, 173n3:2, 176n2, 178n10
Cheyenne War of 1864, 174n7
Chimney Rock (trail landmark), 47, 51–52, 177n5
The Church of Jesus Christ of Latter-day Saints, 171n18
Civil War: animosities leading to, 18–19; conspiracy theories surrounding, 206n1; Hickman service during, 136; Johnston as general during, 8–9; Kearny as general during, 173n3; Lane service during, 170n12; memory of Utah War

overshadowed by, 3, 11, 151; Quantrill as Confederate guerilla, *xi*; Rennick as Confederate guerilla, 7, 23, 131–32, 144, 203n14; WC's role during, 4, 114, 122, 142, 157

Civil War (Confederate) military units: 6th Regiment, Missouri Infantry, 203n14; Quantrill's raiders, 131, 132, 203n14. *See also* U.S. military units

Clark, Anna, 17

Clark, Arthur (Mrs.), 113–14

Clark, Arthur M., 148

Clark, Corphelia Jane "Cora": courtship and marriage, xiv, 17–18, 100, 106–7, 145, 157, 165; death and burial, 113, 148; fiftieth wedding anniversary, 108–9, 114; making a home and family in Ames, 110–11, 145–48; publication of WC's manuscript, 148, 205n42; "westering" travels with WC, 161–62

Clark, Frank, 111

Clark, James A., 114

Clark, "Old man," 25–26

Clark, Orson, 114

Clark, Pliny, 17, 145

Clark, Samuel, 17

Clark, William: coming of age and leaving home, 17–18; about the reminiscences of, 4–5

Clark, William, across the Plains to Utah: befriending his traveling "chums," 18–19, 173n5; encounters with buffalo, 33–36; encounters with Indians, 32–33, 48–49, 51, 173n2, 176n2; encounters with wolves, 52–53, 178n8; gunshot wound, 62, 181n5; hiring on with RM&W as teamster, 19–26; illness and inability to eat, 27–31, 33, 44; map of the travels of, 6; termination of employment at Ft. Bridger, 60–61

Clark, William, captivity in Utah: captivity under Bill Hickman, 67–80; contact with Brigham Young, 80, 137–38, 160, 207n7; heading for California, 61, 63, 64–66

Clark, William, continuing to California: befriended by Bishop Redfield, 81–83; getting a pass to travel, 80, 160; the journey to, 14, 83–87, 94–99, 141–42; passing by Mountain Meadows Massacre site, 91–95; San Bernardino, arrival in, 93, 99, 200n20

Clark, William, the later years: account of work and travels after Utah, 142–44; arriving back in Wisconsin, 106–7; gold mining activities, 144; marriage and arrival in Ames, 107–11, 145–48; obituary and burial, 112–14, 194n11; "westering" travels with Cora, 140, 161–62. *See also* Ames IA

Clemens, Samuel L. (pseud. Mark Twain), 81, 144, 207n7

Clinton v. Englebrecht (1872), 137

Cody, William Frederick "Buffalo Bill," 132–33, 134, 149, 159, 161

Connor, Patrick Edward, 136

Cooke, Philip St. George, 61, 202n3

Corn Creek Indian Farm, 195n14

Cottonwood Canyon/Springs, 82, 97, 103–5, 190n11, 192n4

Court House Rock (trail landmark), 47

Crete NE, 26, 172n27

Crooks, Cooper, and Collins. *See* Turner-Dukes train
Cumming, Alfred, 13, 191n13
Cummings, James W., 178n1
Cushing Memorial Library & Archives, xiv, 9, 154–55, 206n46

Daily Alta California, 93
Dakota War of 1862, 32
Danites: as descriptor for Hickman and Rockwell, 67, 69, 78, 137; meaning of, 191n13; role of, 78
D. A. R. (Daughters of the American Revolution), 135, 163, 205n42
Davis, Jefferson, 184n1
Decker, Charles F., 75, 127
Decker, Lena Young, 75
Delaware River, 25, 172n22
Deseret News, 189n7
Destroying Angels. *See* Danites
Dickey, Richard Rush, 81
Disneyland, 143
"Doo-Dah" (Nash, song), 68, 185n5

Eads, Bill, 29, 173n2:3
Eardley, James, 185n7
Echo Canyon, 38, 60, 62, 67–68, 132, 134, 136, 181n3, 185nn6–7, 186n9
Eckels, Delana R., 125–26, 169n7
Eckelsville UT, 123–24
Egan, Howard, 141
Elliott, John M., 193n16
Enoch UT, 193n8
Evans, C. E., 206n46
Ewing, Thomas, Jr., 131
Eyring, Henry B., 90

Feldman, Henry, 74–75, 187n1
Fetterman, William J., 178n10

Fillmore, Lemuel, 140–41, 144, 175n2
Fillmore UT, 80, 83, 86–87, 191n15, 193n9, 195n14
Finlay, William Porter, 176n3
Finley, Gideon "Gid," 193n5
First Sioux War (1854–1856), 46, 176n3
Fish, Joseph, 195n16
Floyd, 134
Floyd, John B., 124–25
food and edibles ("grub"): buffalo meat, 35, 44, 174n5; canned goods, 33; frog legs, 25–26, 172n26; oxen used as, 182n10; poor quality and variety, 21, 25–26, 27, 29; purchased from settlers, 24, 27, 28; saleratus bread, 55, 65, 171n14, 179n4; salt as a preservative, 174n6; vegetables, 56; WC's illness from, 27–31
Forbes, Henry, 139
Fort Bridger (UT), 50; established as trading post, 182n7; Nauvoo Legion burned down, 57, 189n10; overwintering of the Expedition, 60–63; overwintering of unemployed teamsters, 183n13
Fort Casper (WY), 54
Fort Fetterman (WY), 53, 178n10
Fort Kearny (NE), 50, 173n3:3
Fort Kearny (WY), 173n3:3
Fort Laramie (WY, formerly Fort William), 47, 49, 50, 52, 177n4
Fort Leavenworth (KS), 50; planning the Utah Expedition, 174n6; RM&W at, 15, 18; Utah Expedition's departure from, 39, 122, 170n10; WC and chums' arrival at, 19–20; WC and chums' departure, 22, 24–25

216

Index

Fort Springville (UT), 193n7
Fort Supply (UT), 57, 184n1, 189n10
Foster, Stephen, 185n5
Frank, Albert Preston, 100, 128–30, 158, 173n5, 182n14
Frank, Helen McQueen Thomson, 129–30
Frank, John, 173n5
Freeport IL, 18, 151, 157
French, Charley, 38

"Gentiles" (non–Latter-day Saint individuals): attitude toward, 68, 72; being able to identify, 76; permission to cross and exit Utah, 92–95, 188n5; protecting the wives from, 139; as term, 8, 185n4; treatment of, 76–80
Ginn, John I., 92–93, 148, 158, 161, 207nn7–8
Ginn, William I., 127, 162
Gladstone ND, 148
"The Glorious Gospel Light Has Shone" (Johnson, hymn), 193n8
Goetzmann, William H., 161
gold/gold mining: California gold rush, 3, 74, 103, 168n2; WC's gold scale and equipment, xiv, xv, 135, 153, 163; WC's search for, 17, 18, 98, 144, 152, 157, 171n15, 205n32
Goodwin, Oliver Perry, 176n2
Gove, Jesse A., 177n5
Granger WY, 56, 179n7
Grant, Ulysses S., 39
Grasshopper River, 25, 172n22
Grattan, Joseph L., 176n3
Great Salt Lake, 174n6, 185n3, 186n9, 187n11
Great Sioux War (1876), 47, 178n10

Green River, 8, 13, 56, 58–59, 123, 130, 179n7
Green River district, 57, 179n3

Haight, Isaac C., 94, 196n7, 197n13
Haila, John A., xiv, 164
Hamblin, Jacob, 92, 195nn15–16, 197nn8–9, 198n13
Hamblin, Rachael Judd, 197n8
Hams Fork River, 60–61, 179n7, 180n2, 182n6
Hanks, Ephraim K., 186n10
Harney, William S., 176n3; as command of Utah Expedition, 176n3; Indian massacre at Blue Water Creek, 47, 68, 176n3; relieved from expedition command, 180n2
Harney Massacre (1855), 47, 176n3
Harper's New Monthly Magazine, 183n17
Harper's Weekly, 95
Harris, Susan K., xiv, 205n42
Hastrup, Dorthea, 202n7
Hastrup, Maria, 202n7
Hatch, Ira, 87, 95, 96, 195n16
Hewitt, Randall, 175n5
Hickman, George Washington "Doc," 64, 76, 80, 188n5
Hickman, Thomas Jefferson, 188n5
Hickman, William Adams "Wild Bill": described by Beadle, 201nD1; described by Becker, 184n2; described by WC, 4, 131, 138, 149, 151, 160; about the "Destroying Angel" moniker, 78; holding WC as prisoner, 67–72, 75–76, 80, 127; murder of Hartley, 184n1; murder of the Aiken party, 190n11; murder of Yates, 67, 134; post-war

217

Index

Hickman, William Adams "Wild Bill" (*continued*)
life, excommunication and death, 134, 136–37; about the "Wild Bill" moniker, 67, 204n18; as Young's "b'hoy," 70, 136
Hickok, James Butler "Wild Bill," 67, 173n4
Higbee (bishop), 94
"High on a Mountain Top" (Johnson, hymn), 193n8
Hinckley, Gordon B., 90
"The History of the Expedition against the Mormons in the Year of 1857" (Becker, unpublished manuscript), 187n1
Hobble Creek UT, 82, 142, 193n7
Hockaday, John M., 124
Horse Shoe Creek, 52, 178n7
Hurt, Garland, 54, 69, 83, 160, 183n16, 194n10, 195n14, 207n6
Hyde, Orson, 184n1

Independence Rock, 39, 55, 179n3
Indian Ring (congressional investigation), 39
Iowa Journal of History and Politics, 3, 4, 9, 93, 148–50, 153–54, 169n6

Jackson, William Henry, 15, 29, 34, 41, 79
Jagiello, Edward, 51
Jaques, John, 189n7
Johnny Bull (teamster), 38
Johnson, Aaron, 193n7
Johnson, Joel H., 193n8
Johnston, Albert Sidney: assumed command of Expedition, 180n2; as Civil War general, 8–9; ordering Expedition into winter quarters, 62–63; relationship with WC, 151
"Jolly Tar Whiskey." *See* "Valley tan" (liquor)

Kane, Thomas L., 81–82, 124, 195n16
Kearny, Philip, 173n3:3
Kearny, Stephen Watts, 173n3:3
Kelsey, Benjamin R., 207n2
Kelsey, Benjamin Wilson, 188n4, 207n2
Kelsey, Tiffany E., 207n2
Kenderdine, Thaddeus S., 167n1
Kimball, Heber C., 77, 186n8, 188n3, 188n6
Kimball, John, 188n3
Kingston, C. L., 9, 103–5
Kingston Spring, 105

Lake City UT, 82, 193n7
Lamar, Howard Roberts, x–xi, xiii, 158, 167n1
Lane, James Henry "Jim," 13, 21, 170n12
Laramie Mountains, 47, 52–53
Laramie River, 177n4
Las Vegas, 9, 88, 96–97, 192n4, 200nn16–17
Latter-day Saints, 171n18
Layne, Jonathan Ellis, 185n7
Leach, Celia Amelia Barrett, 121
Leach, Edwin: becoming "chums" with WC, 18, 19; beginning the trek to Utah, 19–26; going on to California, 61, 68–69, 81, 84–86; helping WC during his illness, 27–31; killing a buffalo, 33; serving in the Civil War, 122; WC's reminiscences of, 100, 121–22, 158

Index

Lee, John D., 89–92, 94, 137, 149, 196n7
Leonard, Glen M., 91
Lincoln, Abraham, 129
Liston, Commodore Perry, 96, 197n13, 198n11, 198n13
Little, Feramorz "Ferry," 72, 186n10
London, Jack, 163
Los Angeles *Star*, 207n7, 208n8
Lowe, Percival G., 182n14
Lyman, Amasa Mason "Amasy," 77, 81, 85–87, 95–96, 189n8, 198n10
Lyman, Edward Leo, 103
Lyman, Mary, 191n1

Magraw, William M. F., 207n6
mail service: conflict over Utah, 12; Independence to Salt Lake City, 207n6; Los Angeles to Salt Lake City, 81, 103, 104; Missouri River to Salt Lake City, 186n10; San Bernardino to Salt Lake City, 77, 189n9; St. Joseph to Salt Lake City, 124; Y. X. Carrying Company, 192n4
Majors, Alexander, 15, 20, 39–40, 134, 170n9, 172n1, 172n19. *See also* Russell, Majors & Waddell (RM&W)
Marcy, Randolph B., 64, 181n5
"The Massacre at Mountain Meadows, Utah Territory" (Brewer), 95
Matthews, William, 92{~?~SI: Out of alphabetical order}
Maxwell, William, 68
McCanles, David, 173n4
McCann, Dwight J., 38–39, 41–43
McCarthy, Frank: as assistant wagon master, *xii*, 22, 28; described by "Buffalo Bill," 132–33; described by WC, 138; firing WC and his "chums," 40–41; leaving the bull train, 38; shooting a soldier at Ft. Bridger, 37, 164
McCarthy, William, 48–49
McConnel, Jehiel, 96, 197n13, 198n11, 198n13
McCormick, Washington J., 126
McPherson, William Gregg, 167n1, 168n2
Mexican-American War, 11, 17, 173n3, 176n2, 180n2
Mills, James H., 40
Mills, Samuel C., 51
Mississippi Valley Historical Association, 154, 167n1
Mojave Indians, 195n16
Moon, Hugh, 187n2
Morehead, Charles R., 178n9, 182n11
Morgan, Lodowick W., 161, 207n7, 208n8
Mormons, 171n18
Mormon Trail, 50, 98, 179n2, 182n7
Morrell, Hiram F., 207n6
Mott, John W., 127–28
Mountain Meadows Massacre (1857): account of the atrocity, 13, 64, 74, 196n1, 196n7; attitude toward non-Mormons, 77–78, 139–41, 190nn11–12, 196n1; cause of and controversy over, 88–90, 195n16, 198nn12–13; cover-up and dealing with survivors, 197n8; described by Aiken, 92; described by Ginn, 92–93, 161; described by Nelson, 207n3; described by Savage, 142; described by Turley and Brown, 91, 164, 196n1; described by Ute warriors, 194n10; described by

219

Mountain Meadows Massacre (*continued*)
  WC, 4, 91–95, 103, 149, 151, 159, 161, 196n7; impact on the nation, 57–58, 81; internment and memorial to victims, 89–90, 95; map location on Mormon Trail, 98; prosecutions over, 136–39
The Mountain Meadows Massacre (Brooks), 91

Nash, Isaac B., 185n5
Native Americans. *See individual Indian tribes by name*
Nauvoo Legion: account as prisoner by WC, 4, 67–72, 75–80; attacks against Utah Expedition, 13–14, 54, 57–59; creation by Young, 11, 189n10, 194n10; defenses at Echo Canyon, 181n3; indictments for treason, 124, 190n11; murder of the Aiken party, 190n11, 193n9; prisoner capture and treatment, 62, 74–75, 127, 184n2; prohibitions on alcohol, 187n2; uniforms and clothing, 185n7. *See also* Mountain Meadows Massacre (1857)
Nelson, John V., 207n3
New Mexico Territory, 64, 174n6, 183n17, 194n10
New York Times, 37, 189n7, 189n8, 189n10
New York Tribune, 37

Ogden IA, 112, 148
Old Spanish Trail: mail service to Utah, 189n9; map of WC journey, 98; Mountain Meadows on the, 88; Pomeroy-Kingston story, 103–5; WC journey to California, 9, 75, 139, 192n4, 200n16
Oregon Historical Society, 187n1
Oregon Trail, 41, 122, 147, 168n2, 174n7, 176n3, 177n5, 182n6
Organization of American Historians, 154, 167n1

Paiute Indians, 13, 89–90, 95–96, 195n16, 198n13, 200n19
Paoli WI, 17, 103, 109, 113, 145
Parker, Robert B., 163
Parrish-Potter murders, 64, 78, 139
Pawnee Indians, 32
Payson UT (formerly Peteetneet Creek), 193n7
Phelps, John W., 60
Pierce Franklin, 12
Piutes. *See* Paiute Indians
Platte River (North/South), 32, 35, 44, 47–48, 51–52, 166n3, 177nn4–5, 178n10, 179n2
Plum Creek, 36, 48–49, 174n7, 176n10
Polydore, Henrietta, 126
Polydore, Henry F., 126, 202n7
polygamy, as issue in Utah War, 12–13, 149
Pomeroy (freighters), 103–5
Pony Express, 133, 170n9, 173n4, 174n7
Porter, Fitz John, 61
Powers, George, 92
Pratt, Parley P., 88, 90, 127

Quantrill, William Clarke, xi, 4, 144, 175n2
Quantrill's raiders, 131, 132, 203n14

Read, B. H., 151
Red, the Missourian (teamster), 38

Red Cloud's War (1866), 178n10
Redfield, Alpha Luranda Foster, 139, 192n2, 204n23
Redfield, Harlow "Bishop," 81, 138, 139, 144, 192n2, 204n23
Redfield SD, 148
Redfield UT, 77
Reformation, Latter-day Saint, 127, 190n12
Remington, Frederic, 34
Rennick, Chatham Ewing "Chat" 23, *132*; as bull train wagon boss, 22, 24–25, 28, 35, 45, 52, 55–56, 174n4; as Confederate guerilla, 7, 131–32, 144, 203n14; described by WC, 4, 130–31, 138; encounter with Indians, 51; pressuring WC to drive on Sunday, 39–42; WC relationship with, 29–30, 43, 64–66, 149
Resting Spring, 105
Rich, Sarah DeArmon Pea, 179n4
Rock Creek (NE, emigrant camp), 30, 173n4
Rockwell, Orrin Porter "Port," 67, 78, 85, 127, 136–37, 190n11, 191n13, 192n4, 206n1, 207n3
Roosevelt, Theodore, 169n3
Rose-Baley party killings (1858), 199n15
Roughing It (Clemens), 81, 207n7
Russell, Charles M., 34, *119*
Russell, Majors & Waddell (RM&W): conspiracy theories surrounding, 133–34; establishing the Pony Express, 133, 170n9, 173n4, 174n7; role in Utah Expedition, 3, 19–21; "Rules and Regulations" for bull trains, 39–40, 175n5. *See also* bull trains; *and individual owners by name*
Russell, William H., 20, 39, 133–34, 170n9, 178n9, 182n11

Saleratus Lake, 179n4
Salt Lake City: arrival of Expedition advance party, 58; arrival of Utah Expedition, 124, 125, 174n6, 185n5, 187n2, 190n11; becoming the territorial capital, 191n15; description of the city, 38; "Ferry" Little as mayor, 186n10; Hickman wounded in gunfight, 70, *136*; mail service to, 81, 124, 186n10, 207n6; map of WC journey to, 6, *98*; WC and chums plan to travel to, 63–65; WC as prisoner in, 74–75; WC's departure from, 75, 139
San Bernardino CA, 93; arrival of WC, 200n20; founding of the Mormon colony, 189n8; mail service to Utah, 12, 77, 85, 93, 103–5, 124, 186n10, 189n9
Santa Clara River, 88
Santa Clara UT, 86–87, 139, 195n15
Sargent, Charles E. (Mrs.), 112, 114, 147
Savage, David Leonard: guiding WC and chums to California, 78, 82, 86, 99, 141, 196n7; post-war labors and death, 141–42; WC's relationship with, 138, 189n9
"Say, What Was Your Name in the States?" (song), 18, 169n3
Schmidt (professor), 154
Scott, Winfield, 177n4
Scotts Bluff (trail landmark), 47

Sevier River, 195n12
Sevy, G. W., 128
Shambaugh, Benjamin Franklin, 4–5, 150, 153–54, 158–59
Sheldon, Asa G., 171n18
Sherwood, Martin L.: becoming "chums" with WC, 18, 19; beginning the trek to Utah, 19–26; helping WC during his illness, 27–31; joining the church, 200n1; remaining in Utah, 125–27; return to Wisconsin, 128; WC reminiscences of, 100, 158
Shipps, Jan, 154
Simonton, James W., 140–41
Simpson, James H., 51
Sioux Indians, 32–33, 133, 176n3. *See also* First Sioux War (1854–1856); Great Sioux War (1876)
Siringo, Charlie, 167n1
Smith, Charles Maurice, 123–24, 125–26, 202n6
Smith, George A., 67, 88, 140, 188n6
Smith, George D., 191n1
Smith, Hyrum, 77, 88, 127, 188n6
Smith, Joseph, Jr., 88, 188n6
Smith, Lot, 58–59, 137, 180n7:1, 188n6
Smiths Fork, 8
Smoot, Abraham O., 192n4
Smoot, Reed, 149
Snow, Warren, 75, 127
Snyder, Clarissa R., 205n42
Soda Springs, 60, 62, 181n3, 182n6
Sonora, Mexico, 128
Sons of Dan. *See* Danites
South Pass, 13, 54, 56, 179n6
Spanish Fork Indian Farm, 194n10, 195n14

Spanish Fork UT, 64, 83–84, 100–101, 103–5, 126–28, 129
Springville UT, 82, 142, 193n7
Stambaugh (professor), 131
Stansbury, Howard, 179n2
State Historical Society of Iowa (SHSI). See *Iowa Journal of History and Politics*
Stenhouse, T. B. H., 179n2
St. George UT, 197n9
Stoddard, Judson, 192n4
Sublette, William, 177n4
Sublette's Cut-off (Oregon Trail), 182n6
Sweetwater River, 39, 55–56, 179n2

"A Tale of Adventure" (1905 *Intelligencer* article), 141, 146, 149, 151
Tanner, Sidney, 92
teamster: animosity between the "Yankees" and the "Missouri pukes", 18–19; comparisons among, 21, 27, 28, 115–17; defining the term, 8; drawings of, 34, 79; training oxen to the yoke, 171n18; treatment and abuse of oxen, 175n5; yoking up and driving on Sunday, 39–43; "yoking up" the oxen, 15, 22, 24–25, 41. *See also* bull trains
Territorial Enterprise (newspaper), 81
Texas A&M University, xiv, 154–55, 164, 206n46
Thompson, Zekiel, 128–29
transcontinental railroad, 115, 134
transcontinental telegraph, 41, 134, 174n7
"A Trip Across the Plains in 1857" (Clark): 1905 *Intelligencer* article, 149, 154, 162; 1912 *Intelligencer*

Index

article, 137, 151, 154, 162; 1915 publication of, 9, 151–52, 162; 1922 publication of, 4–5, 19, 148, 154; 1937 holographic manuscript, *xiv*, 150, 154–55, 162–64, 206n46; 2025 editorial decisions and republication, 7–10, 154, 162–64, 169n6; D. A. R. manuscript purchase from Cora Clark, 205n42; donation to State Historical Society of Iowa, 19, 153–54; embellishments and missing information, 157–59, 196n3, 206n1; finding the hidden history, 159–60, 164–65; validation of the WC reminiscences, 161. See also *Iowa Journal of History and Politics*

Tulsa (OK) race riot (1921), 196n1

Turley, Richard E., Jr., *xiii*, 91, 164, 196n1

Turner, Frederick Jackson, 161

Turner-Dukes train, 92, 96, 99, 141

Tuttle, George B.: becoming chums with WC, *xii*, 18, 19; beginning the trek to Utah, 19–26; rescuing brother from the Army, *xiii–xiv*, 122–26; WC reminiscences of, 158

Tuttle, Ira O., *xiii–xiv*, 61, 100, 122–26, 128, 160, 203n10

Twain, Mark (Samuel L. Clemens), 81, 144, 207n7

Twelve Mile Creek Indian Farm (UT), 195n14

Union Pacific Railroad, 115, 134

University of Texas, 206n46

U.S. military units: Fifth U.S. Infantry, 183n17; First Wisconsin Cavalry (U.S.), 128, 203n10; Fourth U.S. Artillery, 60; Second Dragoons (U.S.), 61, 63, 124–25, 159, 182n9, 203n3, 208n8; Tenth U.S. Infantry, 61, 180n2, 208n8. See also Civil War (Confederate) military units

Utah Expedition: command by Harney, 176n3, 177n4; command by Johnston, 180n2; conspiracies and scandal surrounding, 206n1; departure from Fort Leavenworth, 39, 122, 170n10; formation and travel delay, 11–14; lack of adequate planning, 174n6; marching through Salt Lake City, 124–25; overwintering at Camp Scott, 13–14, 37, 182n13, 200n17; overwintering at Ft. Bridger, 61, 122–23, 174n6; overwintering at Ft. Laramie, 177n4; recollections of the experience, 159; reinforcements from Texas and California, 88; resupply from New Mexico, 64, 174n6, 183n17, 194n10

Utah Historical Society, 187n1

Utah State University library, 187n1

The Utah War: background and causes of, 11–14, 194n10; conspiracy theories surrounding, 133–34; lack of historical material on, 3; production of ammunition for, 200n16; Young's Sebastopol strategy, 57, 127, 189n10

Ute Indians, 194n10, 195n14

"Valley tan" (liquor), 76, 80, 187n2, 188nn3–4. See also alcohol/drunkenness

Valley Tan (newspaper), 187n2, 188n4

Van Vliet, Stewart L., 20, 58, 59, 170n11

223

Van Winkle, Rip, 59
Vegas Springs. *See* Las Vegas
Vengeance Is Mine (Turley & Brown), 91

Waddell, William B., 20. *See also* Russell, Majors & Waddell (RM&W)
Wagner, Dave, 38, 132
Wakarusa War, 170n12
Walker, Ronald W., 91
Walker, William, 176n2
Wasatch Mountains, 142, 186n9, 187n11, 194n10
Watt, George D., 181n3, 185n7
Weber River/Canyon, 71, 186n9
Weld, Harriet A. "Hattie" (Mrs. Charles E. Sargent), 112, 114, 147
Wells, Daniel H., 136, 185n7
Wesson, Lorenzo, 172n26
"westering," WC's life as a story of, 161–62
Western History Association, x, 167n1
"The West of the Imagination" (documentary), 161{~?~SI: Out of alphabetical order}
"Wheatland", 139
White (RM&W wagon master), 38
White, Joel W., 94, 196n7
White Crow (Cheyenne chief), 176n2
Wiegand, Conrad, 191n1
Williams, J. Griffin "Griff," 81
Williams, William Sherley "Old Bill," 81
Wilson, Alexander, 202n7
"Winter Mormon", 200n1
Wister, Owen, 161
wolves/wolf packs, 52–53, 89, 92, 95, 105, 178n9
Wounded Knee Massacre (1890), 32

Yates, Richard E., 67, 134, 136–37
Young, Brigham, 198n12; association with Mountain Meadows Massacre, 89, 139, 197n13; declaration of martial law in Utah, 13, 57, 64, 160, 183n15, 188n5; final days and death of, 137–39; forming the Army of Israel, 67, 193n9; forming the Nauvoo Legion, 11, 189n10, 194n10; indictment for treason, 11, 183n15, 188n5, 190n11; informed of Utah Expedition, 186n10, 192n4; prohibition of alcohol, 187n2; relationship with Hurt, 193n16; relationship with the Indians, 198nn12–13; relationship with WC, 80, 137, 160, 207n7
Young, Brigham, Jr., 72
Young, John, 138–39
Young, Joseph F., 72, 128
Y. X. Carrying Company, 178n7, 190n11, 192n4

www.ingramcontent.com/pod-product-compliance
Lightning Source LLC
Chambersburg PA
CBHW031128160426
43192CB00008B/1149